Halcyon Worlds

Sophie Kilic

Published by Honeybee Books
Dorset
www.honeybeebooks.co.uk

Copyright Sophie Kilic © 2017

The right of Sophie Kilic to be identified as the author of this work has been asserted by her in accordance with the Copyright, Designs and Patents Act 1988.

No part of this book may be reproduced in any form or by any electronic or mechanical means including information storage and retrieval systems without permission in writing from the author.

Printed in the UK using paper from sustainable sources

ISBN: 978-1-910616-75-8

Introduction

Halcyon Worlds is a lyrical celebration of Dorset, allowing the reader to escape into places of unchanged timelessness and beauty. The word Halcyon comes from the Greek Alcyone, a mythological kingfisher which calmed the seas. 'Halcyon days' in the traditional sense have come to relate to times in the past when things were perceived as better, calmer, happier. Yet I believe this is an illusion and that if a place provides us with a joie de vivre, a sense of escape and excitement or a feeling of security, whatever the weather, and if the past indeed influences the present, then these halcyon worlds can exist in the now.

This is a journal to dip into and savour in small bites. In visiting different places around the county, it primarily explores the natural environment and considers man's attitude towards it and experience of it through the centuries. At the same time, however, it shows that there is often a distinct blurring between past and present so that time can be intangible and that man and child can perhaps even exist simultaneously. As childhood is a fleeting moment, it considers the juxtaposition of evanescence and permanency, sometimes highlighting this by depicting places which seem contrary to the notion of a halcyon world.

Much of this book was written on location, jotted down over the years in a notebook as an artist will use a sketchpad. It therefore comprises a mosaic of memories and writings on location, following a vague, monthly chronology structured around the meteorological seasons. Its main aim is to evoke, in the words of Lawrence Durrell, a 'spirit of place' and a sense of experience captured by all the senses. For those who have been to these places and encountered the same atmospheres, it hopes to strike a chord of empathy, serving as a sweet recollection of many similar memories. For those who haven't, it hopes to stimulate a sense of curiosity.

Over the years I have not only had the opportunity to grow up and reside in Dorset, taking an active part in certain aspects of its culture and community, but also to explore it extensively, becoming more intimate with the amazing variety of characteristics which can be found in such a small county. I have my parents to thank for this, for they always invested time in my brother and I, generating and stimulating a curiosity within us and encouraging us to explore and understand the surrounding natural environment both in terms of its historical past and its tangible present. It was one of the most valuable of life's lessons, for experiencing the natural world enables us to step outside ourselves, our confines of daily life, and gain a vision of something much bigger, more profound and permanent.

The Dorset landscape, itself an open air history book revealing how past has shaped the present, testifies to a legacy tracing back from the prehistoric eras including the times of the Durotriges, on to the Roman, Saxon and Medieval periods. Not only is history strongly evident, but the county also possesses a stunning and unique natural beauty of beach, forest, heathland, chalk downland and pasture with a spectacular array of flora and fauna suited to these different habitats. Being primarily a rural county, without even a motorway, and the only large conurbation being situated in the east, it is thus the perfect county to escape from the stresses of modern life and to enjoy the beauty of nature. I hope it will always remain that way and consider it a privilege to have been born and bred here, and to still be here, despite having spent ten years living away, which only served to draw me back again.

Halcyon Worlds

Paintings by the author

Kingfisher on the Stour

Shrimping at Kimmeridge

Wimborne Minster floodlit

Kingston Lacy

Spring

And was not the spring with us, and the whole land preaching of resurrection, the birds singing, trees and flowers waking from their winter sleep…..

J Meade Falkner. [37]

March

Sheep

March the first, meteorologically officially the beginning of spring. Daffodils have succeeded snowdrops, and crocuses have sprouted through lawns forming mats of yellow and mauve. My husband, brother and I are driving through Dorset in the direction of its county town where, at Kingston Maurward agricultural college, the annual lambing is underway. We are with my young nephews, who excitedly anticipate the event, wishing that the journey were not so long. One of them, however, admits that the countryside flashing past is very beautiful and notices birds of prey gliding in the blue sky above the fields. This is Dorset, holding a fascination all of its own which is appreciated by both young and old.

Many families with young children, like us, have come to see the lambs, enjoy the tractor rides and feed the animals in the animal park. Despite the clear chill in the air, the sun shines strongly golden, awakening hope and hinting at that long awaited ebullience which saturates the atmosphere in springtime. We watch ewes tending their lambs, which skip around on frisky legs too long for them and look at us with fresh faces full of innocence and curiosity. Never sitting still, they lead each other on, climbing onto the immobile backs of their stoic, long suffering mums, prodding with tiny hooves before bouncing off again- real live woolly jumpers! Everything is new for these lambs, a world which is there to be explored. They know no guile, are full of trust, have no understanding of anything amiss.

Despite the crowds, there is an underlying backdrop of peace at Kingston Maurward today. Birds sing in the trees, animals carry out their established routines and around us the gentle green contours of the earth quietly undulate, delicately gilded in a strengthening sun, while more sheep graze their pastures. Dorset is a farming county and therefore since the Bronze Age, or perhaps even earlier, man has had a close, virtually symbiotic relationship with life stock and the land. Sheep not only grazed, as they do today, maintaining pasture and downland, but played an important role in the Dorset economy. Daniel Defoe, writing in the early eighteenth century, stated that at this time, approximately six hundred thousand sheep were apparently grazing the downs within six miles of the town of Dorchester. Although he was not one hundred per cent convinced of the truth of this statement, he confessed that from his own observations of the surrounding countryside, he felt inclined to believe it [27]. Here at Kingston Maurward, we are embraced into the heart of that countryside while all continues as it is accustomed. The sheep still graze, although perhaps not in such profundity, men beat molten metal in the traditional forge with a regular, monotonous, satisfying clang, piglets greedily suckle sows, a group of excitable goats is led away to be fed, ponies and donkeys graze, chickens peck.

Around the park, the trees, still in winter attire, stand naked and stark, yet it will not be long before they bring forth new leaves and start to utilize the energy of the sun which already begins to warm the grassy slopes. With this creeping warmth comes something of the same paradise which, for me, pervades rural places. Watching the pleasant cycle of routine and the gentle way of life, it is as if we have left all problems in the past, and as we stand in this brave new present, the carefree now is full of new life and hope. This is indeed an exciting world full of wonder and novelty, waiting to be explored and sensed - what better county to experience this than in Dorset!

(2014)

Whitcombe

The church of no dedication stands alone outside the hamlet of Whitcombe not far from Kingston Maurward. Its abandonment is most likely due to rural depopulation, which occurred over much of Dorset in previous centuries, so that Whitcombe, now perhaps most renowned for its stables, exists today as a shrunken village, a picturesque cluster of cottages nestling near an old tithe barn. On this pensive day which hints of spring, the solitude of the church seems all the more intriguing; the grey limestone of its exterior gilded in wan sunshine, enticing us. We enter the churchyard through a small gate in an eighteenth- century wall which circles the enclosure. An atmosphere of peace overwhelms me, for framed in the overhanging boughs of an evergreen oak, is a pastoral idyll, the air soothed by the crooning of pigeons, the fields around the church, where one can see the bumps and lumps of former village dwellings, now grassed over and grazed with sheep. A village laid to rest. I imagine how it once was; perhaps a close-knit community where people lived off the land, close to nature and close to each other. Perhaps though, we romanticise about village life, assigning it to the halcyon days of old, forgetting the harsh reality of living off the land.

Entering the church through a tiny, simple porch with low doorframes and an ancient wooden door, we are greeted by a peaceful interior with evidence of a large medieval fresco; faces frozen in time. The white walls of the twelfth- century nave exude a purity and simplicity, reflecting natural light which flows through clear glass windows, contrasting the dark wood of the roof beams. As our eyes become accustomed, more faded frescoes seem to emerge from the walls in various places. The large and obvious one, which we saw on entry, depicts St Christopher and has maintained a rich colour in places. St Christopher holds the Christ child and apparently there is also a mermaid holding a mirror in her right hand. As I cannot make her out, both her presence and significance remain a mystery to me, as much of a mystery as this lost village and its abandoned church without a name. Other frescoes in the church depict a series of decorated arches which could resemble an altar screen according to the Churches Conservation Trust, which cares for this building.

Tiny windows frame sheep grazing the green outside. I imagine once, people would have seen cottages there. Nature has now reclaimed them, covering their remains so that they leave only a tenuous legacy of buried memories. The frescoes, mostly faded, are equally tenuous, yet having been revealed, they seem to cling on as the faint recognitions owned by a people of the past who saw them there. Apparently uncovered around 1912, they would not have been seen by the poet William Barnes, who preached his first and last sermons in this church in 1847 and 1885 respectively [29]. Barnes was also rector at nearby Winterborne Came, another ghost village whose fourteenth- century church, St Peter's, is equally abandoned and is described by the Churches Conservation Trust as being 'the quintessential country squire's church' [22], presumably because of its location in the grounds of the elegant, mid eighteenth -century Came House and the fact that it contains various impressive memorials to the Damer family who owned it. The church records also show that a Napolean Louis Bonaparte was the witness to a wedding here in 1847.

There are countless examples of shrunken or lost villages all over the county, usually identified by roads leading nowhere, holloways, solitary churches sometimes with adjacent manor houses, isolated farmsteads, and their names. The causes of such demographic movement and change are complex and varied. The Black Death was partially accountable. Coming on ships to Weymouth in the thirteenth century, it devastated the population, leaving some villages without inhabitants. However, there were many other factors playing their part at that time such as unfavourable climatic conditions, making it hard to grow food and thus weakening the poor. Centuries later, the enclosure acts also played their part, forcing people off the land or leading them into poverty and exploitation by landlords. As sheep farming also became lucrative, much formerly arable land was turned over to pasturing sheep, the wealth from which generated further income for landowners to build large houses and parklands. Many of these parklands required the clearance of existing villages in order to create pleasing rural vistas, examples of which will be encountered throughout this book.

Winterbourne Farringdon was once a village near Whitcombe and Winterborne Came. It is now completely lost. The only physical testimonies to its existence are the ridges and hollows in fields, caught on aerial camera at sundown and the solitary remains of the church of St Germain. The east gable, all that is left of this medieval church, stands forlorn and forgotten in verdant surrounds. It is, to me, a symbol of the way in which tradition and with it belief is departing, for many have abandoned them. Yet, like the gable, they still stand, threatened but not defeated, holding on throughout the generations.

*

William Barnes is buried in the churchyard of Winterbourne Came under a Celtic cross. He died in 1886 at the age of eighty-five. While alive, he inhabited the rather original and curiously eccentric-looking rectory, both roof and veranda heavily thatched, from under which peer small, leaded, gothic-style windows. Despite leaving school at thirteen, Barnes became a prolific poet, writing much in Dorset dialect. An intellectual, as well as a philologist (a word he would not have liked, due to its Greek origins), with fluency in several languages including Greek, Latin and Persian, he acquired a profound knowledge of etymology (or what he would have preferred to have called word-shapening) and supported the expulsion of words with Greek and Latin roots from the English language. He suggested, for example, that *emphasis* should become *speech loudening, democracy folkdom,* and *hydrophobia* should become *water awe* [7]. Many other such examples of Anglo-Saxon style variants are found in his book *The Outline of English Speech Craft,* published in 1878. The book also examines and questions grammar and syntax as well as the way in which words should be pronounced. I find it strange that someone who was clearly a writer and lover of words, would want to somehow impoverish the English language, for, although these examples do not show it, the anglicised forms of many of the words in his book are not always translated as a concise, single word and often do not hold exactly the same meaning as the words which they are replacing. I wonder if they were taught to his students, for he was also a school master, establishing a school firstly in Mere and then in Dorchester.

Barnes, however, is most well-known for his poetry and in the small church of Whitcombe, a poem entitled *The Spring* is pinned up on the wall. While reflecting his faith as a country pastor, this poem suggests that past generations not only found God in nature but perhaps seemed to be more observant of and in tune with its seasonal aspects than the average person today, finding joy in the details of the natural world which they inhabited.

When wintry weather's all a-done,
An' brooks do sparkle in the zun,
An' naisy-builden rooks do vlee
Wi' sticks toward their elem tree;
When birds do zing, an' we can zee
Upon the boughs the buds o' spring, -
Then I'm as happy as a king,
A-vield wi' health an' zunsheen.

Vor then the cowslip's hangen flower
A-wetted in the zunny shower,
Do grow wi' vi'lets, sweet o' smell,
Bezide the wood-screened graegle's bell;
Where drushes' aggs, wi' sky-blue shell,
Do lie in mossy nest among
The thorns, while they do zing their zong
At evenen in the zunsheen.

> An' God do meake his win' to blow
> An' rain to vall vor high an' low,
> An' bid his mornen zun to rise
> Vor all alike, an' groun' an' skies
> Ha' colors vor the poor man's eyes:
> An' in our trials He is near,
> To hear our mwoan an' zee our tear,
> An' turn our clouds to zunsheen……………..

(2016)

Gussage Saint Andrew

The passion cycle of medieval frescoes in the twelfth- century chapel of Gussage St Andrew is surely worth mentioning not only for its age but also for its significance at this time of year with Easter approaching. Dark-drawn lines leave traces of faded forms in the fragments which show events leading up to the crucifixion. The fact that these pieces remained hidden and secret through the centuries until 1951 when they were discovered in this tiny chapel in a hamlet away from the world, makes them all the more compelling, allowing us to step back in time to wonder as those twelfth-century pilgrims did; those who had no Bible translated for them, but had to rely on visual representations in order to understand.

*

In an ancient forest near Gussage St Andrew we watch spring stirring. Birds sing unseen in a tangle of trees and despite the wind racing through their branches, the atmosphere remains calm and tender, like a mother waiting for her child to take its first steps. Sunshine turns to showers and back again as an assortment of green shoots push their way through the forest floor: crowns of dog's mercury, fleshy shiny spears of wood garlic, and the leaves of bluebells. From everywhere new life feels its way into the world and we watch the forest floor; a brown base of winter leaves becoming a carpet of green. Moss adds to this, blanketing tree trunks and logs, covering shoots which rise from the ground to create strange standing sculptures.

In a clearing the sun shines on peaceful patches of snowdrops. A blackbird sings. Deep within the moss and leaf-litter, red cups of orange peel fungus seem placed like fairy-goblets, warm and bright. A woodpecker taps, the onset of spring spoken in every resonance, and a woodpigeon adds its warm serenade to a season of wonder and anticipation.

(2017)

Living Dream

Last week the mournful, ethereal call of a tawny owl leached from my subconscious into reality. It's haunting, lonesome cry was of a different world, and hovering in no-man's land between dream and wakefulness, I was transported, in my imagination, to a mysterious moonlit forest. Once awake I was compelled to listen; the call commanding, causing a delicious comfort to ripple through me. It was four in the morning, the moon bright and full, framed in skeletal, silhouetted branches outside the window and I was alone with the night in an amazing moment which gripped me, for as our house is located right on the edge of suburbia, I never expected to hear an owl here.

It called for an hour and I listened, enjoying every echo and indulging in the atmospheric experience, despite lack of sleep. At five o'clock its call faded and I drifted into dreams again, by seven, when I awoke once more, the moon had also dissolved into the morning light, a pallid orange disc, equally ethereal and graceful as it sank behind the silhouetted trees on the western horizon.

Tonight the owl is back, its calls cutting through the evening darkness. Only seven in the evening and it is already hunting. This time I go out, carefully, quietly so as not to disturb, walking through delicate sheets of mizzle beneath the oak tree's silent shadows. It thrills me to walk there, surrounded by the night, surrounded by the owl's compelling call; raw, elemental. The night is icy, and some would say that the tawny's call is chilling, eerie, matching such an environment, but to me there is something warm, resonant and secure about it. It seems to represent strength and permanence, bravely resisting the threats of urbanisation as the owl ventures within built-up boundaries. It thus bridges a gap with the natural world, a world which can be experienced even in the suburbs. I find this reassuring and like a magnet; the owl's cry attracts me, drawing me back to a delicious sense of peace and belonging which I cannot usually feel in built up places.

(Ferndown, 2016)

Arne

March 2012 feels like summer. At Arne, silence shimmers and sizzles, providing a lazy backdrop. In the foreground the air seems to buzz with energy and exuberance. A squirrel busies about beneath trees at the RSPB hut, and my husband and I watch a kestrel's nest on the resident webcam, the parent bird dutifully attending to the voracious appetite of its brood. Despite there being a significant amount of people at the hut, once we have all disbanded, each taking our own paths, we meet practically no one.

A woodpecker's twang resonates through a forest of silver birch while small songbirds flit about branches, their voices bright and ecstatic beneath a blazing blue sky. Sunlight swathes tree trunks in gold and amber light, playing patterns with dancing strokes and a pair of low-flying ducks unexpectedly sweep through the forest.

On soft sandy paths we walk towards the shore inhaling rich, earthy base notes of dry heather and bracken with a sweet top note of coconut. The gorse is blossoming in full, fragrant force while insects buzz about it, their energy emphasizing a dichotomy against the breathless silence. We head down an enticing path towards the sea, compelled like children on long school holidays with really nothing better to do than to explore for endless rapturous hours. The limpid sea laps its gentle dreamy monologue at the shore, blue wavelets spreading diaphanous layers like sheets of silk. Walking along the stretch of sand that curves round to form the beach, we then climb up to the cliff top to look down through flowering gorse to the hulls of pristine boats moored serenely in unbroken blue. Blue behind yellow; the intense clash of primary colours is elating. Beyond the gorse, sea and sky lie the islands; heavily vegetated natural forms filled with wonder. It is as if paradise were laid stretched out before us! The only sound that disturbs us now is the faint drift of a boat's radio wafting up in waves from the water below, a group of gulls bickering on the beach and the odd insect, whose sudden buzz past my ear always takes me by surprise.

Something tickles my leg. Looking down, we watch a team of wood ants scurrying, dragging objects twice their size along the sandy path. I marvel at their synergy. Behind us, pinecones snap and crack in the heat. It has reached the mid-twenties. This could almost be the Mediterranean and the deer have hidden away.

Bournemouth Beach

I walk alone on Bournemouth beach, tide out, soft sand pitted with pugmarks from dogs, the dendritic foot patterns from wandering gulls and hollows of human feet. Although plenty of people walk here, the whole atmosphere is one of calm reflection, intensified by the pensive soliloquy of the sea, an unabated breath which washes with a sleeper's regularity, inducing lethargy. The sea itself spreads out majestically towards Old Harry Rocks so completely flat that sunlight sparkles silver on its aquamarine surface, silence only broken occasionally by a clamour of gulls on the shoreline.

Peacefulness resumes and the sea, now striped with soft shadows of grey blue ink, occasionally crashes with deep resonance, as if expressing its soul. I continue to wander in the sunshine, yet clouds bubble up behind me and faint shafts of sunlight radiate apocalyptically to touch the unruffled sea's surface. Shadows cross the sand for an instant before the sun breaks through again and the sea lulls back, licking its lazy calm onto the shore. A man and his dog walk single file along the silvery rim of shoreline. Apart from them there is hardly anybody about, the highest densities of people congregating near the cafes and entrances to the chines. Few walk so far. I want to walk on forever, watching the changing light cross the surface of the sea, now smudged with turquoise and indigo. I want to see silver sparkles dance, and listen to the call of the pigeon float from the cliffs where the gorse buds. I want to walk on and on. But time beckons, work awaits and so I turn around, a chill breeze on my face, and reluctantly wander back.

(2013)

Fiddleford

A narrow path wanders past thatched cottages, leading beside a small stream to Fiddleford Mill. Birds echo each other's songs brightly in the naked trees and the last snowdrops cover steep verges, surpassed by sunny celandines and nodding daffodils, sunlight shafting through their petals. The air stirs with the familiar smells of spring- a confetti of blossom leaving trails of honeyed scent which contends as a winner against the whiff of wood garlic, although I cannot see the latter yet in flower.

The path comes out onto a quiet road streaked with the shadows of the trees above. There is something nostalgic and timeless about wandering this way, as if it has never changed. The old mill stands bathing in brilliant sunlight, which enhances the irregularity of its ivy-tumbled, rough stone walls, the moss-covered slate roof and the rustic wooden door. It is completely picturesque and compelling so that curiosity creeps up inside me and I begin to wonder about its past. So peaceful is the spot, the mill with its collection of rough-stone barns, that I imagine it has been like this forever, although now it is retired, no longer in operation, perhaps it languishes in the sweet, idle nostalgia for its industrious past. The first mill to be mentioned here was in the Domesday Book in 1086, the current building dated 1566 [14]. I have been told that it was once probably used for the storage of contraband, which had been transported up the Stour. Smugglers aside, I imagine those who worked here must have been kind and trustworthy country folk, for the atmosphere seems peaceful, satisfying; as if an honest wage was made through good work, but I am probably romanticizing.

Perhaps atmosphere provides a more accurate testimony than we realise, for I hadn't noticed, until leaving the mill, that there is an inscription set into the wall which confirms the feeling of satisfying peace mentioned above. Arresting my attention and causing me to peer hard at its cramped, gothic script, the inscription talks of friendship and cordiality between the miller and those that come as friends. The miller goes on to say

> for the tale of trothe I do always professe….
>
> If falsehood appere the fault shal
>
> be thine and of sharpe ponishment think me not unkind.
>
> Therefore to be true yt shall the behove [to] please God chiefly [that liveth] above. [14]

The message is one of truth, honesty and hospitality. This miller of 1566 would therefore have been horrified to think that the mill might have been used to facilitate fraudulent pursuits in years to come [63].

Adjacent to the mill, the manor house, built between the fourteenth and sixteenth centuries, looks out across the Stour, peeping through the catkined fronds of willow and the wispy, silvery heads of tall grasses that line the foreground. It bathes softly golden in the sunlight, beautifully blended into its backdrop on the riverbank, elemental colours and complementing textures. Although these buildings are marks of man, they are so old, worn and mellowed that they have become an integral part of the natural landscape, adding rather than detracting, bringing something of a beautiful balance and harmony, fusing past with present to create a sense of timelessness. I believe that a building has to be old to do this, for a modern edifice has hardly stood the test of time to be missed.

Modernity does exist here, however, in the subtle form of a hydro-electric generator, which turns beside the mill, showing that life continues and that every century brings something new and important to a place. Although the mill is no longer needed in the traditional sense, and the manor house has been divided into smaller residences, they remain unchanged on the exterior, still existing in harmony and unity and maintaining a completeness and contained sense of satisfaction which is enhanced by the blazing blue sky and the light, dancing breath of spring air infused with sun.

(2014)

Hammoon

I walk through the wooden gate of the thirteenth- century church at Hammoon, on which is carved 'enter into His gates with thanksgiving.' I am indeed full of thanks for this wonderful day which sustains a buoyant brilliance, warm and resonant with birdsong. It feels refreshingly cool inside the church, the sunlight clear, softly gilding the stone floor, illuminating the carved wood of the pulpit and the simple altar. The sweet, shrill, repetitive, call of a bird outside picks persistently at the interior of this tiny church- an interior, which is stilled like a heart at peace within itself.

Coming out of the church into the sleepy sun-drenched lane, I spy the Tudor manor house a few doors down, an intriguing architectural curiosity built around 1500, plain and rustic but boasting an ornate, two-storey porch, which was added slightly later [63]. This incongruous mix of architectural styles is further emphasised by the presence of a large thatched roof which appears to shade the upper windows so that they seem like eyes peeping bashfully from beneath a thick fringe, making the manor deliciously characterful, yet understated, being built unobtrusively at the corner of the village. In the strong sunlight its corallian limestone façade exudes the soft, muted creamy gold of mellowed age and warmth, having lost the pride of its youthful, important past.

Its early history was opulent. Owned by the Mohun family (the name of the hamlet, being a combination of the Saxon *Ham* meaning *enclosure* and *Mohun* [52]), it was one of many manors in Dorset and Devon given to them as a reward for assisting William the Conqueror. After ceasing to be in their possession, the manor house at Hammoon eventually decreased its status, becoming a farm, and is apparently still used as one [63]. The first time I heard of the Mohune family, was when I read J. Meade Faulkner's book *Moonfleet* as a child. I wonder if Faulkner had known about this family name and slightly altered it to use in his novel. He may have even known about this house, for it was later owned by a John Trenchard, presumably of the Trenchard family of Wolfeton near Dorchester, and whose name is also shared by the main character in *Moonfleet,* although this could be a coincidence.

We wander away from the church, past an organic dairy farm. To our left, chickens cluck and peck around in a garden ablaze with daffodils. Following footpaths out into the fields we walk without jackets in the shadow of Hambledon Hill, revelling in the subtle warmth of spring, the air effervescent, like champagne at a party ready to pop. Nature seems to tremble as if waiting to burst into the full force of life: birds have begun to sing, flowers to open…

Hambledon Hill, slightly hazy despite the distilled light, is speckled with sheep; the soft, flowing lines of its ramparts suddenly discernible, making this immediately identifiable as being from the Iron Age, which has left its legacy in various earthworks all over the county. It is strange to think that before the fields in which we walk were fashioned, these fluid contours were re-enforced with ramparts. They were here even before the Normans conquered and the old church and manor were built. The Mohuns would surely have seen the same sight if they had care to come this way.

Our path takes us out onto a disused railway track where wild primroses climb the banks and the branches of the trees strike an interlocking web of shadows, a complex conundrum of light and shade. Peacock butterflies sun themselves and cabbage whites flitter about. The fact that their airborne lives are so short, rather contradicts the traditional symbol of the immortal soul, which butterflies stood for in ancient Greek and

Roman mythology and in early Christianity when they were considered as a symbol of the resurrection [4]. Yet as I watch them now, fluttering about the embankment on such a heavenly day, the sunlight catching their wings, they are indeed living miracles, having come into being through transformation and metamorphosis. Life is a miracle in all its forms, and so much marvel and wonder which we encounter in nature is taken for granted; the designs and fragrance of flowers, the intricacy and complexity of a skylark's joyful call weaving threads of sound through a blue sky, sunlight and shade, all contained in the cycles of the seasons. New life, birth and even death are perhaps the most poignant in springtime. Now another miracle manifests right in front of my eyes, for despite the fact that man once carved a railway line through this landscape, the oppressive presence of the train perhaps frightening wildlife, the track has now become its haven.

The railways, often opposed by local people as they were considered in their day to be a threat, actually brought change and progress in the form of industrialisation and a better standard of living, thereby transforming life forever. However, this came at a cost, for the poor and very young were exploited, their effort comprising the backbone of the industrial revolution, without which no wealth would have been generated for the nation. I think of this as we walk along, and am profoundly grateful to those people. However I wonder whether it was really necessary, once the nation had become industrialised and wealthy, to close many of the railways in the name of cutting costs. Because of this, which mainly took place during the nineteen sixties, we have at least been left with a network of recreational trailways around the country and this trailway is no exception. It has seemingly stepped back in time to pre-industrial days, a well-trodden path, which echoes simultaneously with the silent tread of time and the perpetual motion of life and as we resume our steps along it, the butterflies continue to dance in the sunlight, baby goats call from a farm, snowdrops dip their dying heads but celandines and daisies lift and turn their full, bright faces towards the sun.

(2014)

*

Living also in the shadow of Hambledon Hill is Stepleton House of the lost hamlet of Iwerne Stepleton. As the road bends around parkland to avoid cutting through the houses' estate, I think of a weary, bone –juddering, horse-drawn carriage clattering the final steps of a seemingly endless journey. How welcoming this place must have been even through the mixture of hope and apprehension which a young Italian teenager might have felt. In 1766, this fourteen-year-old of the name Mutius Philippus Vincentus Franciscus Xaverius Clementi (better known as Muzio Clementi) left his silversmith father along with his family and the bustle of his native Rome to reside in this sheltered, verdant spot in the heart of Dorset. His patron, Peter Beckford, country squire and owner of Stepleton House, had spotted Clementi's musical talent and potential while travelling in Italy. As a lover of languages (speaking four fluently) and the arts, he felt that he could help further Muzio's future by bringing him to England.

It is impossible to know the true feelings of this Italian musician. Perhaps he was overwhelmed on first sighting of the house; a comfortable country abode of graceful symmetry and elegant proportions, quintessentially English in character and nestled in gentle green and wooded surrounds. It must have surely struck a chord of inspiration, providing a peaceful and learned environment for composing and practice, the whole balanced exterior of the house alluding to a harmonious order behind those calm ashlar walls. The Dorset sun, not being as hot and bright as in Italy, perhaps created a more placid ambience. On the other hand, the tranquillity and remoteness of this rural retreat could have also filled this teenager with a dread of isolation and boredom, a pining for the colour, warmth and vibrant spontaneity of his native city and culture now a world away. Unfamiliarity can bring on a strange feeling of insecurity; it seeps from the clouds on a dull day and is intimated in the wind. However, rain and truculent weather cause the landscape to exude a greenness of an intensity which perhaps rivalled anything he had seen at home. This could have seemed strange and strangeness can either stimulate apprehension or curiosity. Therefore, we have to hope that homesickness was perhaps tempered by novelty and that the excitement of a new experience opened an enquiring mind in the knowledge that this place somehow brought opportunity.

Whether country life suited or not, Clementi nevertheless remained at Stepleton for seven years, working hard to perfect his art while no doubt providing in- house classical soirees to entertain Beckford's esteemed guests. With a resident musician of such promise on location, Stepleton must surely have earned a reputation for culture and fashion. I imagine the graceful notes of the piano twinkling across the grounds, mingled with lingering laughter from an open window on summer's evenings or the same window shrouding candlelit concerts which glowed through closed curtains on winter nights. Behind that window, I imagine an elegant room full of women sporting towers of powdered hair and adorned in heavy rustling silks, accompanied by corpulent men, rosy-faced and sucking on pipes, clapping appreciatively and enthusiastically at every interlude while the young pianist paused. Some of the younger women, no doubt secretly tried to catch his eye. As an Italian and a talented musician, he would have appeared exotic, accomplished and therefore probably very attractive to them. However, under the surveillance of their parents or older brothers, they would have had no chance, as musicians were considered of a lower status and not a suitable match for a woman of title and wealth.

In 1773, aged twenty -one, Clementi moved to London, the centre of the musical world at that time. There he became something of a celebrity; the most sought-after piano teacher in the city as well as soloist, composer and director of the King's Theatre ensemble of musicians at the Haymarket. As his fame spread, he became internationally renowned, being of particular inspiration to the young Beethoven. He apparently possessed a technical brilliance and even took Mozart on in a piano 'duel' in Vienna in 1781. Later, back in London, however, it is thought that he faced further competition from Haydn who resided in the city from 1791 to 1792 and again in 1794 to 1795. He nevertheless retained his reputation as a piano instructor and produced several major publications during the early nineteenth century until his retirement in 1830 when he moved to Lichfield and then to Evesham [25].

It is also interesting to point out that as well as being a remarkable piano tutor; publishing books on his technique which would have probably helped educate many of the young women of society in their accomplishment of the instrument, there are also instruments bearing his name. One of these pianos is housed at Jane Austen's cottage in Chawton.

Clementi is buried at Westminster Abbey and his marble reads 'The father of the pianoforte. His fame as a musician and composer acknowledged throughout Europe procured him the honour of a public interment in this cloister. Born at Rome 1752 died at Evesham 1832.'

When the fourteen-year -old first arrived in Dorset he could perhaps only dream about such a future and it is also perhaps fair to say that without coming to Stepleton with its lack of distractions, and with a wealthy patron providing opportunities for introducing Clementi into high society, this young musician might not have established the foundations on which to build such success in the city and in turn make his valuable contribution to musical history for over sixty years of his life.

Winterbourne Tomson

A journey into the Winterbourne Valley on a calm morning flooded with sunshine is idyllic. Impulsively we follow the road, seeing a sign for an historic church, and stop outside St Andrew's in the hamlet of Winterbourne Tomson. Lush clumps of daffodils flank an old brick and flint wall. Everything is radiant in the sunshine; shadows crisply defined so that the flint and heathstone, used to construct the exterior walls of the church, stand out in characteristic definition and exude a well-weathered age.

This is an enchanting spot, which draws one into a dream: a farm, an old manor house, a few thatched cottages and, silent in the sunshine, the single-cell, humble Norman church, standing completely simple and elemental in its design, the Norman apse at its east end, elegantly diffusing the sunlight which fades softly into a slight shadow around the curved surface. I am overjoyed to have stumbled by chance upon such an obviously old and architecturally interesting church, which I never knew existed, and which yields more surprises.

We wander through the sun-soaked, grassy churchyard, flanked on one side by a picturesque old cottage and a tree about to erupt with pink blossom. Across the fields and through the trees in the distance, tower the chimneys and gables of Anderson Manor, a Jacobean manor house, which takes on all the elegant proportions and symmetry to make it aesthetically and completely satisfying. Young inquisitive cows from the neighbouring farm push their black and white faces up to the fence which lies adjacent to the church door. My husband, who has worked in dairy farming, talks to the cows and they seem to respond to him as if he had a special way with them. There is a look of gentle trust in their large, limpid eyes and they push their noses through the fence. These calm creatures provide a contrast to the clamouring cries of rooks, whose raucous cacophony sears the still air.

We leave them in the strong sunlight and push open the wooden, nail -studded, eighteenth- century church door. The interior stimulates simultaneous feelings of surprise and delight as we are greeted with pure simplicity: white and wood. Slim oak beams follow the short length of the ceiling and then cross, following the curves of the barrel roof and the apse, decorated at each intersection by a carved boss. I recognize the stylized petals of a rose, a swirling shape perhaps resembling a knot. The whole ceiling reminds me of the skeletal hull of an overturned boat, maybe an ark. Pure sunlight shafts through side windows across slightly sloping walls, white walls washed with lime. All the wood supporting the structure of this place is riddled with worm, pitted with little porous holes. Although restoration was undertaken in 1931 with money raised from the sale of Thomas Hardy's architectural manuscripts, and recent restoration has also been carried out, this wood remains wonderfully worn and old. The sparseness and simplicity of this church seems to suggest the faith of the local country people. Devoid of ostentation, dark Victorian wood and heavily carved decoration, the interior breathes a light airiness of hope without the stifling suffocation of religion. The fitted furnishings here comprise simple, early Georgian boxed pews, screen and pulpit made of panelled oak, bleached by time, and donated by locally born William Wake, who became the Archbishop of Canterbury from 1716, when he was fifty nine, until his death in 1737 [23].

As we turn towards the open door to leave, the sun floods in from the bright outside like light flooding into a soul. Beneath an old, worn, wooden gallery, I see a single bell rope which must link to a bell in the weather boarded bell-cote. I do not want to leave, and I dally in this living museum where time has stopped for centuries, savouring its sanctuary of simplicity and stillness while the displaced and distant cries of rooks pervade the peace, reminding us that the world outside ceases to stand still. This interior is a beating heart of trust, a testimony to silent, steadfast faith, a symbol which proves that faith can survive in quiet hope and perseverance, despite being on the brink.

Through flat fields in the vicinity of the church, winds the small winterborne itself. The river, only fills in the winter months, hence being called winter bourne, or winter stream [52]. The flat plain of the valley sweeps away silently while some swans paddle in the remainder of the February floods. Presumably the village was once bigger, perhaps covering some of these fields, the other side of which, lies the A31, seeming distant, belonging to another world. And as I stand here in this present, savouring the trio of cottage, farm and manor with the little church, unique in character, basking in blazing sunlight and rubbing shoulders with contented cows, there is nowhere I would rather be.

(2014)

Corfe Castle

The view of the ruined old castle at Corfe stands out against black clouds as sunlight floods full onto its face. We are heading for Corfe Common, which sweeps proudly away to the south of the village, having managed to escape the Enclosure Acts of the eighteenth and nineteenth centuries. One of the purposes of these acts was to prevent land from becoming over-grazed and impoverished, as well as to encourage people to work for their keep rather than to use common land to graze their animals and collect fuel and turf. It was with the Enclosure Acts that many of the hedgerows arrived, these rich and valuable sources of biodiversity, which are now ironically threatened again as a result of intensive farming practices. It was also with the coming of these acts that many of the poor left, driven off the land, to seek work in the expanding industrial cities. In Dorset, however, industry had not developed significantly and the county remained primarily agricultural. As the Enclosure Acts meant that land was now owned, poaching became a punishable act and farm labourers were forced to work for a pittance in order to try to feed their families [31]. It is interesting to note that the first Enclosure Act in Britain actually occurred in 1604 at Radipole, a green enclave, once a village, on the outskirts of Weymouth, where Norman church and churchyard are contiguous with the impressive gabled sixteenth- century manor house and pathways wander down past the River Wey as it flows into the RSPB nature reserve of Radipole Lake.

Back at Corfe Common, the close-cropped turf, grazed by centuries of life stock, is still frequented by a few ponies, flicking their tails and looking at us with gentle, searching eyes. Sun floods the slopes, illuminating lines and contours on this well-trodden territory which, in low light reveals deeper secrets, for at that time, one can discern the furrows of medieval tracks pressed indelibly into the turf. These are described as 'hollow ways', and mark the rutted courses that were habitually taken by carts and sleds pulling stone from the quarries to the south, across the common and up into the village itself to be worked by stonemasons, as medieval archaeological findings would suggest, before being transported inland [26].

Sunlight and cloud shadows play chasing games across the Purbeck Ridge today. A small settlement, more a collection of farm buildings and a big house, nestles in the valley, softly gilded by sunshine beneath the ridge's strong shadow. The large, old farmhouse marks the existence of one of the many lost villages in the area, probably once a Saxon estate. As the light changes suddenly, the valley is plunged into shadow, a spread of gold diffusing across the ridge above it.

To our south rises the tower of Kingston Church surrounded by undulating sweeps of verdant pasture, the trees stroking the green slopes with elongated shadows like long lashes sweeping soft cheeks. A chiffchaff sings brightly and we are soaked in sunshine, which now enhances colours and textures, branches frilled with lichen, twiggy bushes and budding gorse. It is silent here and when the bright toot of the steam train echoes optimistically across the valleys, it is if we had been transported back to Victorian England lying in the cradle of the modern, industrial world.

As we wander back to Corfe down its lazy backstreets of grey stone cottages, each with an attractive spring garden bathing in sunshine, I feel equally lazy. Dwarf daffodils peep from stone- walls alongside grape hyacinths and bright pots of primulas, and the strong breeze sighs through the sunlight. Beyond the cottages rises the comfortable tower of St Mary's Church, looking protectively over the village. The castle itself, once a royalist stronghold and the home of the Bankes family, now stands as a casualty of the Civil War. Just as the common appears so tranquil now, the castle, remaining dignified in its defeat, has resumed an elegance; a mysterious haunting beauty, which stands as an icon against the skyline. The whole village, peaceful on this dreamy day, makes it seem impossible that it was once thronging with war and the centre of so much suffering and violence.

Likewise, it is hard to imagine the constant activity across the now silent common, whose subtle lines only allude to the time when convoys of traffic constantly trailed across its undulating slopes in the form of stone and most possibly contraband (The rector of Corfe apparently was the contraband controller for the Isle of Purbeck [53]). I wonder therefore, if St Mary's was, like so many other Dorset churches, used for storing contraband and whether, as was often the case, ghost stories were invented by smugglers to deter potential witnesses from coming to the churchyard after dark and discovering their clandestine goings-on [53]. We often hold a romantic illusion of the past, tending to assume that it was more idyllic than the present. Perhaps in some aspects it was, however, I am not convinced that it was always the case. With automation and laws to protect workers, we surely receive more leisure time, a luxury that was perhaps not perceived by the majority of villagers past, who tilled the land, managed the forests, brought up large families and, along with their children, toiled for their daily bread. By contrast, we walk at leisure, taking time to absorb the atmosphere of this sun-soaked landscape and I watch a solitary runner appearing and disappearing up and down the slopes of the common, enjoying his recreation. In the past, physical exercise was a necessity, not a pleasure. Modern man has the freedom, enjoying the indulgent peace of nature, appreciating its beauty, revelling in valuable time and space, concepts which perhaps in the past were dulled by the monotony of toiling for daily existence, the endless activity, noise and lack of personal space. To those of former generations, the countryside was perhaps also a place to be feared, a place where lawless people and wild animals lurked, while to us it, and small, aesthetic places like Corfe Castle, seems a secure, delightful escape from the daily threats and pressures of urban life.

(2014)

*

One of my early visits to Corfe Castle was a primary school trip. We were taught that it was once owned by the Royal Family and our imaginations ran wild with the images of prisoners being left to die in desperate dungeons, tortures and bloodshed, boiling oil being poured onto enemies, the sudden drawing of the portcullis, and unfortunate targets being shot at through arrowslits, which were recessed in the embrasures of thick stone walls. On the no less quieter, but perhaps more merry side, we imagined beautiful ladies in lofty headdresses being serenaded by chivalrous men on horseback, rowdy banquets with the bashing of pewter and the passing round of mead, perhaps all taking place under the surveillance of a stag's antlers, the proud trophy of the numerous hunting expeditions which no doubt took place in the surrounding forests under King John. Our school was a creative school, bringing the past into the present through inspiring, evocative teaching, which perhaps contributed to my interest in places historic and archaeological.

Now as I wander around the castle's empty shell, my mind is drawn more towards its fight for survival. No longer a royal establishment, it became the family home of Royalist Sir John Bankes, who worked as Lord Chief Justice for King Charles I. With the Civil War, one can only consider the intolerable situation which his wife, Lady Mary Bankes, found herself in protecting the castle single-handed for three years while her husband was constantly away on business for the King. She not only defended the castle from the constant advances of the Roundheads, but cared for her young children, enclosed within the protective castle walls. Looking up at these walls now, in their ruins, I imagine them once hung with tapestries of complex design which caught the flickering glow of roaring fires from massive stone fireplaces. I imagine the furnishings: rich ornamental rugs, deeply carved chests of polished oak filled with fine fresh linen, huge four-poster beds, which, in former times were the most expensive and prized pieces of furniture in a house, due to the fact that there were no landings so that people had to walk through adjacent bedrooms. I imagine the detail of the embroidery on the counterpanes, the heavy curtains which shut out the light and gave the sleeper privacy. I imagine items of silver, gold and precious stones, gilt frames full of shady portraits, distinguished men and women, some of them royal. I also envisage cellars of liquor alongside supplies and gunpowder for the cannons. However, all this wealth could not have been a substitute for the insecurity which Lady Bankes must have felt as her home was constantly besieged.

From the ruins, one looks down over the cluster of grey stone cottages of the village and St Mary's Church, settled in the green bowl of the valley and nestling below the castle's protective gaze. The church, which was overrun by Roundheads, suffered extensive destruction and many cottages suffered a similar fate, leaving their inhabitants homeless so that they too found refuge in the castle. While most of Dorset had fallen to the rebels, Corfe Castle's impenetrable bastion remained staunchly royalist. It was only after her husband had died that Lady Bankes was betrayed by someone from within the castle itself: a Colonel Pitman, who apparently, tired of serving the king, allowed the disguised enemy secret entrance to the castle, so that it was finally brought to its knees and fell in the early spring of the year 1646. Lady Mary and her children, stripped of their possessions by greedy looters who used them to furnish and build their own country houses, were forced to leave [6]. Oliver Cromwell then ordered the total destruction of the castle by blowing it up so all that is left now is its iconic ruin, hauntingly beautiful on a misty morning, or in any light. Still standing proud, protective, yet defeated, it serves as a solitary lesson that wealth and status are no guarantee of security, and no one in life is exempt from the possibility of suffering and hardship. Fortunately for Lady Mary, Charles II returned from exile and the Royal Family was re- established. Thus she was recompensed, her knighted son building Kingston Lacy as a new family home [6].

Corfe was not the only castle in Dorset to meet its fate in the Civil War. At Chideock, a mound in a field is all that is left to testify to the Royalist castle which once stood there, also destroyed by Roundheads in around 1645.

APRIL

The Blue Pool

We stand at the edge of the Blue Pool, captivated by its capricious depths, which today, in strong sunlight expound a deep, delicious sigh of turquoise. On other days I have seen different shades of blue breathing here, passing through the spectrum of blue green to even blue grey. The pool was once a clay quarry and particles of clay, still present in the water, refract sunlight causing the blue. It is a peaceful place, a place to wander, relax and dream. As we traverse through the surrounding pine forest with wonderful views over sweeping stretches of adjacent heathland, elusive female sika deer peep curiously at us from between the trees. They are so shy that they only catch a glimpse of us before they are gone, flighty, free, disappearing silently and swiftly into the trees. Squirrels are equally nimble, scurrying up vertical tree trunks and springing effortlessly from branch to branch. Freedom feels abundant here.

I wonder if the clay had not been extracted, whether this magical, whimsical place would have ever been created. Doubtlessly not. It is therefore one instance where man's actions have perhaps enhanced the landscape, for this place holds a unique beauty in itself, one which is unexpectedly soft and soothing in the hard, brown wilderness of heathland which surrounds it.

One forgets that all the old houses around the county would have been built from local stone quarried from the hills and the coast. This accounts for the varied characters of villages in different parts of the county. It also shows that man has shaped his landscape to some extent, by gouging great lumps of stone from the ground. The landscape that we see today, therefore might not be quite the same as that seen by our predecessors. Nature is used to reclaim, soften and renew so that the open quarries, the mighty incisions in the earth are 'healed' with green and time. In the case of this place though, the scar has been transformed by water into a world of wonder, reflection and perhaps rejuvenation, providing a beautiful escape, where people of all ages like to come.

(2010)

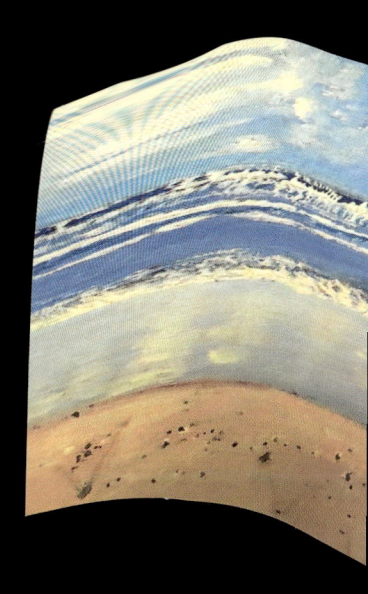

April

Fontmell Magna

It is early April and ducks swim on Collyns Brook at Fontmell Magna. Colours collide in clear waters as trees and foliage become fluid, reflected in the swaying depths like a watercolour which is in the process of being painted. Brown, green, silver and blue, slide and collide before fusing and drifting apart in a constant flow of movement. The song of a chiffchaff is sweet on the air, a tiny wren scuffles in a bush and we are being watched by an adolescent swan with attitude. He asserts himself at first by wading out of the brook to tentatively hiss at us, but when realizing that we mean no harm, he establishes a cool demeanour, cruising casually, as he turns his back and drifts away only to return and watch us again, leaving wide, treacly ripples in his wake.

A quacking commotion reveals two drakes squabbling. Eventually one is chased away and the victor returns to his mate who has been calling intermittently, presumably to him and not to the suitor. They do some headstands together, dipping down into the clear water before retiring to the shallows where she hides in the grasses at the water's edge and he sits outside them uxoriously on guard. He is quite a little hero, a true gentleman. I wonder if they have a nest.

It never ceases to touch me the way in which birds instinctively know how to make a home, sometimes more so than humans with all our intelligence. Just the other day I saw a pair of crows taking twigs from an urban roadside in Ferndown, cramming as much as they could into their strong beaks, so intent on nest building that they were unperturbed as I walked past. While our lifestyle has modernized and changed dramatically through the centuries, theirs is essentially the same, they could be living in any century, following the same cycle of their lives.

Standing here with the sound of the water rushing into the mill behind, the flow of the stream with its interlocking criss-cross currents creating small sparking diamonds of water in the sunshine, I wonder how many ducks have made nests here at Fontmell Magna over the centuries. As daffodils leap from roadsides and the joy of spring is felt all over the old village, blending with the peaceful, historic atmosphere, the thatched cottages and the medieval church, I also wonder whether our lives have perhaps not also stood still a little longer.

(2013)

Fontmell Down and Compton Abbas

From Fontmell Down it seems as if the whole of Dorset is stretched out like a living map before us. On this April day, radiant with sunshine but with a little bite in the wind, I watch shadows shift across hills and valleys with the coursing of the clouds above. The view across Blackmore Vale allows the eyes to roam for miles: a flat valley of tiny fields filtering into a wash of blue at the horizon. In the foreground nestles the village of Compton Abbas. Its focal point is the long slim tower and spire of the church, making it look, to me, as if it could almost be a village in Germany.

To our left, sun-swept slopes plunge down in deep curves to a narrow valley cushioned with bushes and crossed with the lines of trees. There are so many contours and gradients, flowing curves and filtered light providing an aesthetic, organic harmony. The valley bathes silently in the sun, slightly hazy in the ultraviolet, its bushes glittering and shimmering. All stands untouched, soaking up sunlight and silence, sweetened by the odd skylark, the cry of a crow. Only the distant road breaks the spell, that and the purr of old bi-planes winging their way overhead, circling the down and returning to Compton Abbas airfield, the highest in Europe, so I've heard. It feels as if we have gone back in time to the Second World War. Without this constant anthrophony, I wonder what it might have been like centuries before and whether the sounds of spring were richer and more diverse. Undoubtedly yes, for so would have been the eco-system. Soundscape ecology is now used to understand changing habitats, yet perhaps the lack of birdsong today is simply because spring has come late this year; there are still no wild flowers or grasses on this downland site.

Later we visit the village of Compton Abbas 'the farm or estate in a valley' [52], with its intriguing church, all the more intriguing in that it was built in 1868 but displays the obvious signs of Norman architecture about its entrance doorway; zigzag tooth patterns infused in strong sunlight. A quiet, sunny churchyard sleeps in the sunshine, simple and natural, full of clumps of pale primroses, symbols of early youth [48] flourishing alongside vibrant daffodils, symbols of regard [48]. Beyond the churchyard, small pastures stretch away towards Fontmell Magna. The quiet rise and fall of the land, the small silhouettes of vintage planes still turning and wheeling across the blue above Fontmell Down like birds of prey make all seem settled.

I feel the dead are at peace here, happily buried in the soil of the beautiful world which they loved. These are people who could have grown up and experienced their early youth in this village and its surrounds, their legacy now living on amongst the flowers in this peaceful place of respect and repose.

(2013)

Holloway

Early on a Sunday morning in mid- April, my husband and I are setting off for a short break in the West Country. It is a perfectly clear morning, the golden sunlight trailing through trees, flooding bushes and branches with radiance, the air hanging light and carefree with a fresh feeling of excitement and anticipation as we begin our journey. From the road I see Canford School, resplendently gilded in frail morning light. The sun-flooded fields are full of golden-fleeced sheep tending their lambs and the twin towers of Wimborne Minster rise up a little further along the road beyond the sweep of the Stour and its water meadows where we have spotted white swans sitting on large ungainly nests. In a few hours, this town will be ringing with the joyful peals of bells, calling people to the special Palm Sunday service. I remember as a child, being part of the congregation, which before the service, snaked its way around the streets in a hymn-singing procession. Despite feeling conspicuous, I always quite enjoyed the lively, happy mood. There was a real sense of community and I felt as if we were partaking of an ancient custom. In the church, a huge cross, made entirely of spring flowers, had been laid out in the baptistery. It was so bright and fragrant that I found it fascinating. This was also perhaps a tradition passed through the ages as was maybe the hot-cross bun hunt on Good Friday when we went with the adults, on foot across the fields to Pamphill to look for hot cross buns hanging from the bushes.

After an hour or so, our drive to Devon is interrupted by a detour into the depths of West Dorset and breakfast at a bright sunny café in the small, golden village of Symondsbury. Symondsbury is located at the centre of one of the former numerous deer parks which existed in Dorset between the eleventh and fourteenth centuries [44] and is now part of the one thousand five hundred acre Symondsbury estate, a protected heritage landscape. We have come here to walk a few holloways, those paths which delve horizontally and vertically into the depths of the earth, a secret and secluded world of history and nature waiting to be explored. After breakfast, we set off. It is half past nine, we leave a few locals eating in the café, and wander on past a handful of cars, parked on verges outside the church from which the strains of the organ waft loudly and clearly across the sunny churchyard- *'All glory laud and honour to thee Redeemer King'* is the traditional hymn being belted out by this tiny congregation. If their cars weren't here, we could be in the time of Thomas Hardy. The hymn and the birdsong make my heart sing in response, a joy reflected in the flood of fresh morning sunlight which flows over all surfaces and seeps through the petals of daffodils in the churchyard. We continue on our way.

Inside the holloway, or shute, as it is sometimes called, we enter a private, secret world, shared by a few chiffchaffs whose sweet, persistent disyllabic call carries through the stillness. The path has sunk down so that the sides are only a couple of meters high, covered in the green leaves of spring foliage, ferns and moss. It is like walking through an idyllic dream, which is not fully understood, softly treading back and down through layers of time, a place lying undisturbed through the centuries. And suddenly on this beautiful morning, the shrill bleating of a lamb cuts through the silence, pulling us back to the present outside world. Climbing to the top of the bank, we look across a spread of green fields which sweep away in enclaves and undulations. From the field a ewe stamps at us, protecting her two white lambs, chubby and curious. She stamps again, agitated and we retreat back into the holloway.

Later along the path, sandstone walls rise many meters high so that we seem to be walking through more of a gorge than a pathway, and although it is supposed to have been worn by constant human traffic traversing the same route through the ages, I find it hard to believe that this was entirely man made. I wonder if perhaps these early people might have found the track of an ancient water-course, which would have been easier to follow, a channel carved through the soft sandstone by waters racing to the sea. I have no idea, but I am overwhelmed by the sense of complete self-containment and calm which this thriving eco-system expounds.

Today bright sunlight enters the holloway through gaps in the interlocking tree canopy above. The leafless trees allow sharp sunlight to flood through their branches, creating beautiful flowing networks of shadows across sun-gilded sandstone walls, over the golden sunken floor, and across the fecund vegetation which clasps the shallower sides of the holloway. Silence. Gold light locked with shadow in a chaos of complex colours, textures and patterns, the writhing contortions of roots, rough surface of stone, ferns glinting silver, green; primroses, bluebells, wood garlic clinging to the banks. Where these banks are shallower, coppiced trees with satin- smooth silvery trunks grow along the top, where the banks are higher and darker, the twisted tree-roots seem to wriggle their way free from the earth, like badgers emerging from a set, or rabbits from a hole (and there are many intriguing holes in the bank, leading into the interior world of warrens with their shadowy, intricate mazes of rabbit pathways). It is as if the secrets of the subterranean world are being exposed as the trees tunnel beneath, seeking water with their curious labyrinths of roots like arteries and veins. Without roots, they cannot survive.

For a moment, I see this as symbolic of man, who possesses an innate curiosity for knowing his roots and understanding his origins, knowledge of which perhaps brings him more emotional stability and identity. Then as I look up at a tiny chiffchaff singing on a branch with all its might, I realize it doesn't rely on roots, for it will have probably migrated all the way from the Mediterranean or West Africa; a tiny bird going it alone in a big world, each journey such an amazing, unsung miracle. We forget that a bird's experience of the world is completely different from our own, for they have the ability to perceive the Earth's magnetic fields, as well as possessing natural skills in astronavigation, using the stars to guide them on their instinctive journeys across continents.

Drawing my mind back to the depths of the holloway, I am attracted by its silent seclusion away from the magnitude of the world, the quiet excitement of stowaway protection. I wonder how many people have hidden here in the past and for what reasons- persecuted recusants, smugglers escaping the law. Even while the sun shines and the greenery glistens, no one knows we are here. Shards of sunlight play patterns with shade, and the bird still sings its heart out against the deep echo of bumble bees droning around the rock faces where the strata is clearly exposed and may even contain some fossils. Geologists maintain that these rock layers, like tree-rings, can reveal the age of the place and, in the case of rocks, account for various stages in its pre- history, expounding stories, birthing theories. I wish I knew for certain the truth of how these pathways became such deep, wilderness places and who walked them. As well as the possibility of smugglers, sneaking secret contraband up from the nearby coast at West Bay or Seatown, perhaps these paths were also used by villagers going about their daily business to other villages, by farm-labourers, drovers herding animals, by church-goers and priests. But now the paths stay silent, only leading the way back in time to a present land of no apparent purpose other than for growing crops and grazing life stock. Did there use to be settlements here which are now forgotten? Perhaps long lost villages which are now turned over to fields, their secrets buried beneath the earth.

The walls remain many meters high, adorned with exposed tree-roots, which hang in dark, strangely grotesque loops and swirls. Fresh sandstone lumps litter the path, evidence of a recent landslide, yet on a sunny day nothing feels threatening or dangerous. In some places I notice that people have carved their initials into the soft stone while carved eyes and faces watch us secretly. I wonder what man's obsession for making his mark is. Perhaps it is simply a disregard for the natural and beautiful, a way of defacing it (or adding faces to it!) or perhaps it is to conquer a wild place, to claim something, to hold an association, a 'territory'. I remember some Spanish friends once showing me ancient petroglyphs hidden in secret, almost inaccessible caves somewhere in the Pyrenees. We entered the caves by means of a ladder vertical against a sheer rock face, a rather vertiginous descent. These obscure images, amongst other symbols, which I have since forgotten, were predominantly of stick-like men and animals, presumably depicting a hunt. Perhaps the pictures themselves connected the cave dwellers with a sense of identity or self-expression in the same way that graffiti does today.

Coming out of the dark 'cave' of the holloway into the bright, sharp sunlight is like being abruptly woken from a beautiful dream into an even more beautiful reality. It is perhaps akin to the sleeping beauty waking to find her prince, for the reality of the outside world is radiant and intense, fusing with the experience of the holloway and leaving one feeling wholly exhilarated. We feel like explorers returning from a faraway place, full of adventures and discoveries. It is not only an experience of something amazing, but an exploration of the senses and an activation of the imagination which is so satisfying, and there are many of these paths to discover. As they converge, I can't help wondering once again if perhaps there was an important place here, a meeting place, a trading place, a village in which all these roads met, left in a world past, abandoned to time. This is only a speculation and I might be totally wrong, but it does seem so strange that these paths seem to stretch so far into nowhere, converging at certain points along their way.

In another holloway near Chideock, we need wellies. A stream is coursing down Hell Lane, an incongruous name for a path which was purportedly once a pilgrim route down which early Catholics walked from Symondsbury to Whitchurch Canonicorum, a nearby village famous for its saint Candida and her healing powers. The medieval shrine and relics, the only intact relics in England, except those at Westminster Abbey, are still kept within the walls of the church. We do not have time to walk all the way to Whitchurch Canonicorum, and we do not have our wellies. Before leaving, we stop to listen to a song thrush singing energetically from a blossoming tree along the path. White blossom against blue sky combined with the acrobatic convolutions and cadenzas of the bird's clear song is a delight.

We take tiny, single -track country lanes by car to Whitchurch Canonicorum, winding through an area of outstanding natural beauty which rises and falls in green hills and valleys swept with sunlight and shadows as clouds cross. The Symondsbury landmark, Colmer's Hill, crowned with pine trees at its summit which were planted at the turn of the twentieth century by Sir Philip Colfox, [11] looks almost diminished in this vast expanse of the green, somewhere through which run the unseen ruts of the holloways, like veins throbbing deep down in the heart of the earth, secluding precious secrets. History pervades above and below ground, the visible shaping our landscape, the unseen shaping our knowledge and understanding of the past.

I consider this 'natural' landscape and the extent to which man shapes a place. Without our human presence, many places would just 'be' without any history or happening attached to them. When man interacts sensitively and aesthetically with his environment; the tiny pretty village nestling in a green enclave, the manor house peeping between the trees of a wood, coppiced trees, fields, tumuli. When places evolve gradually through time and are not suddenly brutally uprooted by the ugly onslaught of industry in the name of progress, while seemingly seeking to destroy anything aesthetic or historic in its path, then the landscape and atmosphere work together in the most exquisite harmony.

Passing through the tiny, sleepy picturesque hamlet of Ryall with its old stone cottages and spring flowers, we arrive at Whitchurch Canonicorum. The church of St Candida (or St Wite), built between the twelfth and nineteenth centuries [16], comprises a mixture of stone, which has the similar, but less golden effect of the Inferior Oolite stone of which the church at Symondsbury is constructed. On this blazing sunny day, we stand outside while the interior of the church resonates with the voice of the vicar delivering a sermon, the strength and authority of his voice once again transporting me back to the Victorian era when fire and brimstone was preached. The churchyard, as with many churchyards, is peaceful, sunny, echoing with the cries of rooks and the croon of the ubiquitous collared pigeon.

We wait for the service to end, watching two donkeys being led up the road, apparently part of a Palm Sunday procession. As we wait, I begin to realise that if our ancestors had not put their faith in Jesus who rode that original donkey into Jerusalem preceding His crucifixion, none of these churches would have been built in this landscape with no pilgrims or priests to help shape holloways leading to certain shrines. It is interesting to think that the paths which people take throughout their lives, spiritually, literally or figuratively, have a direct impact on the lives of future generations. Their paths shape attitudes and beliefs, mould cultures and landscapes, forge identities. The members of our families are like links in a long chain stretching back and back through time. Their individual actions affect us personally, especially the actions of our parents in determining where and how we grew up.

The thirteenth- century shrine of Saint Candida, or St Wite (her Saxon name) is found within the church. The three oval holes, made for the purpose of inserting diseased limbs for healing or handkerchiefs or prayers, appear functional and purposeful. Many pilgrims in the past made their way to this shrine for healing or to the well at nearby Morecombelake. I imagine them, before the days of medicine, wending their way through the deep holloways intent in their purpose. Today we tend to leave cities in order to wander country paths purely for pleasure, leisure and the quiet, spontaneous experience of the natural world and its small miracles, which perhaps for some of us, bring us closer to God. These pilgrims of the past, by contrast, walked with purpose and conviction; their goal at the end of the road being the hope of a physical miracle, which would, in their eyes, bring them closer to God and perhaps change their lives forever.

(2014)

April

Circles

The A35 runs through an area of outstanding natural beauty, a paradise for photographers but also archaeologists. Not only is there Maiden Castle, the organic ripples of its ramparts best seen emerging in the evening light, but there is the nine- stone circle at Winterborne Abbas, lost in an enticing woodland glade and one of five prehistoric stone circles to be found in Dorset.

Further along the road, the humps and bumps of Winterbourne Poor Lot Barrows stud the surrounding landscape. This morning, sheep graze oblivious of this Bronze Age burial ground, early sun-shafts stretching obliquely across the grass and through their fleecy forms. According to English Heritage, the area comprises a significantly high density of barrows [35]. I have seen aerial photographs of the smooth, green landscape, long shadows of trees sweeping the countryside's graceful undulations, more shadows collecting in dips and curves while circumventing domed, sun-exposed surfaces, and can see that there are several types of round barrow. From my days as an amateur archaeologist with a local group, I can identify, with a little difficulty, their different shapes: bell, bowl, disc and pond. The latter being almost a phantom impression pitting the smooth surface of the green, like a dent in velvet, so that you have to look twice to see if they really exist. Long light and shadows illuminate these shapes and forms and create an atmosphere of intrigue. Who was buried here? How did they live and die? In what way did they think? Apart from the general consensus that it was Bronze Age man who was responsible for clearing much of our forest, over -grazing and farming much of the land, leaving topsoil depleted, we can only ever speculate on the answers to these questions, and even with archaeology, we will never truly know. The secrets lie buried along with bodies beneath silent tumuli, their ancient memories moulded into the earth so that only the landscape testifies to the truth of their existence.

(2014)

Tarrant Hinton

In the heart of the beautiful Tarrant Valley one reaches the pretty village of Tarrant Hinton, its old thatched cottages built on a side street huddled around the churchyard. St Mary's Church, built of grey stone, is heavily battlemented- rather incongruous with such a peaceful and idyllic setting. Today the churchyard basks in brilliant sunshine, sweetly nostalgic while the Tarrant takes its course beside the main street, flanked with daffodils, the sunshine searing through their petals. Ducks wander upstream, gliding through glistening waters. An old farm stands at the end of the village: Sunlight on old stone, the silent hissing of electric pylons. From somewhere a cockerel crows.

Tarrant Hinton is now famous for the Great Dorset Steam Fair. I remember going there several times as a child when it was held at Stourpaine and wandering, overwhelmed, around the vast array of tents with their allure and bright lights. Everywhere was excitement for a child: colourful carousels, barrel organs playing music, plenty of rides, stalls and games, candy floss machines spinning out miles of pink and white sugary fluff, the cloying smell of sausages and burgers being grilled, soft drinks, ice creams. The steam engines, standing with their tall chimneys, seemed austere, almost sinister to me, despite being painted and polished. I remember the warm, slightly sulphurous smell of steam, heavy and intoxicating, burnt coal mingling with the charcoal-grill smell of sausages, the pungent smell of beer, jolly music from gaudy fairground organs, the chatter and banter of people having fun. Nowadays I believe there are live music tents with bands as well.

Between Tarrant Hinton and Tarrant Gunville, a green wooded valley is swept with sunshine and brushed with shadows where the sun filters through naked trees which edge its perimeter. The air carries the echoing bleats of sheep and lambs. At the far end of the valley stands a big house, which, as we discover, is the rectory of Tarrant Gunville. The church associated with this establishment stands at the end of a long path flanking the wall of the rectory grounds on one side. Walking it is like embarking on a secret discovery and when we pass a Victorian lampstand and enter the churchyard through a metal gateway, it is as if we have trespassed on a little world contained within itself. Two wood pigeons; smart, plump and dignified in their dog collars, are grazing there but take fright when we enter and wing away with a flustered flap. A rabbit also hops off, the bob of its tail retreating into nearby bushes. Despite a chorus of rooks, the place is peaceful. The church of St Mary, also with its gargoyles peeking down from windows and doors, apparently dates from the thirteenth century so that despite being almost entirely restored in the nineteenth century, many of the original architectural features have been kept intact.

Sunlight flows deliciously across old stone, spilling onto sleeping graves, plunging primroses into pools of light and dancing through daffodils. It floods into the old porch, illuminating a small spring flower display, which indicates that there is indeed a community here, although the village, with its thatched cottages and old almshouse is completely silent and we see no-one.

Beyond Tarrant Gunville lies the small village of Stubhampton after which the road cuts through green valleys bordered by wooded copses. Silence rebounds upon silence, creating a vacuum of magnified peace, again only interrupted by the bleats of sheep and lambs, which ricochet around the valley, and the rasps of pheasants in a nearby thicket. Above us wheels a raptor, freely coursing the currents, serene against blazing blue. It almost seems to float in a different world, elevated on a dimension high above our own, yet sustained by the silence just as ours is. Suddenly it plunges, entering our world, diving into the green valley with the sheep, before rising up again, wings spanned, heading out towards the forest. Time has ceased to exist here. No cars pass us and it is only the languid drone of a plane passing high above that brings us back into the twenty first century. It is as if for an instant before, the dimensions of time coexisted with the dimensions of space, forming one world into which things from other dimensions could enter: the bird high in the blue above plunging into the green valley, the plane entering timelessness from modernity, and yet all existing simultaneously in the present; different dimensions fusing to create the complex, wondrous atmosphere of the whole.

(2013)

Spetisbury

We pull up in Spetisbury, from the Anglo-Saxon *speht*, meaning *woodpecker*, and *byrig* meaning earthworks [52]. Although only April, the day is sizzling with an estival heat, everything brilliant and clearly defined. As we walk across the fields, I catch a snapshot glimpse of the church framed in flowering blackthorn. We walk on past an old mill and through its garden, serene in blazing sunshine. Bright kingcups shine abundantly around water; a profusion of plants casting lazy, layers of light and shade and all the time a vibrant, shimmering green intensity. We amble through a field fringed with more blackthorn and down an old road near the hamlet of Tarrant Crawford where a strong breeze blows so that slopes of daffodils wave their yellow heads and majestic trees creak.

At the end of the path in complete seclusion stands the twelfth- century church of St Mary, the last remaining legacy of Tarrant Abbey, which once stood on the same site. Lonesome yet serene, it seems to silently reflect on all it has witnessed of people past, standing quietly and inconspicuously by itself while bees bumble about and daffodils dance in the churchyard. I am delighted to have stumbled upon such an unexpected place; one that I had never known was here. We enter its silent sanctuary, immediately being powerfully embraced by quietude, the air infused with damp and age. Sunlight shafts through windows bringing spring freshness and marking the floor with symmetrical shapes of light, but it is the fourteenth- century frescoes which bring a real dimension to this understated church. As our eyes become accustomed to their phantom impressions, we see them ranged in two tiers, the upper apparently depicting scenes from the life of St Margaret of Antioch and the lower depicting morality [24]. Time stands still, frozen in faded frescoed faces, which have stared unseeing through the centuries in this secluded sanctuary away from the world. The interior stillness is an unabated breath which respires almost imperceptibly and with which sounds from the outside world meld; the optimistic persistence of a chiffchaff, the swell of the breeze through branches. As inside all old churches, there is a sense of security, continuity, a feeling of faith followed through time; it is felt strongly here.

Apart from the frescoes, there are ancient coffin lids and wooden box pews complimented by a sixteenth- century wooden roof crowning the nave. I am so grateful to organizations such as The Churches Conservation Trust for protecting such buildings yet sad that, although England has a bigger population than it did in centuries past, many such churches are no longer used as an active place of worship.

Reflective from the experience of the church we walk away in silence. Outside, the sun is blinding, a contrast from the dim interior, insects buzz about and birds sing. As I turn, the church retreats back into itself. We climb an exhilarating slope. Green stretches before and behind, the church recedes, its long rectangular tower still visible, snug in its surroundings. Eventually we return to Spetisbury, approaching over the fifteenth- century Crawford Bridge, with its nine arches. The Stour glides past silently, glistening with sunlight, while the golden-green, lazy lawns of large houses stretch sleepily down to its edge. We re-enter the village, with its pretty cottages, and head along a path for Spetisbury's disused railway line, imagining ghost trains echoing in the silence. Birds sing in high embankments at the top of which we look across to Spetisbury's rings- the Iron Age hillfort from which it was given half of its name.

(2012)

Walford Mill

At Walford Mill, old, peaceful, now used as a craft centre, we sight an otter. This athletic creature, perhaps full of the same energy and exuberance which is breathed by the sun-saturated air, now frolics and twists before turning and slipping away to swim, a streamlined furry body cutting through the cool, clear waters of the Stour. It seems the epitome of freedom and reflects the carefree joy and giddy ecstasy of a spring day when the air is laced with intoxicating floral scents, and everything appears pure, fresh and brightly defined in strong sunlight. We are privileged to have seen this normally nocturnal creature during the day, and are somewhat surprised, which makes it all the more wonderful.

Inside the mill, everything stands quietly still. Beautiful arts and crafts, bright bags made of hand -woven shot silk, smoothly turned wood, ceramics and jewellery with a contemporary twist; a collection of creative outpouring, perhaps inspired by days like this and by nature, as many exhibits use natural materials such as wood or stone. Now they wait like pulsing hearts, which have calmed themselves through the fulfilment of frenzied expression, for inspiration can flood through the veins with the same pounding intensity and exuberance as the strong sunlight which now floods through the mill window, but cannot retain its intensity indefinitely. Once satisfied, it sits in sweet, silent contemplation before once again striking the heart and causing the artist to create another piece in order to fulfil it. These pieces therefore are the result, holding a lasting testimony to that free-flowing, carefree inspiration and joy, which, as in the world outside, is transitory. For when the clouds come and cast dull shadows, so the day will also die down, becoming bland, washed-out. Ecstatic, enhanced emotions will then be stilled, subsiding and drifting away. Not drifting as the otter, which joyfully and freely propels itself away, but in a gradual, subconscious and almost imperceptible way, until one is staring, unimpressed, at plain paper, on which no words can be written, or a blank canvas, on which one cannot paint.

(2011)

Sturminster Newton

Silence engulfs the roar of the river Stour as it cascades behind the old mill at Sturminster Newton, sending rainbow mists spreading through shafts of sunlight. The mist refreshes my face as we walk over a small foot-bridge which takes us to the riverbank. The mill watches on, comfortable, self-contained; an aesthetically pleasing L- shape of worn red brick like a friendly, weather-beaten face nestled in its green surrounds, beyond which stretches a six-arched medieval bridge, completing the picturesque. Indeed if we had been walking here two hundred or even three hundred years past, we would have encountered the same familiar face, perhaps slightly more youthful amongst the trees.

There has been a mill on this site since Domesday, but the present mill was built in the late seventeenth century with additions made in the nineteenth century [14]. We wander along by the banks of the Stour, studded with celandines as bright as the blackbird's song. This is where the author Thomas Hardy once walked and also William Barnes, both writers no doubt inspired by these beautiful surroundings. It is often possible to observe kingfishers flitting in and out of the riverbank but there are none today. Only the sunlight ripples across angled tree trunks which grow from the banks, stretching up above the Stour which runs, glittering below. As the wavering light rebounds simultaneously off all surfaces, it is like a repeated pulse releasing waves, which reverberate as a trembling echo, constantly moving outwards and disbanding into silence.

(2013)

Waterson Manor

On a bright sunny evening we drive down from the Piddle Valley towards Blandford. Green fields are studded with grazing sheep nurturing their lambs. Cows graze in others, the evening light glowing along their flanks. Suddenly, as we pass, my eyes catch a glimpse of a manor swathed in golden evening sunlight which, with the snapshot that I see, seems to illuminate the smooth, sweeping stone curves of its southern façade. This is Waterstone Manor and at this moment it seems to be one of the most beautiful manor houses in Dorset, more beautiful on this evening than I have ever seen it in any picture.

I remember having tea here with my parents and great uncle as a very young child of about three. My great uncle, an artist in South Africa, had come over to visit us and having sold paintings to the family who lived there at that time, had made their acquaintance. My hazy recollections are of sitting in an elegant room, which seemed quite dark and overpowering to a three-year-old, despite its large, curtain-swagged windows. Everyone was very kind to me, offering sweet drinks sucked through straws, and little cakes, while shadowy portraits watched me from the walls. I remember sitting, perhaps on a window seat, but certainly peering through a large, long window at the exciting spread of bright sunny lawns outside and wishing that I could go out to them.

(2013)

Castleman Trailway

The air hangs, a close atmosphere laden with a glaring green intensity and drugged with the dusty, heavy pollen of laurel flowers. Above me, the sky curves its close canopy of glooming grey, suspense-evoking rather than threatening, as if one were contained in a tent and by contrast, everything beneath it sharing my space seems magnified: Dandelions bearing their blazing golden crowns, the dusty croon of a wood pigeon.... Then comes the peaceful patter of soft rain through trees on the Castleman Trailway, as soothing as the clear fluidity of the blackbird's song which bubbles up like a spring and penetrates the early evening gloom with optimism and joy. It makes one feel content to be here in this comfortable, contained environment which, despite the damp, and the powder-rimmed puddles, echoes with exuberance.

Milton Abbas

Sitting on a ledge in Milton Abbey porch, the air saturated with warmth and sleepy silence, I let the sun's rays finger my face as they filter through the doorway which frames a fringe of naked trees sweeping down surrounding hills to clothe the perimeter of the abbey grounds. On this drowsy afternoon the atmosphere is magnified beyond reality so that

I can hardly believe that I am here in such an idyllic location and that this beautiful weather has finally come. The dreamy voices of pigeons carrying across the valley, moulding with the curves and contours of the wooded hills enhance this feeling and only the sudden and boisterous buzz of an insect flitting through the lazy stillness brings me back to reality. Insects buzz about a different clock, their sense of time diminished to the proportion of their size. As we while away the hours in idleness they do not waste a moment of their short lives. Plants work at a slower pace, imperceptible to man. Dwarf daffodils and hyacinths bloom in pots at the doorway of the porch.

The mellow warmth of ham stone, reminiscent of Sherborne Abbey, inhibits austerity and encourages intimacy. Inside this beautiful fifteenth-century building, the smell of cold damp is quickly lost in the light, lofty airiness which travels up and up with cavernous echoes marking every footfall, every movement which we make. I dare not speak as my voice expands to reach the vaulted ceiling and is carried around in resonance before falling back down again. Sunlight floats through clear glass, marking the shadowy impressions of leaded windows across white walls and washing over the marble tomb of Joseph Damer and his beautiful wife Caroline; lifelike effigies of elegant repose, dressed in their eighteenth-century finery, the wash of white sunshine enhancing the flowing folds of their garments. Joseph, Lord of Milton, the eponymous founder of Milton Abbas, acquired the abbey estate in 1752 and made radical changes, destroying the nearby village of Middleton because, according to a friendly villager we encountered an hour earlier, the inhabitants of Middleton had been suffering from a type of malaria due to the low lying location in proximity to water. Damer had therefore instructed the building of a new village in a new location; Milton Abbas, a street of cottages in a wooded valley with an artificial lake leading up to the grounds of the abbey and Damer's new mansion, also set in a connected wooded valley and all designed by the landscape artist Lancelot 'Capability' Brown.

We had met the old man, friendly and jovial, in the centre of the village. He said he was part of a village play that was being performed in a small theatre set up in what looked like the old alms house. He informed us that all the cottages in the village were identical inside and would have housed two families each in Joseph Damer's time. Some of them are still divided up to this day. The line of white, flat-fronted thatched cottages, so unusually similar for that time that they could be the computer designed houses of a modern housing estate, create order in this chocolate box village, yet I imagine that life would have been noisy, chaotic and overcrowded. Illness would have easily spread in such conditions and it must have been impossible to sleep well. It would have been difficult to have had any privacy with the exception of solitary walks in the surrounding countryside. It must have been hard for anyone with any natural creativity or a reflective temperament and I wonder how poets and artists would have been able to find space to think. Now the village is an artist's dream. The man informed us that in addition to the overcrowding, there would have been a lot of gossip, everyone knowing everyone else's business. Today I imagine that along this row, everyone would still know everyone else but with a healthy respect. There were several people out, chatting cordially, popping into other people's houses. Our man left us, informing us that there was to be a photo shoot. He said he always talked too much, to which a couple of ladies at the other side of the road who were waiting for him, agreed. The fact that people know each other was reflected in this friendly, contained village atmosphere and although I am local to Dorset, I felt like a welcomed visitor here.

Another old man was mowing the lawns of the churchyard as we walked by, my nostrils imbibing with relish the warm, almost citrus smell of cut grass. The lazy burr of the lawnmower melded with the sunshine and the line of white cottages foreshortening down the street. Behind each house rose a terraced garden studded with clumps of yellow primroses and daffodils.

Along from the village we followed the small wooded path beside Capability Brown's tranquil, dreamy lake to the abbey. Sunlight spun a diaphanous web of ultraviolet onto its surface, melting into an oily meniscus so that the thick water rippled with a milky calm as ducks or swans glided through it. A solitary man fished, surrounded by sunshine in a golden enclave where new leaves burst from trees. Grey geese gathered on the bank of the lake and cackled. Further along the path, gentle inquisitive ponies grazed the green turf, wandering over to be stroked on the nose as we passed.

But all this happened earlier. Now we are at the abbey itself and time has stood still in this glowing porch until I hear familiar voices reaching through the silence and footsteps scrunching the gravel path outside. Standing up I meet and greet an old family friend and another musician who I know. They are playing in a concert here and we have met purely by chance. They wonder why I am not playing my viola too. I am happy that I am not. I would not want to be inside on such a beautiful day, even if it were to play music. I watch the soaring sky above, cloudless blue with the promise of summer. It enhances the stonework on the tower which climbs up and up to an infinite eternity. We exchange gossip and then they, bound by time, head back to their rehearsal while we wander back down the dreamy wooded path, heady and carefree in the timeless sunshine.

(2013)

Plush

Someone has left a scruffy wooden chair in front of an old thatched cottage in Plush. On the chair lies a tatty, well-thumbed book with dog-eared, curling pages and bent spine, an old hat trimmed with grasses lies on top, holding them open in suspense, as if the reader had to go inside for something and never returned. Tubs of daffodils and hyacinths add freshness and colour to the faded still life, completing the perfect picture. I wish I had my sketchpad. Now in the lazy light of evening sun, nothing stirs. Only a young woman cradling a baby silently ambles on the rough, sun- drenched road. There is a livid gold in the air, in the sun, which shines translucent through clumps of daffodils growing by a stream - the clear chattering of sparkling water. Long fingers of light reach out to touch the old stone of an imposing gateway, presumably to the elusive manor house, which remains a mystery down its long driveway. Rooks keep up a constant cacophony in the tall trees adjacent, scarring the silence.

This hamlet, a collection of cottages seemingly unchanged through the centuries, has the compelling power to draw you into itself. So simple it is in its purity, so enclosed in its green bowl of countryside that it feels as if we are enfolded, wrapped up in the centre of a deep sleep, a beautiful dream, away from the world. I wonder what lies behind closed doors, the hearts of the houses that radiate peace into the amber air. No clock ticks, only long shadows mark the hour, the time of day. Perhaps life has stood still here while time gently passes, the story left open on a curling page, secrets suspended until the sun has finished casting down its radiance into the bronzing bowl of the surrounding landscape. It descends with a warmth which flows like sweet liquor about the village so that, having laid sleeping or dormant for a hundred years, Plush descends into deeper somnolence beneath the stars, perhaps only ever to stir at the annual music festival when music from world- renowned classical musicians resounds from the old church and people picnic in its grounds.

(2013)

Evening Run

An April evening run with five friends to Poole Park from Westbourne. The day has been drenched in sunshine, as warm as a summer's day and the evening so elating and buoyant that we feel as if spring is actually in our steps and running seems effortless. Having been cooped up at work all day in such beautiful weather, we are like dogs let off the leash. We pound past well-tended gardens in Branksome Park where breathless white blossoms hang gold-tinted against a cloudless blue sky and comfortable houses nest on large lawns. Magnolias like elaborate candelabras drip with waxy cream and pink, the soothing croon of pigeons pervades pine trees which brush the ground with sweeping shadows and create, within their canopies, recesses of burning gold amidst deep pools of green shade while sugary pink cherry blossoms clash against the blaze of blue above.

We continue running, energized, free, the flow of warmth lubricating our limbs, the dusty heaviness of laurel flowers peppering our nostrils, our ears full of birdsong. At Baiter the water is a lively shimmering blue. Brownsea Island bathes, its sheer sandy cliffs mellow gold, its skyline leafy. The Purbeck hills roll gently behind, soft and understated, their wonderful world of idyllic dreaminess lounging just beyond our reach. Yet we experience it now, running free, and I never cease to marvel at the beauty of Poole Harbour.

Swans glide across the lake in Poole Park, their feathers fringed with golden sunlight. Running back, I revel in the wonder of sinking, searing sunlight which shafts through foliage and leaves its legacy on tree -trunks, each edged in glowing copper. After eight miles we have returned to where we began, our limbs liberated; light and slightly achy with exertion, and our faces glowing like the evening sunshine which causes walls to blush as it tiptoes through the trees.

(2011)

The Beath at Alum Chine

As dawn breaks, a silent world unfolds and an excited wonder grips me like a child. I wander along the promenade at Alum Chine, a place I often come to. This morning in April, the sun rises; an intense glowing ball burnishing the silent sea and refracting into an elusive spectrum of colours almost intangible against the gentle wash of water. The smallest sounds seem to echo as the sky draws upward, an expanding dome filling with light and intensity so that the world takes on ever more tangible dimensions. The soft resonant call of a pigeon floating from somewhere off the cliff tops echoes ethereality. Gulls gather at the water's edge to drink in the new day, their small, sharp faces framed reflections in seawater pools. Sunrise is a special moment in time like the unfurling of a flower or the bursting of new leaves. Blink and it has gone forever.

(2011)

Walk Near Wimborne

Deep in the Dorset countryside, there is an ancient lane, partly sunken, which links two of my favourite villages on foot. Its steep, tangled banks are clad with ferns and ivy, over which the sunlight ripples and sways. In spring, near the entrance to the path, primroses peep from these banks, alongside bright celandines, each its own little sun, giving way to red campion and cow's parsley in later spring and the stray, self-seeded bluebell. The banks, topped by a hedgerow of tangled coppiced trees, where I have identified elm leaves, are also pock-marked with badger's sets and intriguing, smaller holes down which I am not sure what lives. Tree roots grow through these vertical walls, revealing something of the secluded, subterranean world where these creatures abide. A breeze catches new-born leaves to tremble with intimacy and secrecy, reflecting the cosy security of these dens. This path seems to have evolved through the centuries, a testimony to time. I have heard that it is also known as a 'green path', another word for an ancient path, but is also an apt description in itself, for in summer here, the trees, (mainly hazel, field maple and elm,) provide a rich, golden green canopy through which sunlight dapples in the balmy, breathless air.

As one walks, the way becomes deeper, narrower and more sunken so that it lies below the adjacent fields across which drifts a solitary cuckoo's call. A couple of generations back, this sound was apparently common with several heard simultaneously, now it is special to hear just one. Large, yet relatively slender trees tower across the path at an angle, drawing one deeper into its enticing intimacy. Further along the path still, the straight silvery boughs of coppiced trees grow like thick broom bristles from the banks, vaulting above our heads in a pointed-arched canopy down through which sunlight dances and skitters, shooting a myriad frenzied silver darts as these flexible boughs yield to the breeze. As the light travels the length of each one, they seem to be alive and energized as does the whole atmosphere.

The rousing hiss of wind in the branches and the chaotic, darting, laughing light, provide a contrast to an earlier week of heavy rain, when a stream of clear water coursed along this path creating cushioned ripples over ochre stones. In the dull light, the soft atmosphere felt damp and contained within itself, mysterious, magnified and almost prehistoric with ferns stretching out their ancient fronds. The ambience exuded something incredibly cosy and contained in this secret place, providing a degree of protection from the wet world outside.

At the end of the path, the wind has uprooted a huge tree. Recumbent, dignity defeated; its roots are wrenched from the earth, huge clods clinging to them. Such exposure. Efforts have been made to remove it, as it lies straddled across the path, and from where it has been chopped, the rings on the wounded surface show that it must have been very old. We count at least two hundred with difficulty as the rings are compacted close together in places and stained with damp. At well over a meter in diameter, this tree would have witnessed the centuries of sojourners along this path, it would have provided secure homes for generations of birds nesting in its branches and insects in its bark. Insects still scurry about it now, unaware that their home has been destroyed, and the saprophytic fungus, *Daldinia concentrica*, or *King Alfred's cakes*, grows on its furrowed, ivy-covered surface, suggesting that this might be an ash tree. I run my finger over the rough ridges of the tree trunk. These ridges, also worn with scores of small chips and grooves, are long and wavy, weaving in and out of each other to form a complex, almost interlocking diamond pattern. We so often see bark as just a texture, especially when the sun shines on it, and fail to notice the intricacy of its design, its patterns, the differences in texture and colour, the life running through it as it yields to the elements, protecting and strengthening the inner tree. Around us the air is still and silent, I hear no birds; it is almost as if out of reverence for the dead. This is a sad fate, as every ancient tree is precious; an eco-system, a habitat, our heritage. Yet death is part of life; one of many circles or cycles of nature as that of the seasons, the rings of the trees, the food chain (whereby this tree provides food and nutrients to others) the earth revolving around the sun, the moon revolving around the earth, the cycles of the stars, the spirals of galaxies and the dawning of day from night.

Observations of Bluebell Woods

I will let you discover the bluebell woods, of which there are elusive enclaves scattered all over Dorset. The joy of stumbling upon their secret places unaided only adds to the overall wonder of discovering something sublime. I have read in several sources that fifty per cent of the world's bluebells occurs in Britain, perhaps because they thrive in damp conditions. Moreover, the native British bluebell (*Endymion non-scriptus*) is smaller and daintier than its cousin, the Spanish bluebell (*Endymion hispanicus*). The former is sadly under threat from the latter. My husband and I are heading out to a small copse one Monday morning in late April, a segment of ancient woodland where bluebells should be blooming. Blackthorn has burst into flower as we walk through meadows on the way to the wood, its blossom falls like confetti into my hair as I move beneath it.

We approach the copse down an ancient track, more blackthorn weaving a pretty arch under which we pass, and a canopy of new leaves forming a tender green freshness above. Squeezing through a stile we cross a small field, which leads down into the bluebell copse. Normally a wall of fragrance hits us, as the sweet aroma of the flowers seems to be contained, concentrated in this pocket of ancient forest, but the bluebells have not quite opened yet; they are budding, beauty stirring in the soil, small purple parcels all wrapped up beneath coppiced trees. I refuse to be disappointed; this sunny spring day is brimming with buoyancy and the air seems light and fresh. We have the woods to ourselves, an undiscovered secret which promises rich rewards. Silence breathes suspense, as if the wood were waiting for such beauty to be unveiled. Only the constant chatter of rooks in the trees above breaks the spell. Sunlight softly fingers gnarled tree trunks, playing delicate dancing patterns that wander and swirl. I wonder how many people these trees have seen in this piece of ancient woodland throughout the centuries. Our time is but a fraction of theirs, our lives but a brief season. These trees with their deep knots and pitted bark would be, at a guess, at least two hundred years old, and that is not that old for a tree. I wish they could speak, telling me of times past and what each had witnessed in other's lives, the people passing through.

Coppicing is an ancient way of managing woodland, cutting branches back to the tree stump so that new, thinner boughs regenerate. These were often used for making fences, sheep hurdles and other necessary items; wood being a material on which people of the past almost exclusively relied. As well as being useful to man, this management of the trees prolongs their lives and thins the leafy canopy, allowing sunlight to access the forest floor thus enabling flowers like the bluebell to establish and flourish. It is said that if bluebells and wood anemones have both taken hold, then this truly is ancient woodland classified as being over four hundred years old. Wood anemones do indeed grow in certain parts here, their shy, star-like flowers embroidered white on a dark green backdrop, dappled with golden sunlight under the trees. We have established a symbiotic relationship with forests, which, although appearing to be wild places, actually rely on man's management for their productive longevity. Since the Second World War, many of Britain's ancient woodlands have been lost, leaving the surviving remnants to only comprise an area of about two per cent of the United Kingdom. These rich ecosystems of undisturbed soils and biodiversity are irreplaceable; once lost they have gone forever. The woodland possesses a tentative fragility, despite appearing old, permanent and reassuring, and is very much at the mercy of man and his ability to compromise landscapes and facilitate change.

(2011)

*

A week later we return on a balmy day more akin to summer. The bluebells have opened, diffusing their fragrance into the shimmering , sun-scintillated air which mingles many shades while sunlight casts an ethereal, silvery sheen across swathes of blue and plays subtle shadow patterns with the branches above. New leaves break through buds; blue tingles against green, everything jubilant.

Peeping through the trees at the boundary of the wood, I see red cows grazing in front of fields of yellow rape. Blue and yellow; the primary colours that make the green of springtime, red and blue make up some of the varying bluebell hues. These blend with the green of newborn leaves quivering as a calm breeze sighs through trees, and the ferns, standing tall and straight with tightly coiled spiral tops which will slowly unfurl like snails from a shell. Two young girls perch on a fallen log amidst a sea of blue. The sun catches the gold in their blonde hair and the shadows of leaves dance across their smiling sunlit faces as they sit angelically still while their mother focuses the camera. The popularity of this place today has destroyed some of its atmosphere, its sense of secrecy. I find my own place to sit, a secluded corner away from the world and listen. The bantering backdrop of rooks is so constant that after a while I fail to be aware of it. It is the dreamy, ethereal call of the woodpigeon floating through the trees that commands my attention. Visual and nasal senses have been so indulged that it is almost unbelievable being here, and with the pigeon's soft honeyed voice embracing the silence, the dream is complete. I am lost in an idyllic sylvan reverie, my eyes indulging in the aesthetic, light playing in soft silvery waves across an impressionistic sea of blue calm and rippling across tree trunks, weaving patterns. The trees themselves adorned with pretty ivy fronds, everything sweet.

Bluebells symbolize constancy[48] yet I know that they will only flourish temporarily and that we are privileged to share something of their secret world. It is as if we were trespassing on an enchanted wood, which doesn't really exist, yet as my fingers touch rough tree bark, I know that it does. The trees are rooted firmly in this solid, sustainable eco-system, which has delighted us through the seasons for centuries. There are no elusive nymphs, no Pan playing his pipes, just the echo of the pigeon, perfume poured out on the air and sunlight tiptoeing between the trees. This is an Earthly utopia and I sit here, my heart bursting as a blue bud, with joy and thankfulness.

(2011)

*

Some of the most beautiful things are transitory; sunshine through spring leaves, drenching bluebells with dewy light, lingering on tree trunks, a glistening drop preparing to fall, flowers themselves; bluebells only last weeks, then they die down, bedding back into the earth until, a year hence, they raise their humble heads again. That is why it is so important to make the most of every season, for each has its own fleeting beauty which leaves in our hearts a permanent sense of wonder and joy. Trees stand as testimonies to time, owning a different beauty, one which is enhanced by definition, age and permanency, but the youthful breath of flowers, the evanescent ray of light or the momentary expression on a child's face; if not caught, is lost indefinitely.

Dawn Chorus

As dawn light seeps into a voluminous sky, the silence is broken by birdsong; a solitary robin's liquid mercury notes slip through the monochrome silence with their silvery tones. More birds gradually join him as the nocturnal veil of cloud is slowly ripped to shreds, revealing a pallid translucency behind its frayed, deep purple ribbons. By five o'clock, after an hour, the clouds have dissipated; the sky clear and full of light, silence shattered completely by a scintillating backdrop of birdsong, burbling, soaring; colours and textures of separate songs jostling in a harmonious medley of melodies. But it is the blackbird's bright notes which predominate; fresh, resonant and optimistic, reflecting the clarity of the morning air. The chorus is brilliant, exuberant and I would like to think that these birds are singing for the joy of being alive, of seeing another new day come into being, for the mercy of having escaped the predators of the night as they slept in the trees and for the anticipation of a day spent in the full light of the sun.

(2017)

Bulbarrow

From Bulbarrow the western sky growls above a patchwork landscape filled with golden sunshine and stained with encroaching shadows as clouds clench their fists. From this altitude of two hundred and seventy four meters, Dorset's third highest hill, and not surprisingly used during the Iron Age as a hillfort, one can see, on a clear day, across the Blackmore Vale into Wiltshire, Somerset and Devon. The day has been bright with a strong, cold, north-easterly wind but a hazy horizon melds with the surly, scowling sky which rides in from the west and now hangs overhead. Clouds hug hills, and up here it is a different day to the one down below where the sun still stains the flat plains- a patchwork quilt of green fields interspersed with yellow rape.

Although I told you to discover the bluebell woods, the woods here are so extensive that they cannot be missed, for they flick, like a blue mirage, trembling between the trees for over one and a half miles along the road from Winterbourne Stickland. Excitedly we plunge into part of this blue allure, seduced by a heady sweetness. Blue, intensely violet in the glowering light, stretches as far as the eye can see, and we walk in a dream along a forest path. Beech trees are just beginning to leaf, their tentative, fan-like appendages feeling their way into the world, tender and newborn. When wan shafts of sun break between the trees allowing the silver sheen of the beech trunks to stand silky against the blue backdrop, the fresh green of these new leaves become three dimensional, bursting with a vivacity, reaching out against the violet-blue, now subtly streaked with ashen silver sunshine and faint shadows which last a few fleeting seconds before we are once more plunged into an achromatic gloom. The wind bites, yet it is cosy in this wood away from the world, the sky drawing down its blinds, curtains pulled, so that we too feel drawn to the enigmatic atmosphere, secure as if we were in a cave.

Swathes of *wood bells* or *jacinths*, for want of alternative names, sweep down the steep slopes of the hill, dropping away dramatically in endless blue before curving delicately round and up again like in an amphitheatre, its stage set for the imagination to fly far away. These smooth, theatrical sweeps, plunging down to an unseen valley, are punctuated by the same vertical, tall, slender, densely- growing trees, standing like tall pillars of a cathedral, the relentless roaring of the wind causing them to indulge in animated conversation, to whisper and hiss, expel secrets, gossip, sway incessantly. I lean my back against a rough, red-brown conifer trunk, which seems to yield, to breathe as it rocks almost imperceptibly against my back. Its lack of supporting solidity feels strange, unstable, affirming the fragility and transience of this place, an almost mythopoeic world full of unrealities and surprises where the bluebells silently spread their bewitching beauty to a seeming eternity and trees are moving, animated, alive.

In fact this place is bursting with life, the silent, secretive lives of bulbs, which lie dormant beneath the soil for most of the year, to stir in springtime, the trees themselves, whose roots stretch through the inner chambers of the earth like branches above, seeking nutrients and water from the sustaining soil. Then there are the unseen insects and the birds, the animals, which hide away in their secret dens. We look into a hole, which was once the knot in an ancient beech tree, its mossy trunk iridescent in the gloom, but nothing gives itself away, no woodpecker nor owl. The forest seems empty, devoid of fauna, for apart from the odd pheasant clearing its throat somewhere deep within the breathing blue stillness, and a brave chiffchaff, there are few birds singing today. The ones which I encountered earlier, flying over the fields, were struggling against the strength of the wind, being blown backwards as fast as they went forwards.

As for human life, the only sounds are the faraway, delighted cries of children playing with their dog somewhere on the fringe of the forest. There is no one about, just this unbelievably blue make-believe, and us. Humans were here recently though, making their mark, for a pathway of squashed stalks has been carefully forged through the otherwise unblemished blue. It wanders for a stretch into the depths of the forest before the gradient becomes too steep and the land drops away. I am sad to see this path, for trampling bluebells, despite destroying them in their prime, apparently prevents them from regenerating the following year as the act of bruising the leaves breaks down the nutrients required by the bulb. It is therefore imperative that people respect these natural places in order to sustain their secret charms. We are but guests to a beautiful feast of indulgence laid out for the senses. We must drink in the dream without destroying it.

Emerging out into the open is like waking from this dream, deliciously drugged with the sweet scent of bluebells and the tang of wood garlic. The whole place remaining an enigma in my mind, for the serried ranks of trees, many of them coniferous, suggest that they were perhaps planted here. Vestiges of ancient forest exist in the presence of old beech trees on the path and at the woodland perimeter, but its deep heart appears manmade, yet for bluebells to flourish in such profusion would have required undisturbed centuries.

The fresh, brisk, biting gusts at the windswept summit of Bulbarrow bring us into a tangible reality, yet the view below is still breath taking and we are once again compelled, drawn into a new dream as we look down onto the somnolent stretches of Dorset countryside and beyond.

(2014)

*

On Woolland Hill we chance upon 'perhaps the oldest living thing in Dorset' [59]. A yew tree with a crown of an astonishing twenty six meters, sprawls across a bank above us; dense, dark and mysterious. Yet, despite its great spread and even greater antiquity, it remains humbly living out its days without claim to fame or excessive attention, even obscured at one angle by a backdrop of branches, so that we have to look at least twice to believe what we are really seeing. It is hard to comprehend that this enigmatic tree has been living quietly and reclusively upon this bank for at least a thousand years, surrounded by silence except the creaking of wind-worn branches, a brilliant medley of spring birdsong and the vagrant calls of raptors winging their way above the slumbering valley beneath.

Seasons come and go, people pass by and away. At least a thousand springs have been and gone since this tree took root. I wonder how it managed to survive when the majority of trees in the immediate vicinity seem relatively young and the deep paths carved into the earth all around suggest that this landscape has at some time been shaped and changed. One of these paths, on which we are now walking, runs just below where the yew tree stands, as if those who created it did not want to encroach on the tree's territory, acknowledging its antiquity. With age comes respect, even in the plant world it would seem, and perhaps this yew was once revered and thus preserved by the ancient people who lived before Christianity even came to these shores. Whatever its past, it remains in the present, silently concealing secrets beneath its dense crown, a shadowy spider's web of roots and suckers creating a tangle beneath creeping, interlocking boughs.

We leave it to bask in the sun, another silent day dropping away into the ocean of time. It has stood throughout the centuries, unchanged during our entire lifetimes and will continue to be long after we are gone. This slowing of time's continuity makes me feel a fusion with childhood. Rather than looking at life in distinct stages, I imagine each phase as a link in the great chain of time and that in essence, something of the child still exists so that a part deep within us does not essentially change. We are only altered and shaped by layers of experiences building themselves one upon another. With these thoughts, I ponder on the longevity of this tree, sustained by the Dorset earth, shaped by time, yet only having existed for half as long as some of the tumuli on Cranborne Chase. When one begins to consider time in this way, it exceeds the realms of rational understanding.

(2016)

MAY

More Bluebells

May Day and for once the weather is glorious. In many countries today people will have flocked to the countryside for picnics and parties. Here we have had to work all day. My frustration at being shut inside has been exacerbated by the fact that the bank holiday weekend is typically forecast to rain. It is about fifteen degrees today and perfect for an evening stroll.

As soon as we reach the countryside, my mood is calmed and work seems a million miles away. Long fingers of sunshine reach between the trees to Midas- touch everything. Gold flows across the grass, up tangled banks of bursting green, and over tree trunks, illuminating the bark's rough ridges and furrows, highlighting the thick wooded stalks of ivy, which have become a permanent appendage to the tree. It flows like the liquid clarity of a solitary blackbird's song, whose syrup-sweetness contrasts the twang of a woodpecker. Bluetits trill ostinatos from nearby bushes, a pheasant coughs against the spinning-top song of the chaffinch and the rich, comfortable croon of a pigeon envelopes the evening. In the hedge bank grow bluebells, which reminds me that it is their season again and we must return to the copse. Down the lane we walk once more, plunging into an enticing tunnel of new leaves. Blackthorn in full flower blushes in the evening light, draping itself prettily so that it shimmers against the sky's unblemished blue. The air is alive, bringing a depth of dimension which magnifies the intrigue and excitement of an evening walk.

Over a gate we peer, watching ambling fields fade into a shimmering horizon from which floats a pigeon's dreamy call. Horses gently graze; a doe timidly finds her own patch some distance away from them. Once more we wander into the copse. It is compelling to come here in the evening. There is a deeper atmosphere; one of secrecy, expectancy, intimacy. The bluebells are out, their lingering fragrance drifting delectably on the air. A forest floor striped with sunshine is a photographer's dream.

Long, licking rays of deep gold tinge the blue with bronze. Tranquillity, nobody about; rooks let out an occasional caw, not the usual non-stop cacophony, and so the amber air is scintillated by other bird's songs. In surrounding fields, quiescent Red Devon cows soak up the evening sun. Keeping them company is an apathetic bull; 'a red bull', as my husband points out rather wittily.

Streams of sunlight flood the familiar face of a farm cottage peeping between the new leaves, the flowing lines of the fields rolling away; everything is as it has always been, peaceful, permanent so that I remember whatever life's traumas, there are always places like this. Perhaps we have caught a hint of heaven, standing here, silently breathing in the beauty of the evening. Its elixir fills me with an inexpressible joy; warm air infused with fragrance, shafting sunlight and the bird's songs are a caressing balm and I want to wander in this copse until nightfall.

Looking up into the vertiginous heights where the naked treetops meet in a circular crown above the forest and shine bronze against the distilled blue of the sky, we can see why the rooks have been quiet. They are away finding food. One of them appears and swoops down to a nest from which we can hear thin, but distinctively raucous cries coming. Baby rooks. A new generation has hatched and I wonder how many have gone before. I have certainly always known a rookery here and these woods are ancient.

The mosquitos come out to play, dancing in the sinking sunlight, making us scratch. I watch the light descending down the trunks of trees, golden shafts sinking into soft shadows. There is another hour or more of daylight but everything seems slower, as if having bathed in the brilliance and beauty of day, is now winding down to a dreamy dusk when the barn owl might glide gracefully, a noiseless phantom flitting between the trees, and small nocturnal animals will busy about.

It is time to leave and prepare for tomorrow's work. A group of cub scouts arrive as we depart, their rowdy expressions of excitement and jubilance echoing through the copse. Yet the silence will not be shattered permanently, the sun will dip down and the light will fade, the children's delighted cries will linger for a short while, echoing what we adults feel but are too restrained to express, until all will fall silent. The birds will settle to roost, the comfortable chipping of blackbirds dimming with the dusk, and then the moon will creep mysteriously through the trees, sending silver and shadows across the forest floor. The bluebells will sleep with silent nodding heads while the withering call of the tawny owl floats freely through the forest. The children will one day grow older and become preoccupied with life, but this place will always remain to rekindle that childhood dream, allowing us all to leave our worries at its entrance, to unleash our hearts and escape into its secret, unadulterated joy.

(2013)

*

On a rainy day the bluebell woods take on a completely different atmosphere of reflective, pensive calm. Colours collide in an intensity which seems to pulsate like a beating heart, drawing one deeper into itself. The copse is once again intimate, intensified in the glooming light where blue seems bolder and brighter against glowing green and we are enticed into its security like children being embraced into open arms. This time only the blackbird sings, his shrill optimism carrying through the rain. A chiffchaff joins him; a piercing alarm call cutting like clashing colours through the canopy of new leaves and dank light.

I have read that there are an estimated five million bluebells growing here secretly, silently, secluded in this enchanting wood. We are privileged to trespass upon its beauty, to feel its soft security as its days pass in serenity, quietly contained within itself. Today, only the delicious patter of raindrops can be heard through new leaves, the cries of rooks diminished, the blackbird effervescent. An atmosphere of peaceful reassurance stirs in the soul, caressed by the sweet solace that despite trials, here, all is still well with the world.

(2013)

*

When I go down to the woods today I'm in for a big surprise and not a particularly pleasant one. For everyone that ever there was has gathered here for certain (or so it would seem!) The calm, other-worldly serenity has been chased away, the woods becoming a noisy playground and tourist attraction.

Returning later when the crowds have gone, the forest breathes painfully; suffering silently, bearing the bruises and scars of a harrowing day; a woman who has been relentlessly enjoyed without any respect. Many of the bluebells have been trampled, crushed and killed in their prime- flat green patches break into the boundaries of the blue mirage. Paradise lost. I think of what happened in Eden.

There is always a dilemma between encouraging people to enjoy nature and maintaining a fragile, natural habitat. Media and social media enable places to be discovered *en masse* and while everyone has the right to enjoy such a wonderful spectacle; it should be done with consideration for the environment and others. This careless destruction is no doubt a result of enthusiasm, an over-zealous desire to post pictures on social media which show people sitting in amongst the bluebells. By asserting our identity we destroy its identity. I do not know the answer but when I look at the disconsolate wood, battered and bruised, I feel a sadness creep between the trees as the marks of man have tarnished the perfection of this beautiful place.

(2017)

Cuckoo

From a bridge above the Stour I watch the freefalling cotton-wool drift of pollen backlit by the sun. Trout jump with a comfortable splosh and a grey heron is poised, statuesque upstream. The first swallows I have seen this year rest on a power line, preening silently while other evening birds call. The blackbird is a folksong flute, the tune of its dance wandering into the evening stillness. But it is the cuckoo, whose wistful, mesmeric notes float across the river, which takes centre stage. They are a Tudor court recorder; full of mystery yet slightly flat and as off-beat as a pendulum clock. I seem to hold them in my head for they leave such a subtle impression lingering on my imagination, that I hear them long after they have silenced.

(2017)

Lewesdon Hill

The road from Bridport to Broadwindsor skirts around the base of Dorset's highest point. At two hundred and seventy nine metres, Lewesdon Hill, stained purple today by bluebell swathes on its slopes, towers above us. The verges of the narrow road down which we pass present a livid fusion of bluebells and red campion- a modernist clash of colours. Wooded glades whitened with thick, flowering ramsons flick past, filling our car with the scent of spring onions.

We park before sinking and splashing across a soggy field in the direction of Lewesdon Hill. In the next pasture, sunlight licks thickly-bladed grass so that it shines silver. We follow a vague track of squashed, dulled blades; a suggestion of a path marching onwards and upwards. It is a steepish climb, warm in the unbroken sunshine, but we proceed through the tugging, ripping grass, which ensnares our ankles and tries to prevent us from reaching our goal; the hill, topped with a light-filled canopy of beech trees.

Entering this woodland canopy is like accessing another world, one which radiates the sun, its position elevated and thus remote from the world outside, yet with stunning views of that very same. As Sunlight sifts through tender, trembling beech leaves, it licks the russet beech-masted forest floor with golden tongues and casts long, lazy shadows. In hollows and secluded enclaves, bluebells drift like diaphanous veils, creating torn patches of violet-blue silk between the trees.

Up on the summit, which we share with a few other families, we peer down steep escarpments through the contorted, curly branches of ancient oaks and the outstretched palms of the beech canopy, beginning to spread in its verdant layers. More bluebells grow on terraces far below us, violet-blue impressions melded into a tangled web of branches and new leaves. The views above and beyond are tantalizing, spectacular, viewed through frames in the trees. To the south the dreamy patchwork of fields idly spreads to the sea, from another side of the hill we look towards the neighbouring hillfort of Pilsdon Pen. Devon lies in the hazy distance and from another side Somerset. The pretty golden hamstone cottages of Broadwindsor and the tower of its church can also be seen framed through the trees on our descent. It would have been a wonderful place in which to hide up here, to defend and be protected; that is perhaps why the people of the Iron Age probably had a hilltop fort here, as they also did at Pilsdon Pen, two miles away, contestably the second highest point in Dorset.

As we descend, feet sinking into the deep, soft soil, which lies beneath crunchy beech mast, we are being pulled into the secret world beneath, away from the elevated hilltop of light and beauty. This silent underworld is astir; a place of nutrient, which sustains seeds and bulbs and nourishes roots, that haven of hibernation and dormancy with its labyrinth of burrows and black tunnels is silently revealing its secrets as seeds awaken from the dark, wintery depths and seek light at the surface. The soil has been a soft, warm blanket, the beech mast an armoured suit against the cold, and now the serpentine heads of new bracken are pushing through on long necks like monsters rising from the deep. Some are only a few centimetres high; others have risen to a couple of feet and are beginning to unfurl their tightly-curled crowns. In the beech mast, seeds are sprouting, flinging off their cases and growing green shoots, couplets of leaves breaking everywhere through the forest floor. The silent underworld of leaf-decay and buried dead has stirred. Death has fostered life.

It is strange how things go on unperceived in a forest; the stealthy onset of plants, like the invasion of a silent army, and the unknown presence of fauna. According to the National Trust, deer are supposed to be seen here at dusk and we wonder where they go during the day. Surely they are here, secretly watching us, hearing our feet crunch in the beech mast, the click of the camera, our voices whispering in the sun- saturated air. Surely there is a wealth of fauna here, unobserved, yet observing us and standing as a metaphor for this whole place, for from the top, like the ancients, concealed in their forest canopy, we can watch the world through a one-way window but the world cannot spy back.

(2014)

*

I wonder if this landscape has changed much since the time of William Wordsworth who, with his sister Dorothy, lived at Racedown Farm near Pilsdon for two years at the end of the eighteenth century. As a young literature student, I was inspired and captivated by his sensitive and perceptive renditions of personal experience in nature, deploring human disregard for it, whether as man, corrupted by society, or child, who knew no better. Wordsworth stood at the threshold of Romanticism which found its way in emotive self-expression, feeling, and freedom of thought and stood against the reason and logic which so defined Neoclassicism and the Age of Enlightenment. The seeds of these romanticist ideas had perhaps been germinating during the Industrial Revolution (and its destruction of nature), coming to fruition during the French Revolution which, accompanied by horrific suffering, perhaps encouraged the romantics to seek escape and solace in an idealised form of nature and, in the case of Wordsworth, to develop the existing neoclassical empathy for the common man.

As an adult I see some of these ideas projected into modern thought.

It is as if every era sowed a seed which after growth, was grafted into a taller tree. Although I personally consider Wordsworth's glorification of nature and its influence on man to be at times excessive and misplaced, his poetry is not merely escapist, often leaving the halcyon idyll of childhood to focus on the inevitability of destruction and loss. It is this dichotomy between the reasoned knowledge of man and the open, spontaneous expression of child which specifically defines the romantic era.

As far as I know, Wordsworth didn't write about this place but about ten years earlier, William Crowe, rector of nearby Stoke Abbot from 1782-1787, wrote a lengthy poem entitled *Lewesdon Hill* depicting a delightful walk taken here before church during an idyllic eighteenth-century day in May.

The Dorset Gap

An intersection of ancient pathways lies in a secret clearing, seemingly a world away from any other. This is thought to be the convergence of ancient trading routes and drover's ways, meeting at the Dorset Gap, a former hub, which now expounds an overwhelming silence in its green, expansive solitude. The footsteps of centuries past have faded away with time so that only their memory stands at this crossroads, just as time stands still, waiting. This place was waiting undisturbed long before I was born, waiting with its box of notebooks for passers-by to record their thoughts. I had never known about it until I discovered its secret, for it is remote, only found by following the ancient footpaths which weave their way like threads through the green heart of the countryside to converge here, linking lives and times past, linking lost worlds at this meeting place. Although united, each path remains distinct, individual, holding a unique character and even displaying predominantly different flora in its small satellite eco-system.

A green, sunken path tiptoes enticingly through the trees, steep banks suggesting that it was once heavily frequented and that the incessant treading through times past, of people, animals and carts would have caused deep erosion. A canopy of new leaves rising high above the path causes us to enter a lofty, enticing tunnel, which seems to glow green on this overcast, muggy day. Surely, with a path as sunken as this, and the humps and bumps of a medieval village still visible beneath the fields near Higher Melcombe, now reduced to only a farm and manor house, this was evidently once a place of much greater significance and population.

The path to the north of the gap leads to an isolated eighteenth- century farmhouse. It is a secret, sinuous mossy path thickly flanked with flowering wood-garlic, which grows up the steep slopes between the trees, giving the air a sharply acrid, overpowering tang. The atmosphere is heavy, comfortable, as if embracing you into itself; a thick, warm jumper, where one feels beautifully stifled. Through new leaves, I catch tantalising views of the surrounding countryside spread out in a patchwork plain beyond and feel as if I were happily at home with overprotective parents, watching from a window at the elusive world outside. Perhaps this is how a young bird feels when it is preparing to fledge.

The western path leads to a settlement called Folly, which again supports a single building, once a pub. This path initially wanders through a small beech forest where drifts of bluebells seem to float across the forest floor, a captivating blue mirage, intense in the dreary light. The air exhales their sweet scent and everything seems sublime, innocent, fresh and aesthetic. At the edge of the forest, where the boundary woodbank rises beneath old trees, red campion and bluebells provide a collision of colour, and where I peep through a cleft in two robust branches of an ancient tree, a frame is formed around another secret spread of bluebells, which seems to stretch forever. Leaving this world of wonder and enchanting seclusion, we walk on across open fields, following the path marked the Dorset Ridgeway, which eventually takes us to Folly.

The path to the east of the Dorset Gap, leading towards Bulbarrow, is again completely different in character, for this is an elevated ridge of chalk, almost like a spine from which the other paths radiate like ribs. This is the Wessex Ridgeway, apparently prehistoric, leading on towards Hambeldon Hill into Wiltshire and following part of the ancient Iknield Way which terminates at Hunstanton. It certainly feels prehistoric up here, wild, windswept, open, and elevated, the terraced slopes resembling the ramparts of a hill fort (a small Iron Age hill fort called Nettlecombe Tout does indeed lie in the very close vicinity). Instead of cosy, glowing and intimate tracts of beech woodland brushed with bluebells or the overpowering, green groves of ramsons, this exposed, chalk grassland terrain supports cowslips and orchids, protective in a different sense, for it is strong and stands against the elements in a completely contrasting landscape with wonderful views over towards Bulbarrow and down over the farmstead of Higher Melcombe. A local old man, whom we met at the gap, told us that from the ridge on a good day, one can see right across the Blackmore Vale into all the neighbouring counties.

Back at the gap I stand once again at the cross-roads wondering who walked here in the past, how many people came from miles around to meet and trade. For this was evidently a hub of activity, now left abandoned along with many of the surrounding ghost villages, which are now not even hamlets. It is proof that no marks which man makes are irreversible and that busy, bustling places can be reclaimed by nature, for now this is a small world caught up within itself and its memories, standing remotely and peacefully, resounding with silence. This is a silence which echoes off itself as the intense green glow of the trees rebounds off the retina. It is secret, bewitching, alluring, intriguing and causes curiosity to step out of the shade and try to discover secrets which are barely expounded in the silence. Many people have passed through this place, for thousands of years their footsteps have taken a steady tread along the same pathways which remain the testimony to their existence. The people are long gone, dead and buried beneath the earth and without the mystery of this place, would now be forgotten forever.

(2015)

Hod Hill

Near the village of Stourpaine, down a dappled forest path which gives glimpses of enticing views from between the trees, a stirring wind sighs, rocking dappled shadows and scattering sunlight across the ground like shards of a shattered mirror. At the end of the path, a gate brings us to the edge of Hod Hill; deep ramparts creating furrowed shadows in the strong sunlight while trees whisper their timeless calm, tossing their own shifting shadows across curving edges to fall away into the furrows. This is an ancient atmosphere saturated with stillness, turbulent times set to rest. We walk up through the ramparts and over the top of the hill to reveal a landscape which shows an ever-changing, verdant face as the wind brings clouds to cast intermittent shadows across the bright intensity of a sunny smile. The village of Stourpaine lies behind us, nestling in its green valley, the church tower above a jumble of rooftops beyond which lies the green, patched carpet of the fields.

Hod Hill was used as a hillfort in the Iron Age as well as in Roman times. Being a chalk downland, it hosts a wealth of flora and fauna and is grazed by sheep and cattle. Unfortunately we have missed the cowslips, which I have been told grow in extensive swathes across the top of the hill. Today these seem to have been replaced by buttercups. At the opposite side of Hod Hill lies a copse; deep and dark. Silver sunlight swirls through branches and along trunks as the trees whisper and rustle. It evokes a sense of excitement and mystery, as if holding history's secrets inside it. We skirt the side of this copse and come out through a gate from which we climb again; more beautiful and exhilarating views of Blackmore Vale spread below. But realising that we are going the wrong way, according to our guidebook, we soon retrace our steps back along another woodland path, which skirts all around the side of the hill, eventually leading us back to Stourpaine. Sunshine glows through green leaves, casually daubing the path as it meanders alongside the river, the water, sparkling and playful as we look down at it through towering masses of hogweed and other green foliage.

This path, through fecund woodland, also seems to lead us on a clandestine adventure to something out of bounds, frowned-upon; leading, in its sweet, whimsical way to a guilty secret, carefree in its innocent seduction. Eventually it comes out between fields and we notice the thick, eerie cat's cradle webs of ermine moth caterpillars draped in ghostly abundance about the hedgerows like spider's webs in an illustration for a haunted house. Beneath the webs, all foliage has been ravished, chewed down to bare, skeletal stalks. Naked devastation: nature destroying nature, a complete contrast to the thriving, glowing life of the riverside path.

The village is nostalgic today, as if going back in time to a world without complication, to a world of black and white, light and dark with no complex shades of grey and hidden hues to be discerned. The parish church of Holy Trinity, almost completely rebuilt in the nineteenth century, stands quietly on the edge of tranquil pastures where inquisitive young cows leave off grazing to stand in a line and look at us through eyes, oozing curiosity. We see them resume their grazing as we enter the church, full of light as the sun floods through clear-glassed, leaded windows. Light within, green without, and the soft hush of contained, contented peace.

(2011)

May

Dancing Ledge

I have come to do some rockpooling at Dancing Ledge. A hazy blue sky is swelling with the cavorting, acrobatic songs of skylarks as we cross the grassy slopes to descend to the ledge. Puffins apparently breed here, if you are lucky enough to see them, and sometimes dolphins can be seen arcing in unison through the sea, but today the sheer cliff walls, created by extensive quarrying until the 1930s, are being scaled by climbers while groups of young swimmers in wetsuits brave the seas, which swell and pound into the deep recesses of the cavernous cliff bases. There is too much noise and human activity for puffins and dolphins today. Despite the people, this place still seems wild and desolate- bleak, blank rock, facing the elements, hard and unyielding even on a mild spring day where sunlight is strained through a muslin sky. When it does yield, divulging its hidden fossils in a splay of shattered rock, it is because the land has slipped, could even kill.

We stand above the ledge, looking down onto its flat plateau pitted with rock pools. It is like a stage set for dancing, but whether any dancing actually took place there on its slippery, irregular surface, is not really known. What is known is that it was a popular landing place for smugglers who could then drag the contraband three-quarters of a mile up the hill to be stowed in Langton Matravers [53]. The descent is a scramble over the rocks- fissured, fragmented, blotched with lichen, the landscape hard and hostile, yet one associates it with easy, carefree days. The small tide pool cut over a century ago into the ledge for swimming, once served a local preparatory school. I imagine the happy children released from the confines of the classroom and running through the fields on a hot sunny day to plunge into its cool, salty depths. Children in wetsuits swim here now- others are fishing with their fathers. Surprisingly none of them are rockpooling, a pursuit which engrossed me as a child. I was captivated by the tiny worlds, microcosms of life, miniature, self-contained ecosystems thriving within their own small spaces like natural aquariums. My brother and I would spend hours investigating the rock pools while on holiday in north France, and no doubt in Dorset too, although as to exactly where, my memory fails me.

Today the pools are disappointing. They appear murky and sterile, lacking the usual brightly coloured combination of red and green weed which links hands to sway in the tiny space of clear water alongside the odd tiny crab or fish. Today the sun is not bright enough to plunge its rays, torch-like, into the calm, receding depths so that wavy, watery patterns shift and drift on rocky sides, looping playfully in twisting ribbons of light across the contents of the pool and reflecting on faces which peer intently downwards from above. But looking closer, one sees that these pools are still very much alive with thriving communities. They have been colonized by periwinkles: whorled, spiralled, striped, variegated; their diverse colours subtle, muted but coordinated- chocolate brown, mud brown, grey, russet, ochre, cream. They cluster together at the pool's edges, perhaps stranded, or as if daring to dip their toes into the pool's opaque depths. Some of them are solitary, scouring the pitted rock base to feed on the algae which clings there. The other inhabitants of these rock pools are limpets, ridged lines on their shells radiating from a pointed apex like a star, some sit on the rock bottom; others are positioned so that their pointed hat breaks through the pool's meniscus.

Each pool is an individual world, similar but unique in shape and size and sometimes species. One pool is full of green weed, which opens like fans, waving, and leaving bubbles on the surface. I wonder why this pool also supports plants as well as molluscs, which hide beneath the weed's waving fronds, while others do not. It is possible to spend hours peering into these pools, to become fascinated by their little worlds, to allow one's imagination to run free and to be delighted by such a small creation contained within itself, oblivious of the outside world. They appear calm and contained but actually for prey in their necessary food chain, they are a trap from which is it impossible to escape until the turning of the tide when the sea washes through them.

Dancing Ledge and the whole of this wild, harsh coast is a strange juxtaposition of hard and soft, endurance and comfort. Although it could be dangerous, grim and foreboding, it also seems to hint at happy memories, of fun days out- swimming, climbing, rockpooling, fishing and wandering the miles and miles of undulating green coast path on carefree sunny days with all the time in the world. It is hard to leave. John Betjamen came here, for he wrote a poem about it, *Hearts Together*, in which he recollects indulging in childish pursuits and feeling emancipated. As I observe three euphoric young men, who must be at least in their very late teens, laughing, bantering, pushing each other, taking selfies, I wonder whether it is not perhaps the atmosphere which makes them feel and act this way, bringing out the unrestrained child and that perhaps Betjamen, as a young man, not a child, experienced the same reaction.

We are leaving now. Scrambling back up the sheer rock face from the ledge and up onto the cliff top. We will leave these pools in peace, to indulge, to bask, to bathe in the soft sunlight, which now gently spangles their rims and causes algae and weed to flourish. We will leave them to continue their contained cycle of survival and secret life.

(2014)

Purbeck Coast Path

Walking along the coast path from Winspit towards St Aldelm's Head; late spring feels like summer, wrapping us with warmth. Sea pinks always bring associations with carefree childhood holidays and they flower in profusion along the cliff top and down the rocky scree of the cliff face itself. Amongst a wealth of beautiful flora, bird's foot trefoil clusters in bright sunshine patches, ox-eye daisies stare wide-eyed from their cliff top position while we watch a pair of great black-backed gulls tending their chick on a rocky ledge. It is a privilege to catch a glimpse into their secret, intimate world, a world of reproduction and survival which continues simultaneously with our own, as do the lives of many other birds at this time of year, and to which most of humanity is oblivious. Despite being aggressive predators, these birds show a gentler nature when doting on a defenceless chick, an instinctive bond of duty shown by both parents, which I find both moving and humbling. The ledge on which these amber- listed birds have set up home, appears both comfortable yet vulnerable and I hope that there will not be storms.

Not more than fifteen minutes later, having watched the gulls, photographed flowers, peered into wavering mirages, and followed Adonis blue butterflies chasing each other through grasses, the carefree cusp-of-summer mood suddenly changes. A sea mist casually drifts in, billowing smoky sheets across fields, subduing brilliant buttercups and the tall proud columns of viper's bugloss. The sea becomes a blank void, its reassuring, regular breath muffled beneath us, a presence heard but not seen. Everything seems contained within itself, each retreating into its own little world. Birds stop singing, silence descends, making the atmosphere seem wild and deliciously hostile. The mist provides a diaphanous cool, refreshing our faces as we walk the last part to the chapel; an apparition, compelling. I want to reach it, to prove that its strength has not melted away in the silent mists of time. The only sound apart from the distant sea is the steam train, its remote, measured puff echoing through the smoky swirls of mist. We have lost concept of time, distance and space, all is so suddenly and uncannily still and unfamiliar, yet there is reassuring movement within the coast guard watch tower as those stationed there survey the indefinable, expressionless fusion of sea and sky.

Inside the chapel the usual swell of the sea is inaudible, no wind buffets about the open door, but outside a brave skylark takes up its tune of vibrant cadenzas, a brilliance chiselling the silence like graffiti on old pillars. A bluebottle buzzes busily, its intrusive echo reverberating around stone shadows. It is of course irrespective of time which stands still holding its breath in suspense until the mist has passed. But the skylark has released something. There is no longer hostility or tension despite the tangible battle of heat with haze, for once back outside, I feel the warm, calm beat of sun burning through the vanquished shroud of sea mist. By the time we are back in Worth, sitting in a small vintage tearoom garden with tea and cake, blue skies have returned and the air echoes with the dreamy warm clarity of rock doves calling from rooftops. This is surely the sweetest end to a perfect day!

(2016)

Purbeck Ridge

I always love walking the Purbeck Ridge, that great backbone of land which lounges across the countryside like a recumbent giant, and whose nonchalant, outstretched silhouette can be seen from high points across the eastern part of the county. Nonchalant is the word, for here the atmosphere is engulfed in a calm which allows us to lose ourselves and look down into other worlds and at the whole sweeping panorama spread before us.

We have walked from Corfe Castle down thin lanes, exploding with foliage. Leafing trees provide secret shelters for birds, which sing undercover, without the danger of exposure; chiffchaffs, blackbirds, the usual songs and calls. Ivy clings to tree trunks, nettles grow tall and lush, sporting white flowers, the lacy caps of cow's parsley reach out of verges to touch us, red campion blends into a backdrop of various blossoms which leave a white trail of petals on the ground.

Up West Hill we climb and out onto the Ridgeway where the clipped green grass is studded with buttercups. Silence. We stand watching birds of prey sweeping and soaring down into the valley. They seem to me, the epitome of freedom. Cows and sheep here are also free to roam and graze as part of the National Trust's 'amazing grazing' programme. Two Hereford calves look at us curiously as we pass, peering with innocent eyes. A flock of sheep, white and shorn, sit idly amongst the buttercups ruminating. Behind them, down in the valley nestles the village of Church Knowle, old buildings of grey Purbeck stone huddling around the comfortable church of St Peter with its square tower. It oozes history, containment, stability. I have visited the village on several occasions, to admire its historic buildings, and in the winter, to sit by a roaring fire with friends or family in the New Inn. The village is an inspiration: exuding warmth, security, history and peace. From up here, it blends beautifully into the backdrop of steep green slopes, which rise up again behind it, the tower of late nineteenth-century church of St James', Kingston, crowning the horizon like a stork sitting on a nest.

Below Kingston, one can see the patchwork of fields pockmarked with bushes and lined with hedgerows; some being boundary hedges marking the perimeters of Saxon settlements which no longer exist. Devoid of hedges lies the clean sweep of Corfe Common behind whose horizon drags the puff of white steam as the train, its whistle shrill and distant on the still air, races along towards Corfe. Here we stand on top of the world in our own, elevated dimension. To the north, we see the heathland spread of purple, brown and green towards Wareham, the tower of St Mary's just discernible against the backdrop; the harbour's flat wash of silver, the distant, urban world of the Poole and Bournemouth conurbation so far across the sweeping expanse, so alien to this present place and time, that we cease to be part of them, feel happily detached from them, in a delicious sense of escape.

We walk further along the ridge. Cows stand on an adjacent summit, a Bronze Age barrow, their stoic, stolid silhouettes; big bodies on small legs, almost ungainly and comical against the sobering sky. Below the ridge on which they stand so motionless, I can see that the land has been hewn away at one time, for the escarpment is sheer, the bare face of the stone still exposed. It must be the edge of an old quarry, and I realize that this landscape is not totally timeless and that much is shaped by man and changed.

The same can be said down to our left, for along the length of the valley of Church Knowle, many isolated farmsteads appear to be scattered. Some are attached to big houses, such as medieval Barnston Manor (just outside Church Knowle down below us in the valley and purportedly the longest inhabited property in Dorset [63]) and were no doubt at one time part of small villages of their own. This is certainly the case with Steeple, the smallest Purbeck village, whose sixteenth-century church tower now comes into view, peeping between trees in the same lush valley. The name of the village does not apparently allude to a former church steeple, but from 'steep place' [52]. The church was here before the tower, for it is in itself, twelfth-century. Its unpretentious interior in a tiny, unassuming shrunken village, which some now even class as a hamlet, contains a surprise of historic interest: the Lawrence coat-of-arms which adorns its porch and the bosses on its seventeenth-century barrel roof apparently inspired the American flag. This, according to a very knowledgeable man who I met in Church Knowle, is because the Lawrence family of nearby Creech Grange had, in the fourteenth century, married into the Washington (De Wessington) family whose coat of arms contained stars and stripes. A much later descendant of the Washington family, a John Washington, apparently settled in the USA. He was the great grandfather of George Washington who became President. Thus Steeple, an example of a shrunken village, has retained an understated importance, in possessing the connection with American democracy which it secretly conceals, and proudly remaining while other, neighbouring villages were lost, their remains now only hinted at by the isolated farmsteads round about.

Perhaps in the past, this whole valley wasn't as silent, natural and reflective, so seemingly contained. Perhaps it was more akin to an early rural conurbation, which later disbanded partially due to industrialisation as people left the land to find work. It could therefore be argued that the onslaught of urban civilization and the Industrial Revolution has done more to preserve the countryside than we give it credit for. It is also perhaps thanks to the present conurbation that this place can be so peaceful, idyllic and unspoilt: for one could sit here all day looking down into its sleepy valley, watching the world go by, time drifting silently on the wing of a bird of prey, only interrupted by a random bleat of a sheep or the moan of a cow. Today, however, the day is overcast, the clouds hanging heavily laden, threatening rain. It makes the valley seem even more secluded, cushioned, contained and yet we are on top of the ridge, exposed and unsheltered. It is time to go, following back along the path, which unwinds, like a ribbon, along the soft green contours of the solid ridge itself, leading us back to Corfe.

(2014)

The Undercliff

The Undercliff, leading west along the World Heritage Coast out of Lyme Regis to Axminster is described by Natural England as being 'one of the largest and most important active coastal landslip systems in western Europe', and also 'one of the wildest and most unspoilt tracts of countryside in southern England' [54]. This wilderness lies peacefully above the still calm of a milky sea, which today is perceived only as the faintest wash breathing through the trees. We peer through the green canopy, screening us from sea-views. It seems as dense as a jungle, above and below, concealing the fissures and uneven clefts in the fallen rock, bringing a beguiling sense of calm security in this cataclysmic, unstable landscape. The path seems to stride bravely before us, out along the edge of the world, leading the way through the heart of the wilderness clinging on below the cliffs. It is impossible to leave it, you have to continue, or else turn round and go back; there are no short cuts through the trees, no escape routes.

As we enter the world of the Undercliff on an overcast day, the smooth, stereophonic crooning of pigeons soothes the uneasy tension of muggy air. Chiffchaffs and blackbirds accompany them, juxtaposing the oppressive, moody gloom, which subtly pervades the atmosphere, setting the scene for a gothic romance and bringing with it a lingering sense of prehistory. Perhaps it is also the glooming light which makes everything seem greener, more enticing, looming larger than life a little like the creatures of a past age; the massive insects, the dinosaurs- everything magnified. A gunnera grows in a swampy enclave, huge, grotesque as it stretches out its alien, umbrella leaves through the thickening air. Even the few stray bluebells, the last of this year's crop, appear to blare a brighter blue from their drooping trumpets. Flies thrive in the humidity. Perhaps it will thunder.

Green glares against contorted trees, wrapped with woody, strangulating stems of ivy, which seem to have become part of the trunk, an ornamental appendage, clinging and cleaving, looping and fusing to become an essential dimension and texture. This place is indeed primeval. Horsetails, sometimes called living fossils, the only surviving members of the ancient equisetum genus, grow in abundance alongside ferns, also ancient. Under our feet no doubt lie the fossilised bodies of many marine animals, locked into the layers of Blue Lias rock until it slips against itself and falls away, a mighty upheaval, stirring sleeping giants. This is a reality; landslides are frequent, the perpetual motion of the earth causing a greater diversity of flora and fauna as newly exposed land firstly becomes fresh scrub, later extensive forest of ash and field maple. A landslide has recently closed the path five miles along towards Axminster. We cannot walk the whole way. This is a shifting, unstable world, yet nature gently binds it together, concealing ugly secrets like makeup, covering the scars of fissured rock until they once again wrench open their wounds.

Through the sultry air comes the delicious, comforting burble of a narrow watercourse, its constant stream making its way down from the cliffs above to meet the beach below. These are what cause the land to slip: these and rain. We are walking beneath the cliffs on the land which has already fallen, some of it centuries before, and collected in a large, cascading pile beneath. Nature has reclaimed, made it look mature, established, perhaps more established than it actually is. The whole environment is perhaps not what it seems; perhaps age is not what it seems. Deception here is so innocent, an undeliberate deception, for the greenery has no conscious part to play in it, the wealth of flora and fauna which inhabits this national nature reserve, flanking and encroaching on the concealed path, is merely here because that is its way.

As part of the renowned Southwest coast path, this place is like no other part. It is secretive, a solace, cosy, self-sustaining, an unspeakably natural, untamed, wilful and mysterious world, a perpetual motion through time, a transition, an inspiration. It leaves a big impression on me and I imagine John Fowles was equally inspired by the notion of its subtle deception when, in his novel *The French Lieutenant's Woman*, he created his protagonist, Sarah Woodruff to be not only mysterious, wilful, progressive, representing transition in her own time, but also deceptive. Or perhaps it is just that her character has subtly and insidiously forged an association in my mind, and therefore coloured my interpretation of this place.

We return towards Lyme, the misty silhouette of the dramatic Dorset coastline plunging into the mesmerising milky calm of an almost imperceptible sea, which holds a deep breath of grey light, dissipating at the horizon. It appears transitory, enigmatic, delicate, yet expounds that dependable calm of consistency in its constant respiration. It is then that one wonders what is real and what is illusory. It feels so secure here, so safe beneath the green, gothic -cathedral -arch canopy of this secret enclosure, yet one day the earth above could come crashing down, as it last did on a large scale in 1839, or open up below to swallow us just as an innocuous-looking sea could swell to drown us on a stormy day. A storm simmers in the damp-smelling air, yet now it only adds to the enigma of this place, cosy under the protective allure of the glooming trees. It has not broken yet, nor has it broken the spell or destroyed its calming influence over us.

It is interesting to note that in her novel *Persuasion*, Jane Austen, no doubt influenced by the eighteenth- century obsession for the romance of the gothic, takes an overall more light-hearted approach, describing the Undercliff at Pinhay, as

> Pinny, with its green chasms between romantic rocks, where the scattered forest trees and orchards of luxuriant growth, declare that many a generation must have passed away since the first partial falling of the cliff prepared the ground for such a state, where a scene so wonderful and so lovely is exhibited, as may more than equal any of the resembling scenes of the far-famed Isle of Wight:these places must be visited, and visited again, to make the worth of Lyme understood.

I wonder how many other celebrated people have passed this way, seeing the same coastline, wandering the beaches below and waiting for the fossil-saturated cliffs to yield their treasure. Many early collectors, geologists and palaeontologists came and went, certainly once the fame of an unsung heroine had spread. Mary Anning, a local girl of humble origins who made her living from collecting fossils became something of a celebrity in the geological world of the early nineteenth century. She is reputed for being the first person to have discovered certain complete fossils of a type, including an ichthyosaur, plesiosaurus and a pterodactyl, which she sold to collectors at the time. Her discoveries encouraged scientists and palaeontologists to challenge previously held notions and to hold her in esteem as something of an expert. Her story is brought to life in Tracy Chevalier's novel *Remarkable Creatures* and at the Mary Anning museum in Lyme Regis.

Returning to the secret, shifting world of the Undercliff, so full of wild beauty and wonder while concealing danger, it makes me consider life. We are all walking on the edge of a precipice. One false step or something outside ourselves causing a calamity can send us away from the world which we know and into another unimaginable, with which those people of the past, the visitors, writers, and avid fossil hunters who walked beneath these cliffs, have already been acquainted.

(2014)

Woodland

It is beautiful in the woods today, sunlight dancing through new green leaves, sending soft ripples of light across ferns on the forest floor and causing thick blankets of dog's-mercury to be swathed in silver. Up near the Wiltshire border, we have entered a clandestine world, which has always existed. It is as if, at first, we are intruding upon a place which has found satisfaction within itself, is content to be but then invites us to enter into its joy. The air is infused with a medley of melodious birdsong and I am delighted to hear a yaffle's infectious 'laugh', to be serenaded by a song thrush, to hear the robin's polished song, the see-saw of a great-tit, the warm, carefree crooning of a woodpigeon, and the chaffinch; its spiralling melody winding around a blackbird's notes of shrill exuberance. My attention is arrested by the cuckoo's disyllabic call, ethereal through the trees, and the tawny owl which mysteriously hoots by day. All continue, irrespective of our presence, each in a world revolving alongside our own. The only creature which seems to respond to our steps is a squirrel, shooting up a tree, tail flicking furiously.

Beneath the coppiced trees of this ancient forest, bluebells have flourished and are now fast fading, shrivelling to sink back down to slumber in the earth. A few weeks previously, their oceans of blue intensity, interspersed with bright celandines and gentle wood anemones enraptured, but now it is the wood-garlic which takes centre stage. The forest floor has become a mesmerising snowscape, stretching into infinity as the ramsons spread a lazy, lacy counterpane across it; their alluring sweetness and innocence somewhat juxtaposed by an accompanying acrid scent which steals through the forest. Garlic is known in folklore to be repugnant, repellent and to ward off evil.

Under oak and maple where tree creepers climb and the light filters through translucent leaves, I see spikes of yellow archangel and several species of wild orchid, diminutive against the backdrop of trees, their bashful pink columns rising up secretly from the forest floor as if no one would notice. Wild columbine also grows here; a beguiling beauty, intriguing in its exotic shape and deep purple hue, masquerading poison. A tree-creeper scurries upwards, a great-tit emerges from a tree-trunk hole.

The peace of this place, the stillness and exquisite beauty is overwhelming. And yet the sleepy drone of a plane flying above us establishes the modern soundscape so that the timeless sense is shattered for a moment, perfection marred; and as we walk around the corner, we see a tell-tale pile of feathers and blood; a bird which has been caught, perhaps by a fox last night. Murder and mystery do obviously stalk side by side in the forest, yet perhaps they have been chased away by the brilliance of the daylight and the warding off of the wood-garlic!

All is restored to peace and calm; beyond the backdrop of birds and the lazy buzz of insects in the twenty- degree heat, the only other people we encounter in this enchanting microcosm is a woman with notepad and a photographer with tripod, ambling along with his dog, surely intent, like me, on capturing some of the beauty and purity of this place, the essence of carefree childhood innocence and spontaneity which together seem to hold hands and skip between the trees along verdant pathways on this golden- green day.

(2015)

*

Not far away in north Dorset is another wood completely different in character, flora and fauna. Making the most of the sunny spell and the joy of springtime, we climb up into a mixture of deciduous and conifer surrounded by silence and birdsong. Amongst the medley of birdsong an unidentified caller sustains its sweet mantra of 'deep sleep' so that in this soporific woodland I am tempted to lie down beneath the trees and dream. The reverberating twang of woodpeckers brings me back and looking up, I catch the glimpse of a greater spotted shinning up the trunk of a tall conifer high up, tentatively tapping as he goes and letting out the odd cry. Other birds have evidently made nests which they now protect; the furious castanet click of a wren from a bush, and a blackbird perching on a branch high above our heads, somehow repeatedly making tuck- tuck sounds while his beak is stuffed full, warn us.

Around the periphery of the wood, we look out across buttercup fields. We are on one of the highest points of the Blackmore Vale, if not the highest. An ancient ash tree growing out of the wood bank surveys the scene as it has done for centuries. Its colossal trunk, which I imagine was once coppiced, has grown up in five separate parts, each of significant girth and stretching so high that I cannot photograph the entire tree. I hope it will remain resilient to ash dieback and the emerald ash borer moth, both of which may one day come.

We wander for hours down green, grassy paths between tall trees, watching white butterflies chase. They dart between banks of ladies lace and red and white campion joined by the odd surviving bluebell and buttercup. Life continues here despite everything. After the Second World War, much of the ancient wood was felled for plantations of conifers. Now the Woodland Trust is trying to restore the original habitat. People donate saplings, rising good and strong within plastic tubes to stop the deer destroying them. This new life and regeneration adds a sense of continuity to an ancient place which breathes history with every step and fuses it with the future so that the present feels fresh, alive and hopeful as we wander at the woodland's heart.

(2015)

Branksome Gardens

When it is very hot we sometimes seek the shade of Branksome Gardens; typically Edwardian in character. In May they remind me of the Edwardian garden my family owned when I was a child. Ours was on a much smaller scale of course; planted with bright azaleas, rhododendrons and Japanese acers. It was indeed fashionable at that time and with the Victorians, to import 'exotic' plants from the Far East for their gardens.

In Branksome Gardens there is a path, reminiscent of our old shrubbery, flanked by rhododendron. Entering it is like embarking on a secret world. When I was a child, I not only spent hours exploring the shrubbery, but found a natural cave under a rhododendron bush where the plant curved its huge branches above me like the vaulted roof of a crypt. It was my secret world for thinking, writing, dreaming. No one would find me there. I especially loved it when it rained, listening to the soft flick of raindrops on leaves above my head, yet staying dry. In the lugubrious light of rainfall, the magenta colour of the flowers would intensify, glaring in the backs of my eyes, and so the comfortable feeling of mystery and secret seclusion would intensify as well. The shrubbery was not only a paradise for a child but for adults alike and it is interesting how man has always had a love of secret places; it stimulates the sense of discovery, evokes feelings of intense security and brings out the curiosity of a child as well as quickening the imagination. I believe the child lives in the man just as much as the man is in the child.

Back in Branksome Gardens the sunlight is bright and hot, enticing the fragrance of pinewood to seep from tree trunks. I walk along the shady, dappled path and listen to the rich purr of bumble- bees hovering over purple rhododendron flowers, watching their furry brown bodies disappearing into the bell of the flower to collect the nectar. I admire their industriousness. It is a particular joy to see them, as bees are so seriously threatened. No one would think that such small insects act as the basis to our food chain and if they were not around to pollinate, we could suffer food shortages.

It is a pleasure to walk in these wooded gardens at the heat of the day under the cool shade of tall pines, which were presumably part of the original pine forest, much of which was planted by the early settlers of Bournemouth. So secret and contained is it that I sometimes forget it was created for the pleasure of the public, as was Bournemouth Gardens further along the clifftop. Both gardens combine nature with fantasy. In Branksome Gardens we wander by a stream with a small, artificial waterfall, which tumbles over manmade stones. In Bournemouth Gardens there stands a folly. Imported plants are also strategically planted to provide backdrops of colour, foregrounds of texture and a sense of the exotic.

By this period of history it would seem that people had more leisure time, certain laws regarding working hours had been established and the Education Act of 1870 deemed it necessary for children to be educated rather than to work. One can see black and white photographs of elegant Edwardian ladies with long skirts, parasols and hair scraped up wandering in the gardens with smart gentlemen in hats. There are also many black and white pictures of small children in the central gardens, under the protective gaze of adults, playing near the Bourne Stream, ribboned girls wearing white aprons over dark, knee-length dresses, little boys crouching over on chubby legs to poke at small boats with sticks. The central Bournemouth Gardens on these pictures seem as busy and exciting on a sunny day as they do today. Branksome Gardens are perhaps a little more secluded. We only ever see a few people here. They are a call to the wild, stepping back in time to an era of measured elegance, a fantasy creating fusion of colour, and a piece of living, breathing history, designed for the leisure of their time and lasting through our own.

(2011)

Martin Down

I must stop at the border where Dorset meets Hampshire and north into Wiltshire at Bockerley Dyke. The five and three-quarter kilometre long hump of this ancient linear earthwork indeed leaves a testimony to times past as it runs its fluid contour through the countryside, marking out a section of the border between Dorset and Hampshire through Martin Down. Cranborne Chase itself stretches out far beyond like the open pages of a history book displaying numerous tumuli, hillforts, Roman roads and manor houses. Along Bockerley Dyke the rounded humps of tumuli are no exception to this history, and a Roman road (Ackling Dyke) cuts through on a course down from Old Sarum to Exeter via Badbury Rings and Dorchester. This place is beautifully summed up by H.J Massingham who wrote; 'Man has added it [Bockerly Dyke] to the landscape, nature has accepted it and time has brought it into peace' [49].

The downland landscape along this border would have become so after being cleared by Neolithic farmers around five thousand years ago and has been extensively grazed ever since. Here is a wild, clipped countryside where skylarks shoot into the sky in a delirium of dizzy sweetness, where gorse, redolent of coconut, embalms the air and cowslips grow in abundance. Yellowhammers perch on bushes, pairs of cabbage white butterflies chase in courtship, a cuckoo's call echoes across the down through a backdrop of birdsong and if we are lucky, we can detect the gentle purr of a turtle dove also wafting through the wefts of song. According to Massingham, the downs also once rang with cowbells [49], an aspect of soundscape now silenced.

To the west stretches Dorset; chequerboard fields eventually reaching Shaftesbury. To the north lies Wiltshire; Salisbury Plain and the wonderful, mediaeval city of Salisbury itself. To the east is Hampshire, the beautiful, unspoilt villages of Martin, Rockbourne and Breamore, which trail the borders of the New Forest, their ancient thatched and timbered cottages over -satisfying a delight in the aesthetic. It is between Whitsbury and Braemore that enchanting enclaves of bluebell woods peep through the trees with their comforting blue as we plunge down single- track leafy lanes, a vault of vibrant green arching above our heads, the air infused with the fragrance of spring. More such swathes of blue can be seen on the road from Damerham to Cranborne, which lies to our south as we return to Dorset again.

The presence of Bockerley Dyke shows that borders and boundaries have always existed here and yet it is at this point that the surrounding counties feel so unified, that it is sometimes difficult to know exactly which you are in as you travel between villages. Cranborne Chase binds all together with its overwhelming feeling of ancient history, a relic of our ancestral past. Empty yet intimate, compelling in its sense of ancient permanence, the earth of the chase spread out before us seems to live and breathe, stirring secrets beneath the soil. It is as if it were a time capsule which has the power to draw us back into itself. When we glimpse this virtually unchanged landscape; the contours of the ancient land, the ridges and furrows, the lines and curves, the rounded humps of tumuli and rolling hills, we share something of a common experience with previous generations. It is when this happens that we connect to a past, lost world which began before history, the timeline of the Earth seems shorter, and for a moment we feel a tenuous sense of understanding those generations long forgotten.

(2016)

SUMMER

….a typical summer evening…,
the atmosphere being such delicate equilibrium
and so transmissive that inanimate objects seemed
endowed with two or three senses, if not five.

(Thomas Hardy, *Tess of the D'Urbervilles*)

JUNE

Running Free

    In the evening I often run along the cliff top to Boscombe where in summer, sea pinks sway against the intense blue backdrop of sea and the evening light causes everything to stand out with crystalline definition. Towards Sandbanks in the opposite direction, I can discern the familiar stacks of Old Harry rocks, etched golden in the evening light before the gentle backdrop of rolling Purbeck hills. I always have a yen to return to these hills as often as I can. Somebody has lit candles on the beach. They stand, tall tapers against the silencing swash of translucent sea, flicking and guttering. As I run on, the wash of nacreous light, which blends in layers upon the sea's surface, intensifies in colour and dusk draws in, wrapping itself about me like a delicate scarf. It is summer and the air is balmy.

(2012)

*

    When running, one realizes that we have lost the art of walking. In trainers, and with such a quick step, sensitivities are strengthened to the differences in terrain over which the feet pass. One feels the delicious comfort of the forest floor - soft and spongy, melding with the sole of the shoe before becoming knotted with unyielding roots which weave themselves in a vast, ancient network under and through the earth, and which we have to avoid tripping over. We wince at the blunt stubbornness of stones which angle up through an eroded pathway, bruising the arches of the foot and striking the toes; we endure the flat thud of hardened, windswept earth on a dry day, and sink into the soft yield of sand on heathland tracks. Sometimes we dive between trees, ducking and side stepping to avoid brambles and gorse, following a thin, joyous depression in the springy turf, a whimsical footway which has been trampled down like tell-tale routes through the bluebell woods. These are perhaps the 'incipient paths' or 'slight footways' which Hardy mentions; the pathways which regular walkers would know well and visitors would pass by unseeing. He explains that

> The whole secret of following these incipient paths, when there was not light enough in the atmosphere to show a turnpike road, lay in the development of the sense of touch in the feet, which comes with years of night-rambling in little-trodden spots. To a walker practiced in such places a difference on impact on a maiden herbage, and on the crippledstalks of a slight footway is perceptible through the thickest boot or shoe.[40]

With the advent of transport it would seem that we have lost that sense of touch, become almost desensitized; our feet no longer being as tuned to nature, to the undulations of gradient, to the change in soil and surface, even the most seasoned walkers amongst us. Perhaps it is only the cross-country runner's feet which still experience something of this sensation. With the loss of feeling has perhaps come the loss of many pathways, remaining anonymous, those which were never really frequented enough to be cut into the earth have perhaps faded through time to become an elusive memory in the minds of those who once knew them.

Picnic Tea

The day is hot and dreamy at Badbury Rings where my friends and I spread a pretty picnic cloth. Along with Clipper tea or a Dorset blackberry brew we have homemade scones, strawberries, clotted cream and Dorset apple cake. We unpack flowery china cups and plates bought for a song at Wimborne market. Empty rose lemonade and elderflower bubbly bottles serve as vases brimming with aquilegia from my garden. Not far from where we sit, blue butterflies flitter ephemerally through grasses while orchids lift their purple-pink heads to the sun, children chase around ramparts and skylarks fill the air with song. Freedom and joy is overwhelming and abundant. It is as if everything continues as it has done through centuries past, inviting us to join it and enter into the timeless experiences of all who have gone before.

(2017)

Discovery

I wander through wind -rippled flower meadows above which swallows skim, darting and dipping, and into which skylarks plunge before rising in a spiral of song. Beyond the Spyway barn, we trek back in time to discover fascinating fossil footprints where dinosaurs once walked. Yet out on the coast path watching wind-tugged sea pinks idly tossing their heads against a backdrop of living, breathing blue, I am so much reminded of happy, hazy childhood holidays and engrossed in the joy of the present that it is hard to imagine a prehistoric past here. Today I spy a bee orchid; a brilliant grinning mask, and a new sense of delightful discovery ripples through me just as the wind chases through the meadow grasses.

(2017)

Phosphorescence

Poole Harbour is a different world: an enclosed inlet looking towards the shaggy rugged coastline of Brownsea which looms, silhouetted out of iridescent depths. I remember one summer night many years ago, the sea flicked continuously with small pulses of intense energy as if an electric cable were carrying a charge under its surface. Appearing calm, tiny wavelets were moving continuously, each creating a dancing display of ethereal, electric blue; something that I had never seen before and have not seen since. Perhaps this was marine bioluminescence, phosphorescence which occurs on water when it is disturbed, and is actually the production of light-emitting phytoplankton. This ethereal phenomenon certainly is said to sometimes occur in other parts of Dorset, such as in the Fleet Lagoon. There is even a word for it in old Dorset dialect-*bremming* [10].

*

There are many secret wonders to captivate us on the Dorset coast at night. An old woman told me that when she was young there were glow worms on the cliffs, winking like stars and a fisherman claimed to have seen the aurora several times while night fishing.

Alum Chine

We approach the beach down Alum Chine, green and leafy in summer, where pools of sunlight collect on the path and excited children, clutching bucket and spade run alongside their parents and dogs, full of the anticipation of the sea. It is still so exciting to catch that first glimpse, that beckoning strip of blue at the path's end. Along the cliff top, Mediterranean-looking trees shimmer in the sunlight and the water glistens like a crystal bowl beneath, enticing. The cries of children on the beach below seem detached from up here, as sound rises and dissipates in the pine- laden air; light, easy and deliciously drowsy.

On a day like today, it is almost unbelievable to think that Alum Chine was once a smuggler's pathway along which silent convoys of contraband would have been transported at the dead of night through what was once then wild swathes of hostile heathland and on to the New Forest and beyond.....

Song Thrush

Somewhere deep in Delph Woods, a song thrush salutes the dawn. I am awakened by its song piercing the delicious dozing twilight and stealing into my subconscious with cutting clarity. It is a delight to dream and hear the vocal virtuosity of this early bird penetrating my state of half sleep, causing it to mingle with the beautiful dream world of the dawn forest. One does not have to be asleep to experience dreams. Now I am fully awake, watching the sun slanting through the trees with fingers of frail gold which touch the belly of a woodpigeon, an ethereal phantom, winging through wisteria-entwined trees on the fringe of the forest, warmly caressing the morning with its croon.

(2013)

Pimperne

Clouds contest with clear skies at Pimperne, sending shadows to drift across fields and hills with the scowl of the sun. The strong wind is almost indiscernible in the sleepy village with its sunny-faced brick and flint cottages surrounding the church and the high walls of its old rectory concealing intrigue behind dark and silent yews. Out in the fields the wind causes green wheat to hiss, sending out a myriad silver serpentine ripples which whisper and float in silky waves across the surface. Rippling fields surround us and the sunlight moves across the green hills behind them like an ever -changing face. As bludgeoned clouds clench black and blue fists to fight back at the sun, the wind chases them away again and so sunlight burns down upon our backs and dapples droves where trees sigh deeply in an agitated whisper, arousing suspense. The air is energetic and everything seems alive, exhilarated, excited to see the sun.

Out by the fields we hear skylarks everywhere, seemingly frolicking in their freedom. Here in a wooded copse that flanks the drove, blackbirds pour out their hearts in a constant conversation. For a few minutes we are plunged into a pastoral idyll, a false sense of summer security, until clouds cast a shadow once more and the atmosphere drops a degree of brilliance as if a light had been clicked off. But it will be back, and it is; on and off and on again so that a while later we can descend back down the hill into the village and sit at the thatched, sixteenth- century *Anvil Inn*. I watch the full strength of sunshine beam through the liquid bronze of my husband's pint. Each bubble a tiny star floating upwards and disbanding on the frothy surface as new ones are produced in a constant tidal flow, hundreds of tiny points of light rising endlessly. It is a bit like the feelings which rise in the heart when one walks in the countryside on days like this. Feelings bubbling up inside like a warm, clear spring, effervescent and full of joy.

(2012)

The River Stour

We walk down paths behind the medieval village of Cowgrove with its half-timbered, thatched cottages and farms from where a cockerel crows, its triumphant cries carrying across the fields. The trees whisper and hiss with excitement and joy on such a warm summer's day, a livid sun turning their leaves intensely green- gold while quivering dapples daub the path. The air, on this June day, expounds brilliance with bird song: a chiffchaff, a blackbird, a mellifluous song thrush. Their songs are as bright as the buttercup fields, which peep through hedges flanking the path. Horses graze gently, peacefully. Along the lazy river glide swans in the silver sunlight and a heron dips for fish; an expert fisherman he swallows them writhing, whole.

Today we can venture right down the riverbank where a platform of tree roots stretches to the water's fluid edge. Silent and secluded below the bank, we watch scrawled lines of liquid-golden water light dancing and flicking through leaves, waving across tree trunks and rising and plunging beneath the shimmering surface of the river itself. A breeze rustles leaves with that calm, easy nonchalance of a summer's day. This is a timeless day, one which evokes senses of sweet nostalgia, connecting us with the shared experiences of centuries. People who no longer live surely saw the same light leaping like laughter below the river bank, felt the same carefree drift of summer carried along on the river's course, the heady flow of balmy, rejuvenating heat, making them feel forever youthful and exuberant as the sun touched their skin many similar summers ago. Perhaps they too were delighted to see the male banded agrion damsel flies (*Calopteryx splendens*) flitting through the bushes by the river bank, appearing like black lace in flight until they land to reveal bodies of metallic green- blue. Everything is abundantly alive and present yet, as we take the path once more, the faint lilt of folk music drifting across the water meadows from Wimborne where the folk festival is in full swing, it is as if we had stepped back to the time of Thomas Hardy.

Back in the modern world, a group of seemingly carefree teenagers wander along the path; three boys and three girls, the latter, fashion-conscious; makeup, long, straightened hair, tanned legs in cropped, denim shorts- appearances already alluding to pressures to conform. If only life could always be as easy and uncomplicated as this path, which stretches freely before them, along by the river and the fields of tall, waving grasses. Another family pass with dog, young children clutching fishing nets. Contented. Further upstream, people plunge into the river with resonating splash, followed by euphoric laughter. It is a cool, refreshing sound, one which has no doubt echoed through the centuries. On the Pamphill cricket green, swathed in leafy sunshine, men play cricket, the epitome of traditional English village life, and on this dream of a summer's day, I am glad to see so many people enjoying themselves.

(2013)

Charmouth

Cold, persistent drizzle greets us in Charmouth, accompanied by a chill, searing wind. We wrap up and wander through the sleepy town, feeling as if we have travelled into a time where modernity and traditional simplicity exist simultaneously. Many of the houses are modern, built in a traditional style with well-attended, flourishing gardens, pretty even on a dismal day. White –wash and small side streets provide a casual, nautical feel and we imagine what the town would be like languishing in sunshine, rather than battling with the elements.

We wander out onto the beach, greeted by the resounding crash of a grey and surly sea. Shingle scrunches as we walk, purposefully, picking through pebbles as we go. About ten other people walk in the same way, dressed in waterproofs, hoods up, heads down. I am now eager to find a fossil. The last time I came here was on a school trip, aged about eight. I have always had a fascination for fossils and was equally determined to find one then. I remember scraping through the shingle for about an hour, feeling more and more despondent as my friends had all found at least one and my teacher dozens. At last she gave me one of her ammonites, but I was so determined to find one of my own, that I wasn't to be defeated. Then, just at the last minute, as we were about to leave, I scraped deep down into the shingle and found a perfect little ammonite sitting, staring up at me, so tightly coiled and damp shiny black; it was more beautiful than anything anyone else had found and I was instantly elated. Back at school, our teacher told us that she wanted us to stick all the fossils we had found onto sugar paper for a big wall display. As far as I was concerned, the glue would ruin the fossils, which I saw as valuable evidence of the past. I refused to let them have my fossil and was incensed about the fate of all the others and the fact that no one seemed to truly care about them.

Today, the same childlike enthusiasm has come to visit me and I find myself uncontrollably engrossed in fossil hunting. We forage at the bases of the cliffs, muddy grey and sticky on this damp day. We scratch through shingle, mounds of it, and after twenty minutes I find my first fossil; a shell. I am over the moon and remember exactly how I felt as a child. A woman walking along, sensing my evident enthusiasm, very kindly hands me a piece of pointed belemnite. This time I feel very grateful and it only inspires me to continue in my own pursuit, resulting in finding another piece of belemnite and an ammonite imprint. There is something very satisfying in finding fossils, the fact that before any historic event was recorded, they were lying here silently in the layers of the earth, not knowing that one day they would be discovered. I find them an intriguing testimony to a past, lost world, a world of extinct species whose characteristics and habitat we can only begin to imagine. These rocks are testimonies to a time so far removed from our own, that they are the only connection, the only similarity fusing that past with our present.

(2012)

Castleman Trailway

An owl glides in front of us up the forest path as we walk in the dreamy dusk light of midsummer. This elusive vision, serene as it silently drifts, seems to fade into the foliage, and aware of our presence, it reappears further up the path before disappearing once more as in a game of hide and seek. We, peering in vain up into the trees, are perhaps not seekers but intruders blundering into its kingdom. This skilled and powerful hunter has outwitted us as it no doubt outwits many a mouse and small rodent, casting fear into their miniature world. Yet despite this reputation, it evidently feels uncomfortable in our presence. How sad that man should instill such fear in wildlife that it wants to escape every time we try to come close to it.

It is eight o'clock and the owl is already hunting. The warmth of amber evening light filtering through the trees casts tints of gold upon their trunks. Foxgloves seem to stalk like predators, their proud, hooded heads rearing up above bracken and other vegetation, the warm evening air soothed with the soporific, stereophonic croons of wood pigeons, the cheerful, flowing melodies of blackbirds, and the fresh, spearmint sweetness of a song thrush whose meandering reverie pierces the heart. Somewhere from the world beyond this wood, the faint monotonous pounding of a disco beat pulses across the wheat fields in weak snatches of sound. Perhaps there is a party up at one of the farms. Nature continues unperturbed here in its sweet serenade of the evening, yet the owl, sweeping majestically somewhere between the trees, lost to sight, is silent. It has evoked an image so brief, yet one which I will hold in my memory forever.

(2015)

Shaftesbury

A strong, hazy sunshine lingers on this late June morning; the type that wraps itself around you in a sticky embrace and silently burns your face. Fields languish in the heat- haze on the journey to Shaftesbury, while the bus which I have taken, bounds, not effortlessly, along country roads. I enjoy taking buses in the country. Everyone is so friendly and usually a free-for-all conversation instigated by the driver ensues. People embark, greeting everybody else on the bus, people disembark and wave as the bus pulls away and we all wave back. I love the spirit of close village community, where everyone looks out for each other, passes the time. On this bus, the driver even takes time to chat to a couple of old women who are waiting at the bus stop for their friend to alight. He has obviously met them before and it is refreshing to see that the impersonal, distrustful city mentality, which naturally exists to a certain extent in the conurbation, has not taken over the countryside.

As we pass through Charlton Marshall and Spetisbury something excites me; the green hills behind the villages are brushed with scarlet. Poppies are growing in abundance, their colour dense and bright, thinning out at the edges as if the hillside has been smeared with scarlet paint. A yellow rape field looms in the foreground; the yellow so intense and vivid that it hurts the eyes. It lounges in front while another red field comes into view behind. These are acrylic, primary colours and there is something surreal about seeing the English countryside so vividly hued. A group of Friesian cows sit nonchalantly in front of the red hill. With this brilliant backdrop and the red and yellow fields clashing so intensely to their right, they are unaware that they have become part of a living piece of pop art, as moving sculptures framing the foreground.

The bus ambles on through more pretty villages, some with brick and flint cottages and others with traditional thatches and roses climbing up, around and all over their plastered walls. Everything is a feast for the eyes with flowers in abundance. The driver banters on all the way; an infectious atmosphere of joviality pervades as various passengers banter back, a bit like a game of word tennis, each trying to outdo the other with their wit. At some point we pass through Blandford, the most intact Georgian town in Dorset, as it was totally rebuilt in 1731 after a fire.

We disembark in Shaftesbury; most famous for its Gold Hill whose photograph has appeared just about everywhere (I even saw it once in the window of a photography shop in Spain) It seems to epitomize the rural, the carefree, and appears picture postcard perfect. Its old, friendly-faced cottages step down a steep cobbled road which seems to lead to the abundant freedom of the green fields and gently rolling hills spreading out beyond like an open book, so near yet so far. From the top of the hill, one cannot see the bottom, which is perhaps why these fantasies exist, for one can only dream, as one does for the pot of gold at the end of the rainbow. Yet what are we in fact dreaming for? The grass for many of us is always greener, and yet this whole town seems to exude contentedness as if it had already found the pot of gold and the greenest grass as it basks in its verdant surroundings. I imagine that nothing has changed in hundreds of years, time trundling on, exuding a wealth of nostalgia and happy memories and I feel instantly sustained by this whole atmosphere; town and country blended together and complimenting each other in exquisite harmony.

From Abbey Walk, the views stretching out across Blackmore Vale are simply breath-taking. A woman remarks 'This is England at its best,' and she is right. I stand drinking in the scene, compellingly peaceful. An incessant, distant drone of some farm machinery rising somewhere from the valley below only serves to exacerbate the dreamy silence and a pigeon croons wistfully, its familiar tone bringing a warmth to mingle with the air on this sultry day. Suddenly the sharp yowl of a peacock slices it, shocking us into reality. Silence is destabilised momentarily before drifting back into timelessness once more. Only the dull clank of an old church bell somewhere behind the abbey keeps note of time; twelve o'clock it chimes and in the height of the hazy midday sun, church steeples and small farms seem to snuggle further into the thick eiderdown of idle Dorset fields, warm and gentle.

I wander around the ruined abbey, once wealthy and powerful, founded in the ninth century and becoming, in 1539, a victim to the dissolution of the monasteries. Now only the foundation stones remain; tangible evidence of the edifice which was once at the heart of this prosperity. I was informed at the abbey museum that Shaftesbury Abbey had owned so much land, not only in Dorset but in Wiltshire and Somerset, that if the Abbess of Shaftesbury had married the Abbot of Glastonbury (to my thinking, an impossibility as nuns, and monks to that matter, were surely to remain celibate) together they would have possessed more land than the King. There is something incongruous about an establishment of such piety, into which women withdrew in order to distance themselves from the temptations of the world, to be coveting so much wealth and power.

The museum provides an evocative insight into the abbey. Stumps of columns and pieces of capitol have been excavated and put on display alongside other pieces of stone with a very informative guide telling us of their former function, their style and from which stone they were hewn. Soft sunlight, slipping through glass, moulds to the contours of these exhibits; shadows shift on a medieval face, crudely carved, and sink into the shapes of sculpted designs.

Outside, I walk amongst the foundation stones, tufted with a profusion of pink valerian. Nature has reclaimed them, transforming them into something beautiful so that the gardens blaze with colour, enticing bumblebees and butterflies. The ethereal call of the pigeon once more enhances the contained and peaceful atmosphere of contentment and although the days of the nunnery are long since gone, a different life continues here amongst the flowers while memories linger fragrantly on the breeze in an air of reflection as soft as a prayer.

In the town a similar sense of stillness remains unbroken by old buildings. Bustle is merely superficial against the backdrop of peace. Taking all the time in the world I browse small shops, pour over handmade jewellery, antiques and books, try a tea room where the warm waft of food is too heavy on such a hot day, and buy up a stack of second-hand Beethoven piano concertos; I am delighted at such a find! The silent saxon church of St Peter stands next to the nineteenth- century town hall, quiet and understated as it blends into the overall ambience of total escape, though what I escape from, I am not sure. Home is a blissful haven suitably far from any sizeable town and as I happily chat to the locals while waiting at the bus stop, I relish the thought of trundling once more through the pretty Dorset villages and to the green beyond…....

(2013)

Ashmore

Ashmore, the highest village in Dorset, lies close to the Wiltshire border at seven hundred feet above sea-level. We have just come from walking the deep and secret valleys near Tollard Royal, an undulating, sun-soaked landscape with forested, soft green slopes grazed by sheep. The sun has stayed in the valleys and clouds cluster above us at Ashmore, enclosing us in a soft sense of permanence there. Certainly it is an old village, possibly Roman, as it lies on the Roman road from Badbury Rings to Bath, but certainly mentioned in the Domesday Book as 'Aisemere' the pond where an *Aise* (ash) tree grows [52]. The village centre focusses mainly on the large dew pond, a rare survivor of its kind, possibly dug in Roman times and lined with clay as water cannot be contained in high chalk areas. It would have supplied the village with a precious resource and would have been relied upon not to dry out. I watch the wind scour its surface, causing silver sheets of shimmying water to fan out across and so break the mirror-like meniscus.

The Filly Loo, the Ashmore village festival, happens each year around the twenty- first of June. It is thought to have associations with the dew pond. The atmosphere is one of anticipation and community as people gather for the festivities and young girls in white Jane-Austen -style dresses dance prettily in step to traditional folk music. As the sun dips down, the atmosphere closes in on itself, becoming more contained and exciting. A traditional dance begins at dusk, men with stag's antlers move slowly past the crowds accompanied by a teasing melody on a solo pipe. The music seems to run away like water and soak into the dark unknown of the night, while the community link hands for the final dance around the pond in the immediate glow of torchlight.

(2016)

Butterflies

We have an ancient forest to ourselves today and walk with anticipation into its peaceful seclusion, wondering what we will observe. Snatches of windswept sunlight cast dapples on the forest floor and spill silver shards across deep carpets of dog's mercury while lone butterflies follow whimsical ways through their fast-fading shafts. As we venture further into the forest interior, we feel as if we have encroached upon an unseen world and we cling to the wonder of discovering its secrets, unwittingly revealing them through every footfall. Our presence causes hidden birds to suddenly appear; flapping away, flustered, emitting alarm calls. Then the tangible stillness falls again, the only sounds being the subliminal background drone of a million insects and the wind rifling through the trees.

The birds do not want us here and we feel, although discrete as we try to be, that we have blundered in on beauty, uninvited like gate-crashers to a feast. We do not mean to spoil the equilibrium, cause any disruption or agitation, yet it is because our eyes relish this feast of nature, savouring every sight and sound, that we inevitably do. Horse flies similarly cause us agitation as they anticipate feasting on our flesh.

In a sheltered ride, butterflies nectar on brambles. We count ten species but it is the silver-washed fritillary sunning its huge, complex-patterned wings, which causes me to look down, and the graceful glide of the white admiral; a black and white enigma soaring high up into the tree canopy which carries my attention upwards. Then, with an elegant white streak retreating into the vast forest, the admiral is gone. We have a privileged view of its private world; one which we physically share despite its seeming so remote. When the admiral comes gliding back to the brambles, almost landing on my arm; so close yet intangible; tantalising as it circles around me, I sense the separation of these two worlds more strongly. Yet it is as if there has been a brief connection on its terms, when it perhaps acknowledged my presence with curiosity rather than fear. A few seconds shared. Then it is gone again, escaping into the freedom of the trees once more; an elusive, ethereal transience to be enjoyed in the present and relished in the memory forever.

(2017)

JULY

Summer's Evening

The ancient copse glows; glowing with the warmth of a searing summer sun; oblique rays fingering through foliage, turning each coppiced hazel tree into an individual fire. In cool shadows beneath the trees, the atmosphere is warmed by the deep and delicious croon of a lone wood pigeon; its soothing, repetitive mantra seems to steal from the shadows, echoing another world; a secret world of mystery and beauty which we are part of and yet cannot completely understand.

*

On Badbury Rings the evening is hot, even an hour before sundown. Butterflies bask on scabious, blackberry flowers and pyramid orchid while the descending sun spills its light across the contours and ripples of the rings, suffusing them with molten gold. It is so still here, the only sounds being the exchange of yellowhammers calling to each across breathless spaces, the pebble-clattering chatter of a stone-chat and the buzz of bees. While a wan moon rises above the rings, breaking into the sky's unbroken-blue expanse and promising the embrace of a velvet-warm night, the ancient landscape soaks up the last of the livid sun as it has done through so many summers past.

(2017)

Cutt Mill

On a warm and sultry day, the air a stifled breath, we walk from Sturminster Newton along the banks of the river Stour to Cutt Mill through waist-high grass that tickles and itches. The exuberance of springtime has fully subsided. Now in silence, only the odd blackbird, chiffchaff and the occasional rustle somewhere below the riverbank elude to the liveliness of spring passed. The river, filled with grey light, glides nonchalantly, thick and heavy as the sky above and as the air, drowsy and humid about us. Tall magenta flowers brighten the riverbank before the path plunges down into a wooded area, becoming an overgrown corridor of leaves woven with the cerise flowers of cottage roses. It glares with a glowing green intensity in the gloom. We are nearing some settlements. A comfortable thatched cottage peers from between the trees.

The path opens out and we have come to Cutt Mill, the sorry sight of an abandoned building; roofless, red brick with empty gaping holes. Yet this was the place where the poet William Barnes apparently used to play so joyfully as a boy [33] and as I take in the landscape round about, the layers of leaves, some silvery, sweeping before a backdrop of darker green and in the foreground grass, reeds and rushes providing differing textures and shades, I fancy that I can hear the imperceptible echoes of children from long ago, plunging into the river with delighted splashes, shrieking and laughing. This, of course, is an impression borne only on the imagination however, I also remember the words of William Barnes, written in Dorset dialect:

> In happy days when I wer young
> An' had noo ho, an' laugh'd an' zung,

The sad, pensive loneliness of the present mill, a sorry figure of what it was once when Barnes used to play there in his halcyon days, seems to stand as a metaphor for much of his poetry, which often looks back to the times of his childhood with sweet nostalgia, the past perceived as superior to the present.

> The works o' man do rise an' vall;
> An' trees the toddlen child do vind
> At vu'st, an' leave at last behind;
> I wish that you could now unvwold
> The peace an' jay o' times o' wold;
> An' tell, when death do still my tongue,
> O' happy days when I wer young.
> (William Barnes- *O'happy days when I wer young*) [8]

There has apparently been a mill on this site since Domesday, suggesting that pathways leading here were used frequently, worn through time by habitual passage and that the mill was thus active throughout the centuries. The fascination of old paths is that they reveal a history of constant human comings and goings, carved in the earth like graffiti for future generations, yet we can only but wonder at who once walked on them, sharing something of their anonymous experience.

The path alongside the Stour is an exception, for although countless footsteps must have traversed its banks throughout the centuries, there is no sign of erosion, no wear and tear, and when the grass has grown long, as it does in summer, it is sometimes impossible to see where the path should even be, so that one is forced to forge one's own way through, creating a disappearing pathway as one parts the grasses which spring back behind. To our right, the Stour seems to have stood still, so slow and languorous is its oily, inky flow, reflecting shadow trees and dark banks in its grey- light-filled depths. Again the words of William Barnes, seem to wash through the stillness, for in another poem entitled *The River Stour*, he alludes to it with affection as being a place of boyhood play.

(2011)

Summer Evening at Arne

As the day begins to drain away to evening we walk by the wash of the sea at Arne. Waves lap gently, regularly fanning out in a thin film at our feet, smoothing the sand at the shore, erasing the wandering, dendritic footprints left by seabirds. Cushion clouds make marbled effects on the surface of the sea, a suggestion of sunset cuts through them rippling pastel pink on nacreous waters. All is soft, safe and soothing; a child being rocked to sleep in parental arms. The wild, lonesome cries of waders drift across the empty space where sea meets sky, hauntingly ethereal and beautiful; and in the mysterious calm which holds its breath with a tangible expectancy, sound snatches in waves, the rise and fall of laughter and wordless conversations. People are enjoying the evening on their sailing boats, moored in the shallows so that long, lazy lines of scribbled masts spear the pastel-smudged sea as it laps its lullaby and we drift into dreams.

As the broken cloud clears, so the sun becomes a blazing ball and we return to the heath to watch it descend over the dark horizon. Then the treacly churr of a nightjar steals out of the shadows, looping in beaded threads around the empty spaces. Such profound complexity of compelling sound, a wandering radio wave searching for a signal while drawing the whole atmosphere into a dense, contained security. It is as if the ring of silhouetted pines that surround us, the dome of twilight sky with its tentative stars above and the black shadow of the earth beneath, are one big cave of magnified dimensions around which the churring resonates and we are standing in the middle, lost in awe and wonder at the immensity of dusk.

(2016)

*

A year later I wander on the same shore, wrapped in the pashmina of approaching night, listening to the almost imperceptible trickle of a listless, chiffon sea which washes in and in, softly stroking the shoreline. The beach stretches away lethargic, no sound of seabirds; only the constant trickle tickling the shore's edges with a whisper, subtle against the scrunch of shells and stones as people pass on the beach behind. In the reserve itself, honeysuckle hangs a delicate fragrance on the balmy air, a song thrush salutes the evening as the last lick of golden light lingers across the landscape and a dreamy duo of woodpigeons croons comfortably from a nearby ash tree. I wait on the beach watching rising moonlight mingle with the sun- blushed surface of the sea, the creeping colours combining in the water's mesmeric movements, fusing and fading, flickering with the moon's wan path. An owl calls out of nowhere, its screeches swallowed by silence. Evening walks contain an excitement, and a sense of mystery, which is not felt during the day, and as everything familiar settles to sleep, there is a growing anticipation of the night to come.

(2017)

Studland

Studland, said to be the Toy Town of Enid Blighton: nostalgic and carefree. Today is a perfect July day, warm with a teasing breath in the air, which rides through leaves, tousling them playfully. As we walk along a path above the beach, the whisper of the trees stirs excitement while shadows tickle their trunks with feathery strokes. Freedom is ageless, timeless: we could be in any century as the stillness of this small village washes over us. Peering between the trees I see the deep sunken spread of sea below- marbled, graduating tones of pink, aqua and green stain the shallows where overhanging branches cast indigo shadows and wash into the tranquil blue of the sea itself. Seahorses once sustained their secret, secluded existence beneath these opalescent layers but tragically, because of their eel-grass habitat being systematically destroyed by the anchor chains of mooring boats, their numbers are in steep decline.

We have just passed concrete wartime bunkers, abandoned on strategic points along the coast path, leaving their legacy of conflict and the fact that things were not all quite so idyllic here. Now their empty shells resonate with the delighted cries of children as a father's voice booms merrily from within, testing the echoing acoustics. Time and nature have perhaps healed the war memories here, the latter growing over its scars. One day, these bunkers may be totally reclaimed by the wild.

Back at Studland, we are now walking towards Old Harry rocks, stopping on the cliff top to admire the view. Away to the right, the strong, forty- foot high chalk stacks of Old Harry themselves rise out of the sea, reflected as bold brushstrokes in its vitreous depths. Here the water is a rich petrol blue, not the opaline aquamarine of the shallows. Its intense colour washes placidly against the bases of the whitewashed rocks, the rocks to which groups of students and families walk like lemmings, gathering at the top for photos, perhaps to show that they have reached the most easterly point of the Jurassic Coast.

A stiff breeze blows across Ballard Down, gently ruffling the sea to shimmer silver across its azure surface and teasing the kaleidoscope of downland flowers; magenta pyramid orchids, the misty blue of scabious, blushing clover, the brilliant white of ox-eye daisies, and vibrant gold dandelions and vetch to name but a few. The amount of flora and fauna per square meter of downland is too numerous to count and is an extremely rich wildlife habitat. Unfortunately much of it has been lost in the last century.

Above the down, the sky arcs in an eternal blue dome, rising ever upwards as do the joyful voices of skylarks. These tiny birds epitomize the feeling of being in this place as they frolic on the currents, twisting and tumbling, full of freedom and the joy of being alive. Swallows too, streak across the cloudless sky and there are always birds of prey out here. On the crest of the down, we sit in the grass and eat some fruit. Below us the sea spreads like a silent, idyllic dream, intangible from the cliff top. We watch the sunlight dance and sparkle on its surface and the serene white sails of lazy sailing boats gliding by, silhouetted for an instant against the sun; white becoming black, before re-emerging into the calm blue once more. Somehow up here on the cliff top time stands still and yet one knows it passes and wants it to stop forever. We are on the outside looking into a beautiful dream and yet we are also part of it, for the sea and coast path exist in unity. The boats below seem detached from our reality and yet they are part of the same scene. It is a strange feeling, which perhaps helps to add to the dreaminess and the sense of escape which this ambience provides. The urban world with all its problems and pressures seems to be far away. I believe deep down that man is always looking to escape from something, to gain more freedom than the freedom that he owns, but he is also looking for something bigger and deeper, something outside himself into which he can step, something intangible which can become tangible by looking into the vastness of creation.

Having reflected awhile, we get to our feet and turn back along the coast path, too lazy to walk to Swanage today. Cyclists whip past us, free-wheeling down the slopes with the freedom of the wind, hang-gliders launch themselves, seemingly walking off the cliff edge and continuing, as they are carried out over the sea, the world floating beneath them as they sit suspended in a little chair. It must be the nearest experience man can get to flying and I only wish we had wings, as, despite the fact that they make it look so easy, I have never been brave enough to try. The land stretches round in a hazy curve to the glittering 'mirage' of Swanage. I remember walking there across the down from Studland beach as a child of eight on a school trip, a memory as vague and out of reach as Swanage seems today.

As we walk back towards Old Harry, I see two children, a boy and a girl also aged about eight, as I was then, engaged in deep conversation as they wander along side by side. So engrossed in conversation are they, that they seem like little adults, undisturbed by their surroundings. In this strange dichotomy, it is they who seem responsible and us, the adults, who feel so gloriously and recklessly free.

(2011)

Beaminster

The sun has reached its zenith over the small market town of Beaminster. It sits, radiating the stifling heat from its golden walls. Its hue, by nature of similar building materials, is reminiscent of Sherborne and adjacent villages in Somerset yet located about twenty miles hence. I am told by a local that most of the buildings here are listed, constructed mainly in the seventeenth and eighteenth centuries after a succession of fires during the fifteenth and sixteenth centuries destroyed what was previously there.

Despite having a population of approximately three thousand, barely anyone can be seen venturing into the midday heat. The streets stand silently, echoing a wave of merry laughter which rises from deep within the Red Lion and suggests where the locals might choose to spend their Saturday. The contrast in terraced cottages; some facing full sun, others sunk in shadow, galleries, small shops, including a grocer emitting nostalgic aromas of warm cardboard and ripe fruit, make us feel as if we have travelled back a couple of generations to when people didn't rely on big brash supermarkets to do their weekly shop.

Up a steady hill we climb, to where the fifteenth- century church of St Mary gracefully rises above the town. From its graveyard I look down onto the road below, curving away with its jumble of pretty rooftops and rose-entwined cottages. The church, also built of the same honey-coloured Ham hill stone, has an impressive sixteenth-century tower with battlements and pinnacles, an array of elegant sculpture standing lofty and gracious as it looks gently down.

Beaminster is surrounded by beautiful, verdant countryside. Rolling hills and golden green fields bordered with deciduous copses enclose what is often known as 'Dorset's hidden valley'. The landscape rolls on and on, away to a muted horizon; silent, timeless, peaceful. Somewhere snuggled and secluded deep within its coombes are the beautiful manor houses at Mapperton, Parnham, Wraxhall, Melplash and Mappercombe. These are the ones which I know about, and I am sure there are more, hiding away like jewels in a landscape which must be part of the crowning beauty of Dorset.

Mapperton lies two miles outside Beaminster down a thin country lane. Cows graze in dazzling golden- green pastures while a wooded hillside climbs away behind. Today the bright sunlight blazes golden through the trees and grass and the cow's tails, which they patiently flick at flies, enduring the heat. The green is so intense that it leaps at the eyes as brilliantly as the full force of sunshine. The road winds past a sleepy farm, and on to the entrance of Mapperton House, with its long, enticing driveway. The house represents a unity of building across three centuries from the sixteenth to the eighteenth [63]. Its weathered, ochre facade of Ham Hill stone, so characteristic of this area of Dorset, exudes the mellowed warmth and contentment of a vintage port. Mullioned windows and twisted barley-sugar chimneys add character and curiosity, infusing within us an intrigue to explore the grounds. Behind the house, one enters a silent walled garden basking in beautiful memories before wandering through an old orangery redolent of soil and idle, glass-warm heat as the sun beams through arched windows. We then descend to a wonderful Italianate landscaped garden laid out below us in formal elegance, full of flowers and bees. This place is not pretentious, but rather intimate. One feels, when one saunters through the grounds, to be sharing in the secrets of a happy family past with an equally contented present. Leaving the formal gardens one can amble freely along dappled forested paths under whispering leaves and finally look out across a valley swept with the shadows of trees. It is a quiet, reflective place; one which is difficult to leave.

(2013)

Kingston Maurward Old Manor

A deep, resounding splash accompanies shrieks of laughter as teenagers mess about in canoes near the old manor house at Kingston Maurward. A glint of sun on bronzed arms and legs, a balancing act on boats between the trees, more laughter; and then the canoes move off, drifting on the river's sleepy tide.

Silence. The river looks refreshing, inviting thirst. This is a real Fentiman's afternoon, or perhaps a Pimm's for those who prefer something stronger. Unprepared as ever, my husband and I share a small bottle of water, sitting on dappled grass which stretches down to the river bank beneath a cool weeping willow whose fresh, lazy fronds caught by a breeze- breath casually sweep aside small partings like door beads to reveal tantalizing glimpses of the manor house itself. Built around 1597 by Christopher Grey, the house was sold just over a hundred years later by his great- great granddaughter, Laura, or Lora, when her husband, George Pitt, decided in 1720 to build a new house, [63] the present Kingston Maurward agricultural college, with its imposing Palladian façade set in a parkland of mature, spreading beech and copper beech trees under which sheep graze and lie panting in the breathless heat. The roots of these magnificent trees resemble the petrified water of bubbling springs, caught whilst rising and trying to flow away, or perhaps they are more akin to welling, oozing mud. Whatever they seem, they feel ancient, as if time has stood still through the centuries in this bucolic idyll.

As we walk around the corner, the whole manor house reveals itself and I look up with wonder at its warm grey serenity, radiant in the summer sun, friendly pointed gables and mullioned windows strong against a brilliant sky. I wonder if it had been a wrench for Lora Grey to part with such a house. I imagine she could have stood in one of those windows looking out over the golden green valleys of her childhood, the river running past, the fields and water meadows beyond. Did she feel torn, a sense of betrayal to her family home? Or perhaps she yearned for something more modern and was excited by the extravagant prospect of a big new fashionable house being built, yet still within close proximity to the old. Although evidently inhabited in 1847 (a blue plaque states that George Singer, the car manufacturer, was born here in that year), Lora had apparently left the old manor to its eventual fate, for after being used for a variety of different purposes through the subsequent centuries, it finally fell into neglect and was threatened with demolition. However, it was rescued in the 1960s by a local man, preserved for posterity and now stands elegant and prosperous in its verdurous surroundings [63].

We cross the river and wander down a long shady path, dappled and cool with steep hedgerows and banks to each side and tree branches stretching to form a roof above us. A deep rhythmic swishing and splashing of legs with waggy tails pounding the water behind the hedge reveals two springer spaniels running the river, or some tributary of it, we cannot tell. The look of doggy delight on their faces makes everyone smile as they relish the cool experience on such a hot afternoon. We experience it with less relish as climbing out; they shake, covering us with brown river water, before bounding off again to plunge once more. They have taken a liking to us, leaving their owners to follow far behind along the path. Every time we hear that plunging splash, we wait for the shake, dodging flying projectiles of muddy water. It is as if they know that we are trying to avoid them and so in their way, try to ingratiate themselves with us. They succeed. Who could resist that naughty, toothy smile of canine ecstasy which spreads across their faces every time they get us wet, or the eager excitement as they stand looking at us with expectant beady eyes, ears pricked up, head slightly cocked to one side. But then we are soft about dogs.

We lose them as we wander into the village of Stinsford and the graveyard of St Michael's Church; an eclectic mixture of styles from the thirteenth to seventeenth centuries, restored extensively in the nineteenth century and topped by a squat, square fourteenth-century tower. This church was where the family of Thomas Hardy worshipped during the nineteenth century and was so much part of his life that it features heavily in his book *Under the Greenwood Tree* as Mellstock parish church. Hardy apparently always wished to be buried with his family in the churchyard, but it was decided that he should be buried at Westminster Abbey. To reach a compromise, his heart was removed and buried in Dorset while his ashes remained in London [36]. Sure enough, we easily find his grave, clean and clearly carved, stating that his heart lies here, that he was the son of Thomas and Jemima Hardy, born at Upper Bockhampton on the second of June 1840 and died at Max Gate, Dorchester on the eleventh of January 1928, and that his ashes rest in poet's corner, Westminster Abbey. Other graves from his family occupy a regimented line near his own; well-maintained and lichen free. Inside the church, there is also a stained glass window dedicated to him, as well as an epitaph to one of the Grey's from the old manor house- Angel Grey, Lora's grandfather, 'Surely the name which inspired Hardy's Angel Clare in Tess of the D'Urbervilles,' I burst out in revelation! But perhaps it was a coincidence. Outside the church, yet another distinguished writer is interred; the poet laureate Cecil Day Lewis who died in 1972 and, according to a woman who I talk to in the churchyard, wanted to be buried in proximity to Hardy, whom he so greatly admired.

This whole place evokes a sense of tangibility with the elusive Hardy, whose revered words linger on the lips of those in literary circles and whose presence is marked in so many places around the county. The village itself; compact and pretty, comprises small cottages, some thatched, others brick and flint, mostly old but the modern built so assiduously to conform to the old style that apart from their fresh faces and the cool sweep of the level tarmac road which runs past them, it would be difficult for the undiscerning to know that they were not old.

The proximity to Kingston Maurward, whose college occupies the land around here; its peaceful, picturesque farm buildings, fields of sheep, a mixture of agriculture and horticulture, the riverside rural village and the stately home is surely the epitome of the English countryside all rolled into a few square miles.

July

Poundbury

The shops and houses of Poundbury stand out with clean, brave definition in the morning light. Despite being built in traditional styles, none are more than twenty years old, as reflected in their fresh facades. In fact, 2013 was the year this town celebrated its twentieth birthday. As a creation of sustainable urban planning, initiated by Prince Charles, Poundbury seems to have been a success. Whether the function of a building is primarily business or residential, aesthetic is evidently paramount, making it a pleasing and healthy environment for living and working. I find this refreshing as so often computer-generated urban sprawl arrived quickly, haphazardly, seemingly without any real plan; engulfing acre after acre of green countryside with no architectural merit to enhance the landscape or environment. At least Poundbury was planned sensitively, and although a local told me that it covers four hundred acres of previously undeveloped green land and will add five thousand people to the population of Dorchester, it provides jobs and homes and is controlled. Its planning suggests a desire for man to live closer to nature as might have happened in a market town in centuries past.

It is interesting how we cling to tradition, or our perception of it. Many of us, myself included, are drawn by the aesthetics of traditional architecture. We also want our own private homes with a garden; a little piece of natural escape, almost a cry against urbanisation, which ironically causes it to spread. Programmes such as *Escape to the Country* encourage these dreams.

Our love of tradition is reflected in Poundbury's modern streets. Yet as I sit in a tearoom, I question how traditional this really is. Afternoon tea originated in the eighteenth century when tea was brought back from the Far East. As sugar was expensive, as well as the ingredients involved in making cakes and savouries, it would have been something only enjoyed by the upper classes. In fact most agricultural labourers, without modern technology, could barely afford to feed their families, hence the rise of the Tolpuddle Martyrs. Many traditions, such as Christmas, with all its extravagance, Sunday roasts after church and recreational walks and picnics in the countryside would probably only have ever been for the privileged in society, and perhaps were not even fully practised until the nineteenth century when people became more prosperous. So what do we mean by tradition and how far do we have to go back to make something traditional? It is almost as if we derive some comfort from something that is tried and tested, something which our ancestors experienced, for after all, our grandparents always liked telling us that life was better in the past. In terms of biodiversity, perhaps they were right, but, as I look around at the smart houses in Poundbury, life must be much more comfortable now.

*

The Tolpuddle Martyrs have become famous in history books for taking a stand against the pittance paid to the average farm labourer. So low were the wages that it was often impossible for them to feed and support their families. As a result of this, some of the Tolpuddle labourers decided to form a friendly society in order to live honestly. The society held regular meetings under the village sycamore but stopped in 1834 when six of its members were arrested and deported to Australia. The government, however, met strong opposition as thirty thousand protestors demonstrated on the streets of London and the martyrs, as the six became known, were pardoned in 1836 and allowed to return home, which they did in 1838. Although trade unions were banned in Dorset, the Chartists had been establishing a successful trade union movement in the north of England in 1838, which became more powerful through supporter's sympathy for the evicted martyrs [31].

Wandering around the same sycamore tree, under which the martyrs used to meet, one can only marvel at their courage for standing up to the government at a time when freedom of speech was perhaps harder than it is today. They showed no violence, only moral conviction. Even though they appeared to lose, as labourer's wages did not improve and there were still no unions, the martyrs created a national awareness which perhaps paved the way for a brighter, more prosperous future.

The Russell-Cotes

I am alone in the garden of the Russell-Cotes Museum. The elegant turrets of the Edwardian house looking serenely down on a garden ablaze with sunlight, a profusion of flowers: roses around arches, fuchsias, magnificent lupins towering up straight and tall. Bees and butterflies flit from flower to flower. Here is a microcosm protected from the hub of the outside world, the blaze and swelter of the beach, the cacophony of traffic, amped music, and shoppers. Yet beyond it all, even this, the blue escape framed in the entrance gateway to the garden is still and calm, lying just out of reach.

I am brought back into the garden world by a wren trilling brilliantly; a bright, sweet virtuoso of complex cadenzas, a fountain of notes as pure as water, a stream of sound. The notes come more than once, tumbling from different corners of the garden and once they come almost next to me, filling me with surprise and delight as the wren perches on the head of a statue about half a meter from me, its elevated position enabling its tune to carry across the garden, as brightly as the summer's day. My ears flooded with this sound of sweet innocence cause my memories to indulge in childhood once again and the garden becomes a secret garden, a haven of sublimity, hidden from the outside world.

(2014)

Connurbation

The panoramic view from my classroom looks over the angled rooftops of the student village shimmering in the silent scintillation of the day, reflecting student experiences of excitement, discovery and the embryos of future dreams perhaps beginning to transform into a reality. But the students have left now and are all on bright vacations, perhaps awaiting the results of exams. Far beyond the rooftops and the glittering spread of suburbia trailing away to the distance, lounges the long, lethargic hump of the Purbeck ridge, stretched out and hazy in the heat- the only aspect of landscape which has escaped the tread of time, the only piece of view from my window left unchanged. It lies intangible, out of time's reach, the place where I always long to be, walking amongst the fields of sheep, trailing through small grey villages, savouring the aesthetic, the brilliant blue of the sea, the nostalgic, dreamy timelessness. Every day can be as youth if you want it to be, and here, although teaching, I am a student again.

In the other direction, the water tower on Canford Heath stands high above a mirage of housing- glittering glass and sleepy red brick- a landscape covered by the conurbation. Thankfully, blocks of housing are divided by clumps of green, clinging on to the legacy of the wilderness which once was; the wild beauty, which has been scarred by the encroaching onslaught of urbanisation. This is a part of Hardy's Egdon Heath, the great heath which stretched from Dorchester to Bournemouth and which he described by stating that 'civilization was its enemy', 'everything around and underneath,' he continued, 'had been from prehistoric times as unaltered as the stars overhead, [giving] ballast to the mind adrift on change, and harassed by the irrepressible new.' He goes on, 'The great inviolate place had an ancient permanence which the sea cannot claim' [40]. However, the 'irrepressible new' has arrived and from my window at the university I can see how overcrowded this part of Dorset has become, with constant pressure on the councils to expand the conurbation further. This, to my mind (the same mind which compelled me, at the age of sixteen, to write to the government to protest about building on Canford Heath) would be disastrous, eroding yet more of the county's original character. And yet, at the moment it is still a beautiful place to be and as I leave work each day, passing gorse bushes which snap and crack in the full force of the sun, past a farm with fields of cows; incongruous in the centre of suburbia, walking back down the lazy, pine- clad, sun- splashed road which evokes something of the serenity of the Edwardian era, and sometimes walking as far as the sea, where the shimmering spread of blue drifts in an endless dream irrespective of crowds that now cover the sand, I never forget the privilege.

(2014)

Evening Walk Near Wimborne

The remnant of a three-week heatwave wraps itself around my shoulders like a ragged shawl which I cannot shrug off. Not a breath rouses the impending stillness of an atmosphere edgy, waiting for rain to come. The entire day has been bathed in a sickly, surreal light with hot sun struggling to burn through a stifling veil. Now it still battles but silver-lined clouds tower, like the whipped peaks of ice cream cones, up into a sky bruised black and blue. These are *Cumulus congestus*, the harbinger of storms.

The 'green way', down which we walk, is dark, mellow and lugubrious. Despite the dry weather, hedge banks are tangled and verdant, dank ferns receding into their shadow while dark nettles reach out, trying to touch us. Along this ancient, sunken path, where streams of winter water have ceased to run, the sun's weak shafts are suppressed by impending gloom. Under coppiced hazels, which meet in a vaulted canopy above our heads, it is almost dark- today no sunlight sends its myriad dazzling golden darts leaping the length of the hazel boughs, as if Eros stood with his bow and quivers, to joyfully target us with shards of light. Instead a scowling, glaring green makes us feel strangely safe down here, cosy and secure. It would be a welcome refuge from a storm and I tingle with a delicious feeling of wellbeing, as if this path, embraced by banks and branches, were a secret cave echoing the steps of centuries past, for many people must have once walked here, perhaps sheltered here.

Out in the open, a nervous rabbit chews a stalk before bobbing away to its own refuge of tangled undergrowth. Flies and bees buzz in the listless heat and the dust dry smell of summer flares in our nostrils. More nettles have assembled serried ranks, standing as straight as soldiers along the banks by the road which leads to an old hamlet. They march right up the bank to meet the hedge and on into the fields behind and it would not be good to fall into their leafy bed. As we enter the hamlet, the first leaden drops of rain begin to fall- heavy, wet; the smell of metal mingled with dry earth. As they fall, I feel the heat rise from the road to touch my bare legs with a whisper of warmth. Suddenly all energy is unleashed and the heavens turn on their taps.

Rain is refreshing and evaporates from our clothes almost instantly. The cosy cottages, mostly farms, and many built in the sixteenth century with their brick and timber walls, nestle snugly beneath thick thatches, peeping through the grey vapour of the storm. Anticipation has reached its zenith and the pressure has all been unleashed so that parched land can sigh with relief, relishing every drop. The rain has become intense now, comfortably pattering through the hedgerows. Cows look contented. As we climb up the hill to our car, raindrops continue to flick through the trees, more softly and silently now. The land has breathed again but I am disappointed that there was no thunder, for last night I heard it rumbling around the countryside, echoing into the deep and secret recesses of the earth while lightning spliced the sky. Now an apocalyptic sun, still trying to usurp the storm, sends down weak shafts through ice cream clouds. The rain has stopped but the earth has found some brief refreshment.

(2013)

Trailway

An enchanting evening. The forest drips green and gold. Fingers of light obliquely touch the trees, casting long shadows and a silvery sheen across plump bracken beds and moulding around a myriad spindly shanks of silver birch. A chiffchaff sings into a clear blue sky and oak trees, towering up along both sides of the path, blush bronze; thick trunks mottled with the smudged, shadowy impressions of branches and leaves. I am practicing photography in the golden spell of this sanctuary, this place of wonder and silent scintillation where every angle paints an exciting picture.

From deep interior shadows, ferns fringe the path, their filigreed, feathery fronds gilded. Ivy hangs like golden chains from branches, swaying with the soft susurration of a myriad shimmying leaves as a silver birch breathes against the blue backdrop of the sky. It is as if the world is waiting, bathing and basking in this golden glory, knowing that the weather will change tomorrow. Red admiral butterflies sun themselves along with an elusive white admiral which glides, phantom-like, from the dark interior of the forest to sit a while on the sunlit path. Dragonflies dart between the trees, some several inches long, and small flies frolic in shafts of sunlight. This is an ethereal forest, adjacent to the old railway line where the train used to chuff between the tall oaks from Ringwood up to Wimborne and beyond. We walk somewhere along this stretch and wander off along other dappled forest paths which take us further into the compelling countryside on an adventure which leads us to new territories. Horses now graze in paddocks around us, their tails mirrored in streaks in the sky as if someone had swept brushstrokes upwards through the cupola of blue, high above the towering trees so that our broadening horizons also encompass new, vertical dimensions. Cirrus cloud and the weather will surely change tomorrow.

(2013)

Sailing Days

One sunny summer's day we take out the boat. I am a fair-weather sailor and so this is perfect. My father, as skipper, takes the helm and after a couple of hours or more of tacking down the coast, we help him reef in the sails and moor gracefully at Chapman's Pool. The air is saturated with silence and we uncork wine and lie back, lulled by the gentle, idle lap of the sea licking the sides of the boat and the soft clink of the rigging. The mainland climbs up in green strides beyond the beach; an undulating coast rising and falling in rolling waves. I launch the rubber dinghy and take it ashore, its puttering engine scarring the silence. Once on shore, enticed by the strength of such steep slopes, I climb, the land almost vertical beneath my feet. The top is exhilarating and I look back down, catching my breath, at the snug circle of the cove with our boat nesting within it. The breeze plays with my hair, cool on my face, before I race back down the steep slope to the sea to be embraced by its refreshing balm. Back on the boat we lie again in the sun watching wisps of smoke rise from the small huts of a fish smokery. It appears so traditional as if we have entered a zone where time has retreated several generations back or even ceases to exist. It is only after lunch when the plates are stowed away below deck and the bottle of wine finished, that we hoist the main sail once more. We have no idea of time, but our stomachs are satisfied.

*

As a child I loved summer days at the boatyard; days of unbroken sunshine when all was busy, vibrant; water slapping in weed-strewn shallows, rocking creaking boats like a soothing lullaby. I remember clutching a cool-bag, waiting with my brother while our parents dragged the dinghy to the water's edge; the smell of sunlight on salted seaweed mingled with the choking stutter of outboard motors, a stutter which, along with cackling gulls, drowned adult's instructions. I remember the impatient smack of flip- flopped feet echoing along the wooden jetty, moving backwards and forwards beneath gently chinking masts, the scuffling of excited dogs, scampering children. I can feel the rough drag of ropes, the bump of lugging bags against scratched brown legs and the crawl across saline-sticky surfaces. I loved the suspended feeling of freedom, the holiday anticipation in peerless weather but I equally loved the empty, pensive boatyard on unsettled days; sun and storm skirmishing while an exciting sea surged; spitting and hissing at the jetty, accompanied by the haunting song of a skirling wind which agitated the masts of the still- moored boats into such a clanking frenzy that an unexpected, comfortable calm crept through me.

Night Places

They sat on the jetty opposite the Haven Hotel, a boy and a girl, appearing lost in a dream as they looked out across a placid sea perfused with a flaming spectrum from the setting summer sun. The first stars were becoming visible, pricking the voluminous sky which still held so much light- all the colours of the rainbow seeming to collide at the horizon, fusing and merging, a kaleidoscope of soft light patterns- melting and dissipating out across the surface of the sea. This sublime world was theirs for the time that it lasted, unbroken, breathless. Only the dark, mysterious forests of Brownsea Island and the presence of this silent young couple cuddled on the jetty looked real and solid against the irresistibly beautiful, ever-changing and refracting mirage that held them captive. When the dark draws in, this image will be lost forever, the marbled colours melting away into the depths of night, and the couple eventually leaving their spot. Yet to them then, sitting together silently, now immortalized, it might have seemed to their young minds that, in the words of John Fowles, 'The world would always be this, and this moment' [38].

*

I love driving through the countryside at night. Atmosphere becomes mysteriously magnified along with shapes, sounds and senses. On the road to Salisbury, Gaunt's Lodge at Stanbridge seems to reach out to us with pallid, wizened hands, a fairytale cottage inviting us inside. It stands as a perfect example of an early nineteenth- century cottage *ornée* [9], so quaint and cosy, huddled under its pristine thatch, both compelling and repelling in the darkness.

Further on, we pass a dark field where the intriguing Philosopher's tower recedes unobtrusively into tree-lined shadows. Built in about 1700, it is the folly where the third Earl of Shaftesbury purportedly philosophized. He apparently believed the building of follies to be an expression of art in nature, helping to recreate a state of the ideal which existed before the time of man [43]. The building of this tower in a field during the dawn of the so called 'Age of the Enlightenment', perhaps made the Earl therefore a little ahead of his time, for his idea seems to have preceded the eighteenth- century view that nature could be beautified through the application of art, requiring a composition with a focal point, such as an old building, to make it aesthetically complete, or 'picturesque' as the term was much later coined.

This idea of enhancing nature by art, suggested around 1705 by the architect Vanburgh, who was in turn inspired by the seventeenth- century landscape paintings of Claude Lorraine, can be seen at gardens such as Stourhead, which evolved throughout the eighteenth century, employing classical temples, follies and an artificial lake, all integrated into the environment to create the feeling of utopia. Wild nature, at this time, and equally during the preceding century, when parklands and gardens were ordered and regimented and nature completely controlled, was not considered to be beautiful by its own merits [45]. But then, as we look at the landscape with its rolling fields, one has to question whether we have all become in a sense accustomed to a contrived beauty, for we live in an ordered society and man has made his mark on the landscape so entirely, that wilderness has been repressed, allocated pockets of space in which to thrive, and although it could break man's boundaries and regenerate itself, it has been banished or contained to such an extent that there is barely anything significant of it remaining.

Back on the road, darkness disguising the fields, I imagine the Earl in his tower on clear and starry nights, contemplating the cosmos in all its wonder, marvelling at the nature of the heavens, practically unchanged since before man came to be. He would have perhaps already possessed knowledge of the newly discovered natural laws of his time, which would have made these marvels seem even more wonderful.

By night, everything seems more wonderful and mysterious anyway. Around the next bend, Orion strides above the silhouettes of ancient tumuli, their seemingly larger, dark humps interring secrets. Illuminated by car headlights, these tumuli stand out stark and silvery against a velvet black backdrop. Under the same surveillance, contorted tree trunks take on new forms, each gnarl and knot defined in sharply ridged shadows in the silver glare. Trees become grotesque and exaggerated personalities so that we are transported back once more to the age of fairy tales. The silent world seems to sleep in a time capsule, past has awoken in the present as present has become past , only the opaque eyes of startled rabbits suddenly moving from frozen, shake us into reality. And so the perpetual cycle of nature, regardless of man's intervention, continues timelessly on this night drive, while most people sleep obliviously.

*

Sitting out under the stars with friends at a local pub. Beyond the banter and rising laughter from the glowing patio, where despondent dogs slouch in the shadows of their companion's convivial tables, is a natural world. A nearly full moon rides high above silhouetted treetops, shreds of wispy clouds scudding in front of its familiar face, yet the stars are twinkling, their pulsating forms the distant echoes of ancient times. I trace the plough; it evokes memories of many faraway places. The wonder of the stars, the night; the awe of its magnitude completed by the trembling cry of a tawny owl, haunting, ethereal as it hunts somewhere in a dark tangle of a thicket. Sitting 'in suspension between … two worlds', as Fowles so poetically writes, 'the warm, neat civilization behind…… the cool, dark mystery outside' [38]. So it is this night.

(2015)

Durdle Door

We prepare a picnic and drive with friends down to Durdle Door. Having parked the car, we make the descent to the beach, looking down on the contortions of times past; twisted rocks whose layers leave a legacy of geological upheaval. Time has tamed, softened hard exteriors and the sea spreads itself tranquilly in the listless, hugging heat. Humidity and ultraviolet have caused a haze. Blue mixes grey in a sweep of sea and sky, yet my skin is touched with a tinge of pink. To seek a sea breeze we move to higher ground, climbing, with our picnic, up an endless slope and onto the cliff top. Sun-scorched grass, resembling chaff, is literally covered with rose-chafer beetles sporting shades of green, purple and gold in their iridescent armour. Sometimes they take flight, purring past our ears, but they are more interested in feeding on small flowers that cling close to the ground. There seem to be hundreds of them but they do not disturb our picnic, it is the frisky wasps that do that. I am not a fan, and their presence makes me hotter and more uncomfortable. A faint wisp of breeze blows in from the cast iron stillness of the sea, yet the heat still hugs us.

(2010)

AUGUST

Milton Abbey

A summer's evening at Milton Abbey, nestled in a silent, landscaped bowl below forested hills. The fusion of flowing sunlight, sweet music and peace completes the harmony of this tranquil setting and as choral voices drift from inside the abbey, I am compelled to leave my friends talking on the grass and draw nearer. At the porch, I hover on the threshold between the sacred and the profane. Outside is the unassuming natural, gloriously bathed in a blaze of sunlight, while from inside floats the most sublime plainsong, pure and clear as it sweeps upwards into the resonant spaces of lofty ceilings, lifting one into a transcending realm. Yet both are intrinsically linked and as voices ascend, reaching these higher recesses, I look up into the blaze of blue sky and think of paradise!

Interior and exterior are also linked by the simple fact that if the abbey were not here in this place, then the natural may also not have been preserved and if the original setting, the beautiful convergence of three wooded valleys, had not been regarded as a suitable place for deep spiritual reflection, then the abbey would probably not have been built here. I wonder how many times such angelic voices have rung out across these silent valleys through the centuries, flowing past the golden gargoyles; soft stone swathed in sunlight, encrusted in age and frozen in time. How many past peoples have looked upon them, as I do now.

I enter the interior of the abbey where the voices still soar on the resonant acoustic. It is deeply uplifting and past blends with a present timelessness, a unity of being at one through all ages. Never have I felt so much a part of this place. The plainsong prayers, beautiful in their simplicity, echoing a forgotten past, remain mysterious although deeply familiar as I heard them sung at Salisbury Cathedral so many times when my brother was a chorister there. A sense of security and comfort sweep over me, not only because of these memories, but because of meaning.

Standing in the entrance by the porch I can see that other onlookers are equally uplifted. We are on the outside looking in. All involved in a summer music festival here, we have spent the afternoon rehearsing for a concert, but this is the evensong which precedes it. Sunlight shafts through windows leaving faltering impressions daubed on ancient walls, silhouetted window patterns in a blaze of brilliance. All is air, light, resonance, space and we stand in the heart of Dorset as we listen.

(2013)

Cerne Abbas

The largest chalk hill figure in Britain at fifty five meters tall and fifty one metres wide dominates the landscape at Cerne Abbas, yet this iconic, two-dimensional, two-left-footed, naked giant, stuck in his rigid, brazen pose as he wields a mighty club is almost definitely not an example of a primitive sense of humour. All brawn and perhaps no brain; the small-headed, huge-torsoed titan, who throws bravado to the four winds yet daintily side steps across the turf, remains as enigmatic in portrayal as he does in purpose. There has been much speculation as to his origins, local folklore assuming him to be an ancient fertility symbol perhaps dating back to the Iron Age while other schools of thought opine that he could be the Roman hero Hercules, so often presented in a similar state of nudity, brandishing a club [12]. Others still, base their opinions on the fact that there are no records of him before the end of the eighteenth century and that he is maybe therefore some sort of satirical figure synonymous with Oliver Cromwell, of which I am doubtful [55].

As we stand in the early evening sunshine, contemplating the giant, sun-bronzed face, sometimes crossed by fleeting shadows so that his proud expression changes, we also ponder the when and the why. What smug secrets does he keep in that tiny head of his? Does he resemble the ancient epitome of manliness? Is the club a threat or some sort of erotic promise? Perhaps he promises protection and genealogical prosperity, for there is something incongruous about the sensitivity of his feet and the waving of the club. Is it all banter and bluster? We shall never know, and our thoughts are now straying towards the hypothetical realm.

When looking at him, the most likely explanation for his existence to me is that of folklore and I like to imagine the childless couples of our superstitious past, silhouettes in the moonlight, sleeping out under the stars within the perimeters of the great giant. Above his right shoulder, the shadows of a small, rectangular earthwork melt into the grass. This is the Trendle, again assumed to be Iron Age, where for hundreds of years, according to a local, maypoles were erected, around which infertile couples danced in the hopes of inducing fecundity. These days it is only visited by Morris dancers. The presence of these earthworks perhaps suggests an ancient connection to the giant but I am only speculating. Sometimes it is more exciting to remain with the mystery. As children, we would never wonder about him at all but would just laugh, completely innocent of the subtler (or maybe not so subtle) implications behind such a gesture, and just thinking him plain rude. In the end, therefore, perhaps he is just some kind of prehistoric joke.

*

On a path which leads through fields behind Cerne Abbas we meet a man walking his dogs. Together we stop and comment on the wonderful, pastoral view comprising rolling hills, patches of copse and fields ready for harvest. Birds of prey wing across this backdrop, plunging down into the gentle valleys and soaring skywards again. The hamlet of Upcerne basks below us in its sunny parkland; a church and a beautiful seventeenth-century manor house, much of which was built of stone from the old abbey. The man informs us that Upcerne had a sad past, for it used to be a thriving village community, relying on the glove-making trade, but the Lord of the manor one day decided that he did not want to be surrounded by a village so ordered the houses to be demolished as well as sending its inhabitants away. The manor house now stands in isolation, no longer in his hands. With its satellite church, the two look slightly incongruous in the surrounding landscape, a landscape which has, reckons the man, been inhabited for over seven thousand years. This is not hard to believe, for there is the giant striding somewhere high above us up on the hill. We skirt around its edge, through chalk grassland blooming with scabious, orchids, thistles and harebells amongst many other flora.

The man with the dogs presumes, as I do, that the giant is older than the seventeenth century and the link with Oliver Cromwell. Apparently, similar figures are depicted on Roman coins from the Mediterranean, possibly Hercules. However, he informs me that there is also a Celtic god, which perhaps gave the name to Cerne Abbas, although I have also read that Cerne comes from the Celtic word *carn*, a heap of stones [52]. The presence of the Trendle, perhaps an even earlier structure, would also suggest a pre-Christian association. Because of this, it would most probably not have been in the interests of the monks at the abbey to have acknowledged the giant, which is perhaps why it was not mentioned in early literature. The man with the dogs goes even further to suggest that the monks may have covered over the giant altogether and that he was only revealed later at the time of Oliver Cromwell. Whatever the truth, it is nevertheless true to say that this ancient landscape has been inhabited and changed through time. At right angles to the path on which we walk, runs the Wessex Ridgeway, in itself an ancient path which links part of the Iknield way mentioned earlier in this book.

Cerne Abbas, itself a picturesque village comprising many Georgian houses with impressive, original doorways, exudes history. With an abbey established in 987, it has therefore been in existence for over a thousand years. Its small streets comprise a medley of old architecture, some of the earliest perhaps being the terrace of Tudor, timber-framed houses, called the Pitchmarket, bent and bowed across the street from the thirteenth-century church. We wander past them, banks of lavender, which grow in front of them, blending beautifully with distressed wood and rough plaster, a wan veil of sun glinting in leaded windows. Little of the abbey remains now, apart from the porch and guest house. Once when visiting a few years ago, we got into conversation with an elderly resident who lived in the abbey grounds. He was tending his garden and stopped to engage us in a friendly and fascinating conversation about his days in the war.

We stop for refreshment at The Royal Oak, where Charles II purportedly took refuge during an escape from Worcester, which involved him hiding in oak trees [47]. Whatever the upheavals of the past, the present seems to have washed over them in a kind of reflective nostalgia, like a watercolour painting, pleasing to the eye. The past has resigned itself to the present, content to savour beautiful memories. The village is in its retirement phase, serene, content, tranquil and secure and as we wander its picturesque streets and the green leafy back paths which wander beside the river Cerne, everything seems so deliciously aesthetic. I can also say that everyone we have met here and chatted with on subsequent visits as well as today, have been so friendly, taking the time and interest to talk. Their conversations are full of colour, like the flowers which tumble from cottage gardens around the village, and they help to complete the image of this picture-postcard place.

(2015)

Minterne Gardens

Hydrangeas at Minterne: the faded- paper- fragility of vintage letters. This 'Himalayan garden' is a dream to walk around; landscaped in the style of Capability Brown at the turn of the twentieth century, a wooded wilderness tamed. Dappled sunlit paths are flanked by tall trees, water cascades into secret pools where dragonflies dart, butterflies flit from flower to flower, warming themselves in sunny glades; all is completely peaceful. Even sheep, bleating from surrounding fields, enhance the stillness. This is an English pastoral paradise fused with a subtle flavour from the orient, as these plants, some most probably brought back from the Far East, as was fashionable in Edwardian times, have now become commonplace in many English gardens.

Many of the trees would have perhaps been here in the nineteenth century before this present garden was created and when the older house still stood. They might have witnessed a mother's face, worn and faded-paper-fragile; the sadness of missing a daughter. This strong-spirited daughter: beautiful, intelligent and speaking nine languages, had chosen to marry a Bedouin sheik and live a nomadic life in the Syrian Desert; a life so far removed that the mother could perhaps never relate to it. The daughter, herself Dorset-born, would have been no stranger to this place and indeed travelled back from Syria to visit her elderly mother before she died, but was destined to return to Damascus where she had settled her home and her heart. Her compelling life is beautifully illustrated in Mary S. Lovell's biography *A Scandalous Life*.

As I look at the present Edwardian house overlooking an elegant, clipped lawn bordered by cream hydrangeas; blousy, delicate heads resembling natural wedding bouquets, I try to imagine the contrast in lifestyle that the daughter would have had to make. As someone who has also lived abroad, I can feel the wrench in her heart as she came home to this comfortable, familiar, easy serenity, the moist green stillness and soft warmth of a Dorset summer, so different from the harsh bright warmth and dust of the Syrian Desert, for which she also yearned intensely. She would have perhaps experienced conflict within herself, a momentary crisis of identity as she reconciled with her family once more. Yet every day activities bring a consoling sense of cultural connectivity. In Syria she would have perhaps drunk tea in tents, sitting cross-legged on exotic carpets amongst a tribe, here she would have taken tea with family, as we do now on the veranda, china cups with homemade cake. Like her, we are visitors here, but for this bright moment in time, we are away from the chaotic outside world, sitting on the inside, cocooned in tranquillity while everything seems deliciously exotic.

(2016)

Shell Seeking

One warm, wet August evening at Sandbanks a friend and I search for shells together along the shoreline. Having been brought in by the tide, they lie abundantly on the flat wash of sand where the sea crashes and retreats repeatedly, licking a long line of foam, which is sucked back with relish. Polished with water, the shells gleam like jewels, even the most mundane of them, so that my friend comments on how beautiful they are. Lumps of stone in shades of ochre, cream and grey lie alongside them. Large, barnacle-encrusted oyster shells with their thick, grey, cumbersome layers without beauty or form, slipper limpets, reminiscent of the outer ear, pieces of razor shell, common limpets in their pointed hats and small cockle shells. All have been deposited by the sea in seemingly drab uniformity until one considers the detail.

A broken mollusc shell reveals a spiral staircase- a labyrinth to a grain of sand or anything else small enough to enter and explore its hidden chambers. I pick up a cockle, its profile like the crest of a wave, its ridged back horizontally banded in grey, black and cream, another in grey, cream and ochre. As I look further, I find each to be unique and yet all blending beautifully together in coordinated colours. We collect small scallops, satisfying in their symmetry, speckled in muted shades of pinks and purples, browns and russets, mauves and greys, the colours blending together as if someone stippled them repeatedly with a paintbrush until all the white was concealed. When looking down onto a limpet, one sees a beautiful star or the rays of a sun as ridges radiate out from the point and down the sloping sides to the edge of the circle. Then there are the small, fragile inners of saddle oyster shells in peaches, pinks, whites and shades of grey. I always sought these as a child, attracted by their oily, marbled opalescence.

Although none of these shells are as valuable as the carnelians which I picked up by the handful as a young child on holiday at Runton, or the small, pastel pink cowrie shells which I found at the same age on the beaches of northern France and have kept by the hundred, these shells, washed by the water, have their own special charm and I collect a few more, wet sand clinging to the inside of dry pockets. Their display in my bathroom at home will serve as a memory of their casual, haphazard beauty abandoned here on the beach, an untamed evanescence, for they will only lie like this until the turn of the tide.

(2008)

Heathland

August is when the heather blooms, great swathes of muted mauve melding with peat brown earth. As sixth-formers my friend Bee and I, torn between aspirations of art and Oxbridge, would sometimes abandon our studies for a few hours and go to Canford Heath with our palettes of paints to sit amongst the heather, revived by the rich, comforting aromas of bracken and peat, and seek inspiration. There we would sit on rugs and idly chat, sketching or painting the scene before us, Bee smearing thick oils onto canvas (I never knew how she could carry all that paraphernalia) and me opting for watercolour in a pad, as the colours came compact in a tiny box and dried almost instantly, making it easier to take the finished product home. Pale golden light smoothed the sides of silver birch trunks and stretched through the heather so that the tiny blooms blushed in pale golden-pink tones. The gorse, no longer in its prime, struck a contrast of yellow, and slender pine trees stood up straight, tall and bushy dark above the low-lying scrub. With such a rich medley of colours, tones and textures the watercolour palette produced something too insipid, while Bee's style was, to my mind, a little too dark, powerful and abstract. I always felt, therefore, that between us, we never did the heath justice, never quite captured the real essence of what was laid before us.

*

The beauty of this heathland world is vulnerable and transitory; a blooming, radiant face frequently becoming grave and ashen and I wonder at the depraved mind of the arsonist who seeks such destruction. During the summer months, all through the time I was growing up, towering plumes of smoke on the skyline over towards Canford Heath were a regular sighting and one of my earliest memories is as a child of two, living in a house which backed onto Delph Woods and seeing flames glinting through the oak trees at the end of the garden while my worried parents prepared to evacuate the house.

This all too common occurrence throughout my childhood was not always put down to carelessness in hot weather, but to deliberate arson. At the sound of sirens and the smell of smoke, I used to fear for the animals and insects which would be losing their lives and remember walking on many patches of heathland where charred remains left black soot on shoes, trees stood as charcoal twigs and there was little sign of life. While graffiti is a small act of rebellion, an intrinsic desire for man to leave his mark, arson goes beyond this; rebellion yes, but the perpetrator of the crime is rarely identified, a cowardly anonymous entity making such a mark that he or she would wish not to be known for his or her actions.

Cranborne

I stand inside the church of Saints Mary and Bartholomew at Cranborne, relishing the sound of silence, for silence shrouds the interior of this old building like a comforting velvet cape, wrapping one in warmth. The musing, slightly mournful drift of a wood pigeon's call is the only sound which seeps, haunting and ethereal, through this silence from the green, leafy world outside. It breaks, yet fuses with the stillness of the interior, bringing a new, transitory dimension to complement the flood of sunshine through stained glass, and contrast the lingering permanence of faded medieval wall frescoes and the continuous strength of stone.

I am aware that I am standing on the foundations of a Saxon monastery. The church, mainly constructed in the thirteenth century, is the only part remaining after the confiscation of much of its land, given to Tewkesbury Abbey at the bequest of Queen Matilda, wife of William the Conqueror. The monastery at Cranborne, thus becoming subject to Tewkesbury, took the status of a priory. Being handed over to the King at the time of the dissolution of the monasteries in the sixteenth century, it was finally demolished in 1703 [13, 63]. Perhaps it is the centuries of worship on this site that gives it such a sense of peace and permanence.

As I leave the church, however, the feeling of what was once and is no longer strikes me more deeply, for this church, with its fifteenth-century tower, appears like a typical English country parish church, a mere shadow of its former monastic self. Similarly Cranborne, now a village of eight hundred inhabitants in the middle of the once great royal hunting chase, used to be a market town of considerably more influence and importance during those times, holding the biggest parish in Dorset. Later in its history, it became a hub for contraband [53].

Behind the church along a narrow, shallow path that cuts across green meadows by the river Crane (from which Cranborne takes its name) one can catch glimpses of the manor house itself, near yet far, peeping from its romantic setting between the leaves of towering, stately trees. It seems settled in its surrounds and is described by David Cecil, who grew up very happily there, as being homely, historic; full of intrigue and imagination for a small child with its turrets, secret staircases and panelled rooms set at slightly different levels [20]. Cecil's ancestor Robert Cecil, first Earl of Salisbury and 'the most powerful man in England' [20] as chief minister to Elizabeth I, bought the manor house from the Queen and had it transformed to incorporate the walls of the original hunting lodge that was completed for King John in 1208. After this transformation, King James I, also an advocate of the hunt, became a regular visitor [63].

The romance of Cranborne Manor is therefore attributed to its history, location, its medley of moods and architectural styles ranging from predominantly Jacobean through Tudor and Stuart. On a grey day I have seen its turrets and battlements look austere, however, as I catch intriguing glimpses of the house through the trees on this day where strong sunlight burns through a veil of cloud at intervals, I see its character changing before my eyes. A translucent veil of cloud washes across the sky, muting the façade with soft shadows, drawing secrets into itself, then the sun shines strongly, intensely, and the façade becomes radiant, golden, as if expounding its secrets into the still summer air and I long to come closer, to enter its interior and savour something of its soul. I am also curious and impatient to take a walk around its renowned and beautiful seventeenth- century gardens, usually closed to the public, as they are today, and usually open when I am at work.

We wander back into the village; aesthetic and historic. All the buildings seem to have been erected over a hundred years ago and many are probably as much as three hundred. The village has assumed a snug, satisfied feeling, as if it has lived and seen life; has owned, farmed and hunted land, done its bit for religion, hobnobbed with royalty, housed aristocracy, dared to play against the law, and has now sunk into a blissful retirement in which it relishes the refined aesthetic of its old age, exuding a general air of comfortable ease and affluence. It admires the formal gardens of the manor, and the flower-filled ones of its pretty cottages, the soft symmetry of Georgian façades, the secrets hidden behind high walls. It seems to savour the serenity of atmosphere while the wood pigeons coo soothingly from every angle and the stately copper beech trees stand leafy and lofty, rustling in the summer breeze. So the town holds together all its memories in a cherished intimacy, like an old person savouring the secrets of the past while watching present time drift comfortably by as gently and contentedly as the river Crane itself.

(2013)

Edmonsham House

The quiet, quintessential English countryside is perhaps best experienced in Cranborne Chase with its ancient aura, pastoral idylls and stately homes, so it is no surprise that we find ourselves on the driveway to Edmonsham House one fickle July afternoon. Sharp spears of sunlight plunge through leaves, streaking the road and flicking the windscreen with jabs of dazzling light. We proceed slowly, while a group of small partridges suddenly scurry from the undergrowth, scuttle a few meters up the road and dive back into the bushes again; comical fat brown bodies on ungainly legs, preferring to run than to use their wings. It is as if we have disturbed them, invaded their peaceful habitat and that they seem to have no knowledge of cars, being taken quite by surprise, despite the fact that the gardens are open to the public most Sundays during summer.

The drive sweeps round to the front of the house, a mixture of periods and architectural styles, dating from 1589 and evolving over time. The grey façade faces south-west, with three projecting, pointed gabled bays flanked by two rounded gables at each end. The red brick wing on the west side dates from the eighteenth century [63].

Across the drive, where a forest path skirts the perimeter, the tiny twelfth to fifteenth- century church of St Nicholas nestles in a quiet enclave. From this approach along the forest path by the back door, it seems to be an undiscovered secret secluded in a sylvan sanctuary and bathed in brilliant golden streams of sunlight through which mosquitoes meander up and down. Flustered leaves change from gold to green, rustled by the breeze.

In the walled garden we admire old fruit trees whose wizened trunks and branches twist with time and age. So old are they that they reach far out along the ground, feeling their way with gnarled, knotted, swollen-jointed hands. Suddenly the clouds begin to draw together like curtains. As the gloom descends, the atmosphere intensifies, becomes magnetic, drawing us deeper into the compelling, silent soul of this place. The first raindrops fall, pounding softly onto leaves and stone, and we feel cosy, contained within these garden walls with the house watching over us. The air smells of water, not the metallic smell that sears the nostrils after a spell of dry, but the smell of saturation. Then the rain becomes torrential and we have to take cover until sunshine returns to beam brightly, resuming its strength, the air humid and steamy. Puddles and foliage dazzle where the light rebounds off their saturated surfaces, refreshed flowers radiate brighter tones than before the shower, raindrops remain trapped in the gentle curves of rose petals, beaded on their waxy surfaces.

At the side of the house towers a copper beech, radiant before a now cloudless blue sky. Sunlight scintillates its rustling leaves, and as a sudden rush of wind comes to toss its auburn head, shivers of sunlight are sent quivering into pools on the ground beneath. This is the surface of a subterranean world into which roots spread and creep, their fronds a replica of that which towers above. Some of the roots have pushed up, manipulating the earth with huge, capable fingers- twisted, knuckled and strong. Everything about this tree speaks of age- its height, its girth, its dignity. Knowing and seeing all, it stands serenely, peacefully, perhaps now in its prime on this exhilarating summer's day where the hot sun blazes, gilding lawns, the green leaves against the copper, casting deep shadows, which plunge into pools of pure white light.

When the wind blows the branches of the old beech, it is as if it is expressing its soul, as if it unleashes, through its rustling leaves, a suppressed sigh of contentment, a climax of anticipation and joy suddenly exhaled so that dapples dance deliriously on the ground beneath the trunk. The warm, drowsy comfort of the ubiquitous wood pigeon's note flows through the air, embracing us with honey- sweetness and calm. Everything seems nostalgic, soporific, indulging in the idleness of beautiful memories yet rejoicing in the brilliance of the present on this glorious day.

(2012)

Poohsticks

We are playing Poohsticks in Delph Woods, standing over the small stream, which glistens as it ambles idly through the wood. My stick is lost somewhere under the bridge and my brother's appears first, as it always used to do when we were children, spending what seemed like hours of contentment doing exactly the same. Somewhere in this wood is a big yew tree, so old and large that when I was a child I was fascinated, yet in awe of it. There was perhaps something sinister to a small child about its imposing, dark-needled canopy, the contorted ridges of its trunk. Now I am still fascinated, but the only awe I hold is out of respect for something that can be alive and yet so old. I too am older now, but as I walk through these woods, I feel the delighted freedom of a child, perhaps more than I did then because now I can identify it.

Although my memories are of my brother and I, I know for a fact that we were forbidden to come into the forest alone. I was told that a body had once been found here and at the tender age of three, not ever having considered that men might kill one another, I was deeply shocked and it left a lasting impression, for although the wood appears full of beauty and innocent joy, I knew then that it was once tainted and sullied by something sinister. This is perhaps the case in all areas of natural beauty. Remote and lonely, perhaps they have all witnessed some secret lawlessness, some of the nefarious undertakings of man. Yet the present has a way of forgetting the past, nature smothering all evidence of evil in its cloak of beauty, and although I might have held some of the natural features of this forest in awe, it was more akin to the excited awe which one gets from reading an adventure story. The towering, pointed stems of foxgloves, dominating the surrounding vegetation and seemingly looking down through their seductive, hood-like purple 'gloves', always filled me with a delicious dread. In the *Language of Flowers*, they symbolize insincerity [48], not to be trusted as they flower in all their haughty splendour. I had the same respect for cuckoo pint with its tempting bright berries, alluring or warning, depending on how they were interpreted. Toadstools were enticing and the strange bracket-fungi formations, which grew out of tree trunks like large plates every autumn, were grotesque. I was intrigued but would never dare to pick or touch in case someone was watching, for they were too unreal to be truly believed, and I felt some alien being must have mysteriously put them there, for to me, they were something out of science fiction. I now know that I feared these plants and fungi because I had been told that they were poisonous. Associations are strong and we do not always remember where they originally came from.

   I throw another stick into the sparkling stream, a stark contrast to the stagnant waters of Dead Man's Lake, somewhere in the centre of the forest, where our black labrador would invariably head to, revelling in the joys of escape and adventure, freedom from the leash. It was in its murky depths that he would inevitably wallow, emerging smelling strongly of sulphur. We used to laugh, but again I felt uneasy, and have never been able to determine where the lake's name came from. My stick moves slowly under the bridge, this time I have won and my mind returns to the present. We are adults now and having childish fun, yet my young nephews do not want to play anymore and suddenly start to whinge with boredom. Perhaps the modern generation is even further removed from the simple joys of nature than my own. Technology has caused more children to stay inside, an easy (and addictive) option to keep them quiet and entertained, but also perhaps considered necessary as parents generally deem it unsafe for children to play alone outdoors. Yet there is nothing like the delicious joy which one even feels as an adult of being by oneself in a secret, natural place.

   We cast our final sticks and leave the bridge, to walk a little further into the forest interior where the boys can kick a ball about on the cricket pitch. Contrary to the stories such as *Alice in Wonderland* and *Gulliver's Travels* where the main characters shrink, I feel as if I have grown, and I have! for when I was a child, the bridge by the stream seemed so high and the water so deep and the walk to the cricket pitch, which is now a mere footstep, seemed sometimes too strenuous for a small child with short legs. In fact Delph Woods are only twenty- six acres in their entirety. Just as size can be distorted, so can fear, and I realize now, on this sunny summer's day, that my misgivings of this forest were perhaps ill-founded, blown up out of all proportion by a child's wild imagination and magnified so that they towered like a tall, dark ogre looking down on someone young and small, a vulnerability which adults, out of good intention, lead you to believe you own.

(2009)

Kimmeridge

The village of Kimmeridge has almost taken on a French feel today. There is something about the intense sunlight on grey stone buildings when one enters past the churchyard from the fields, the bursting colours of summer flowers and the exuberant atmosphere which is partly the hot weather and partly the fact that many visitors seem to be eating alfresco here. There is also that lazy, sleepy indolence behind closed windows while buildings bask in the sun, the strong shadows and golden blush of their rough stone surfaces enhanced by the strong, hot light. Sheep silently graze the browning slopes around the village, many huddling for shade beneath clumps of trees.

As we walk through the village, the feeling becomes more English. We pass a line of thatched cottages, roses rambling around porches and front doors, polychromatic gardens. The sunlight plays on the line of thatch, enhancing its ripples as the roof undulates above upstairs windows creating pockets of light and shade. These cottages are peaceful now but I wonder, within their thick and soundproof walls, how many mothers screamed in agony as they delivered new babies into a chaotic world crammed with people, how many of these then screaming babies survived into childhood, how many children played and cried here, how many shouted and argued, how many people died here. Such was the cycle of rural life, and small cottages usually supported large families.

The road continues down towards the coast and we walk up onto a flower-covered clifftop to Clavel Tower, a folly. Such edifices are so aptly named for their lack of purpose, wealthy landowners often building them as a flight of fancy, having the money to do so. This one, constructed around 1820, comprises a combination of eclectic architectural styles, providing it with an eccentricity all of its own. Gothic windows peer out over a large, rotund columned base, which, to me, makes it oddly reminiscent of a tiered wedding cake. The man behind this curious construction was a Reverend John Richards who took the name of Clavel as he inherited nearby Smedmore House from that family [43]. It is not known why he built the tower except perhaps out of amusement, a trifling fancy. Nevertheless, it stands as a landmark and no doubt assisted sailors and smugglers alike. It also perhaps provided a focal point for the family to enjoy some diversion, a stout walk or perhaps a picnic in the carefree summer months. In 2006, it was apparently deconstructed and moved eighty-five feet inland before being reconstructed again, piece by piece, as there was a fear that it might become a victim of cliff erosion and fall into the sea. It is impressive that this can be carried out so meticulously and that even a folly can now be taken so seriously.

The brisk sea breeze is welcome on the cliff-top, cooling us from the sun's rays, but when we hit a sheltered spot, the heat soaks into our skin making it uncomfortable to climb. One such spot is the steep, ragwort-covered slope up to Eldon's Seat which we ascend as the last leg of our round trip from Clavel Tower. Exhausted by heat, we stop half way up and sit on the slope looking back down across harvested fields, their golden coils of hay placed in neat rows and shimmering in a lazy mirage. Beyond them spreads the flat, endless, trembling blue of the sea, remote and silent, as if we were on the outside looking into another world. Yet we are part of this silence, only broken by the faint murmur of Friesian cows and the drawl of a tractor at a farm down in the distance. We are drifting through a dream up here, on a carefree summer day where, once we have caught our breath again, nothing else matters.

(2012)

The White Mill

The sun is strong behind a glaring grey sky, we walk in the sultry surrounds of the countryside which seem to echo the atmosphere, our ramble taking us across ploughed fields which roll, brown and uninteresting, seemingly waiting for some reviving rain to unleash their earthy aromas. Following paths which now meander across grassy meadows, we suddenly come upon an old, arched bridge, quite by chance. As we approach it, a red brick, almost industrial-looking mill comes into view. I realize that this must be the White Mill, a flourmill built in the eighteenth century and now owned by the National Trust.

The mill is peaceful and pleasant. Used as a flour mill until the end of the nineteenth century. H.S Joyce, the Victorian naturalist, comments in his memoirs on the wonders of a childhood spent living here. I imagine it as I look out of small windows from an upper floor, down over the silent spread of green lawn and the river Stour, shimmering and sparkling silver- blue in the sunshine, which has finally burnt through the sweltering veil of cloud. Joyce maintains that all the animals that lived on the farm at this mill were white [46]. I imagine white cats chasing white mice, perhaps a dovecot of white doves, white peacocks strutting along by the river, an elegant white horse, white cows, sheep (which are usually white!) gentle white rabbits, white goats. The list is endless.

We duck through a low door to enter the wooden mill interior, which, according to the National Trust, contains the original machinery, constructed of elm and applewood. This delicate machinery now stands stationary, having completed its working life. Old grinding stones propped around in odd corners make it feel as if the clock just stopped one day and everything literally ground to a halt. I enjoy climbing the thin, wooden stairs to the upper levels of the mill where we walk across wooden planked floors and peer through tiny windows. On the top floor there is a model of the working machinery in operation, which looks impressive but complicated. I do not profess to be an expert on mills and thus it is better for those interested to visit it themselves. Outside we watch the Stour taking its carefree course and I think of the young Joyce excitedly fishing in its swirling depths. This was the start of his inspiration and enthusiasm for wildlife, which he later drew and wrote about. This river, as was discovered earlier through the poetry of William Barnes, would seem to have provided a source of inspiration for many.

The bridge, under which the river gently flows, is aesthetically pleasing with its decoration of alternate red sandstone and white limestone bricks lining the inside of each arch and divided by cutwaters, which cause the light to flow with a wavy symmetry in the water. Apparently it is the oldest bridge in Dorset, its foundations thought to be twelfth-century, the rest thought to have been constructed four centuries later [51]. It is associated with a folk story. Apparently the villagers of nearby Sturminster Marshall required a new bell for their church and so went to Knowlton to steal one from the abandoned church there. However, the Knowlton villagers were displeased by this action and chased the thieves back to the river at White Mill. The thieves, unable get away, dropped the bell from the bridge, but were unable to ever retrieve it as it slipped back into the water every time they tried to pull it out. It is said that every year, the toll of a bell can be heard coming from under the water at White Mill bridge. I find it strange that there were apparently still villagers living at Knowlton after the church was abandoned.

(2012)

Cloud's Hill

Cloud's Hill, whimsical retreat of T.E Lawrence, and nestled in the rhododendron forests at the edge of Bovington camp could be summed up as a place of escape and peaceful contemplation. The four-room cottage would have perhaps been regarded as a paradise for children on holiday in nature, carefree and without worry. However, this was the home of a man who had served his country, had helped the Arabs defeat the Ottomans to such an extent, that he not only totally identified with them, living as one of them and speaking their language, but had also become their hero. Yet conversely, this was also a man who despite creating this identity, also seemed intent on losing it after the First World War, leaving the Middle East and joining the RAF under a pseudonym which he changed twice. When finally stationed at Bovington with the RAF, Lawrence bought this retreat perhaps as a place to hide or escape from the past and its memories of illegitimacy, war, death, betrayal, disappointment and perhaps even guilt. This spartan place, offering no mod-cons or creature comforts must have provided a solace, a place for reflection and recuperation. Lawrence's health had taken a toll from living as a Bedouin, moving from place to place. Here was an anchor, some stability, a refuge; although it held nothing of luxury or value to draw one to it or to tie one to it. The simplicity of the house with the words οὐ φροντίς (why worry) above the door, seems to mask a life and a person, both of which were much more troubled and complex.

The exterior simplicity of white-washed walls and pale blue paint is reflected in the minimalist but practical interior. It was in this retreat that Lawrence spent time writing and entertaining literary friends such as Thomas Hardy (who lived at Max Gate in Dorchester about seven miles away) and E.M Forster. He apparently never served alcohol here; just tea or water, and without a kitchen, meals would have been a simple affair. A guide informed me that in winter he would have made toast in the fire of the dark downstairs library and that he frequently ate an evening meal at his neighbour's house across the road.

Despite being basic, the house is dark and cosy with the whispered hush of a bygone age held locked inside its four walls, trapped in time. As nothing much has changed since Lawrence lived there, it is indeed as if one were stepping back in time into an age which we perhaps romanticise about as being carefree and happy when actually it was reeling from the impact of the First World War. With the onset of war, times were also changing, teetering on the brink of the technological era, as the gramophone with the huge trumpet and the antiquated typewriter attest. Here is sweetly nostalgic and yet also intriguing, the mind wishes to delve deeper into the life of this highly intelligent man with such an important and prestigious past, a life which seemed so exotic yet ended as something so tangible, human and simple.

We walk from Cloud's Hill to the village of Moreton where Lawrence is buried. The sandy path, part of the Lawrence Trailway, takes us through heathland with glimpses of panoramic views across to the silent Purbeck Ridge, its hump riding the horizon. Although technically in Purbeck, the atmosphere of this place is completely unique. There is no sea here, no comfortable cosy grey stone cottages or warm green fields of livestock. The heath appears wild, although controlled and used by man. Serried ranks of tall pine trees stand as straight as soldiers in orderly plantations, amidst warm, unspoiled vistas of purple heather splashed with yellow as the gorse flowers. Natural pine trees, towering against the cloudy blue, soften the skyline. Even nature reveals the dichotomy of organised, regimented life in the army compared to the escape of spontaneity. Today the sun shines strongly and the heat is intense and close. We walk nostalgic and carefree as if we were walking away from time. Out here is such an escape that one forgets reality.

Near the village of Moreton, the heathland becomes deciduous forest and fields. The path cools in the dappled shade of oak trees, a livid sun still glaring through their leaves. We reach a very wide section of the River Frome where families picnic and fish on the banks and paddle in the clear depths. A group of young teenagers, the girls in short sundresses, hair swept up, the boys in bermudas innocently play pooh-sticks while a woman paddles on horseback, much to the amusement of some small children wading in the shallows. The horse stamps his foot repeatedly, enjoying showering the delighted children with cool water. Everybody laughs and the horse does it again and again, enjoying the water and the attention. This is a popular and sociable spot where families enjoy refreshment on a lazy late summer afternoon.

Back in Moreton village, the church of St Nicholas, built in 1776, nestles in peaceful green surrounds. Behind it stands the stately elegance of Moreton House with its pleasing classical proportions. In the foreground, willow herb is becoming whiskery and wispy although it still flowers pink, and ducks on the river quack somewhere in the green vicinity while the air is soothed by the calm of a pigeon's croon. The church, which was bombed in the Second World War, apparently lost all its stained glass and so the windows were replaced by the renowned glass engraver Laurence Whistler. The intricate beauty and clarity of the windows illuminates the sanctuary with uplifting space and light. As one normally expects an old church to be dark, it is a shock to the senses, almost a revelation.

After visiting the church we walk to the grave of T.E.Lawrence, which is in a newer churchyard across the road. A man who made such a mark on world history has met the same destiny as every other human being and now lies peacefully under a simple white stone in a country churchyard. He died prematurely in a motorbike accident not far from his cottage at Cloud's Hill only four months after completing its renovation. He was forty -six.

Before we leave, we visit the Moreton tearooms in the old school. This peaceful village is buzzing with people today but still holds a calm serenity. The tearooms are no exception and are highly popular. They serve excellent homemade cakes and are a friendly and hospitable establishment where we feel instantly welcome and at home. As Lawrence found escape from the stresses of life, so, on this August bank holiday, we have left work behind to experience something of the same. The feeling of nostalgia and a past present seems to be bound up in this village, and especially the cottage at Cloud's Hill, which remains unchanged since his time.

(2013)

Nethercerne

Nestled in a green enclave by the glittering river Cerne, the church and manor house at Nether Cerne come into view as we wander past a handful of thatched cottages and down a dappled path filled with sunshine. A still summer's day with nobody about, only the lazy drone of a combine harvester coursing up and down one of the adjacent fields alludes to human activity, but this, after all is a hamlet in the heart of Dorset. A sign informs visitors that there are 'free range children and animals', but I can see neither let loose in the quiet road which runs through the hamlet, nor down the leafy lanes. It is almost as if this place and this scene have been trapped in time, a pastoral place where everything has stopped still and remained perfect. Caught up in this nostalgic reverie, I imagine it must be wonderful to be a child growing up and exploring here with enticing footpaths taking you through the Cerne Valley with its undulating landscape of outstanding natural beauty. Climbing steeply up along one of these paths and through a whispering, shimmering copse on this hot, bright afternoon, we come out onto a hilltop summit, which watches over a daze of fields, hills and valleys sweeping to the horizon. It is so peaceful; the world spread out below us, basking in the sunshine; tranquil, reflective. To our left, we see the small silhouette of Hardy's monument spearing the skyline just outside Portesham. The monument, incidentally, was erected in 1844 in honour of another Thomas Hardy, this one the captain of the HMS Victory at the battle of Trafalgar in whose arms the dying Lord Nelson was purported to say 'kiss me Hardy,' [56]. To our right, we look at the patched landscape of fields falling away towards Cerne Abbas.

The manor house at Nether Cerne, comprising an L-shaped structure of banded stone and flint, is not particularly old as manor houses go, being built in the late seventeenth and eighteenth centuries. The church, being thirteenth- century in origin is therefore much older and must have at one time existed in a larger village or on its own although today, the house and church together form such a perfect couple that it would be difficult to divorce them. As Nether Cerne is mentioned in the Domesday Book, it is possible that an earlier edifice existed before the present manor house was built.

I am told that the church had former connections to the abbey at Cerne. Now no longer used, it stands serenely and peacefully in its surrounds, its simple, fresh interior containing a twelfth- century font. Someone has left the door open; a silent testimony to an elusive presence, and has caused a swallow to become trapped. It flies, demented, towards the window, a tormented soul desperate for paradise. I wonder whether the unseen mystery person will come and release it into the glowing utopia that it sees through the panes.

It is difficult to leave the hamlet, this understated emerald jewel in the crown of the Cerne Valley where lush water meadows lounge beside an idle, sparkling river, sunlight creeps through chlorophyll in lazy, leafy lanes, and fields stretch away to dreams. As in so many tiny Dorset villages one feels drugged by the sleepiness, overwhelmed by the aesthetic. Here

I am struck by the absence of people; perceived yet not present. Despite the lack of people, Nether Cerne seems to survive contained and content within itself and I wonder how the population of thirty pass their time and their days. I will often think about this place when life becomes too hectic, knowing that this is one of the worlds of timeless tranquillity, existing secretly within the green embrace of the countryside as it has always done throughout the centuries, virtually unchanged and without a care to disturb or change it.

(2014)

Brownsea Island

August is fast fading and soon will come the September sinking feeling as a new season approaches with its slow wind down to winter. Yet summer is having its final fling, a perfect day in fact for visiting Brownsea Island. Poole Quay has a bright, buoyant, feeling; flags billow before a blazing sky, families walk up and down; excited cries of children blending with an indiscernible drift of voices. The dark shadow of smuggling, characteristic of Poole Quay in the past, cannot even be sensed today. Consigned to winter days, smuggler's tales are best told around a roaring tavern fire. The custom's house stands, maintaining its face of serene and elegant respectability despite the fact that its windows, and the windows of the building before it, often turned blind eyes to the comings and goings of the smuggling fraternity. Now the windows watch equally blankly, staring into the sun, so that they reflect the sky. Perhaps with the sun in their eyes, they still cannot see the people of the present enjoying the pleasures of the good life as they stroll about. From the quayside we board a small ferry, which takes us to Brownsea Island.

We arrive in a different world, immediately transported back to a nostalgic time of childhood abandon and adventure. It is perhaps no wonder then that Enid Blighton was apparently inspired by Brownsea for the setting of *The Secret Island* and some parts of *The Famous Five* [34]. A tinge of autumn tingles in the air with a cool crispness, while the sun floods the small string of battlemented coastguard cottages and the façade of Brownsea Castle standing on the quay. All seem to draw us towards the compelling quiet and timeless simplicity which the island promises, yet I am sure that it has not always been so peaceful, for I am told that King Henry VIII originally built the castle as coastal defence against cross-channel invasion. It later stood for parliament during the Civil War.

We quickly disembark onto the lapping, sunlit quay. Like children, we are eager to explore and follow a less-frequented track which seems to lead us far away from the world and all its ugly problems. Idyllic, timeless, dreamy, we are engulfed in anticipation, as if one were re-entering a lost childhood. I imagine what a wonderful life the islanders must have had in this sleepy abode; children growing up in such freedom and paradise. Indeed, according to information at the island museum, there were islanders here before a Mrs Bonham-Christie bought it in 1927 and, declaring it a haven for wildlife, sent the islanders packing to the mainland. Thanks to her establishment of such a sanctuary, which was later sold to the National Trust, it has escaped development and maintained its wild charm and complete peace, unspoiled by man, but I can't help feeling sorry for the islanders.

Every sight and sound speaks directly to the senses today; the breeze stirring the trees, the faint mewing of a peacock, the breath of silence as if gripped by suspense. Golden light stripes still, straight pine forests and floods heathland paths where heather is beginning to flower in all its purple glory. The air smells rich and woody. Across our path waddle a pair of optimistic ducks quacking and clamouring for food, they are not afraid to ask in their own way, but sadly we have nothing to offer them.

Wandering through a forest of old beech trees whose smooth trunks seem like turned wood in the sunlight and which in autumn provide a blaze of bronze leaves, we spy the tufted ear tips of a red squirrel staring down at us from the canopy. Brownsea is one of the few places in the UK where these creatures still exist, the mainland squirrels having been chased away by the greys. It is a wonderful feeling to catch a glimpse of such an elusive creature before it scampers off into the leaves.

The forest stretches down to a beach. We stand under an umbrella-like canopy of low-lying, twisted trees, which cast dappled shadows on the sand. The constant rhythm of the sea washing in and out lulls us back to an almost primeval time, perhaps before men existed, as if we were the first people to step into this scene, feeling like intruders, not wanting to taint its perfection or invade its hush. Perhaps that is how Robinson Crusoe felt. The coastline wraps around a blue arc of sea; rugged, deciduous, trees tumbling down to the beach, an old, twisted trunk of dead wood lying across the sand. Except for a statuesque peacock, there is nobody here.

We now walk past Pottery Pier, so called because of the nineteenth-century industry that existed here. Potsherds still litter the beach. Beyond stands the Scout memorial. Baden Powell founded the first boy scouts' camp here in 1907. Perhaps that is why one is gripped with an infectious feeling of uncontained, childlike joy and adventure when one walks these paths. I think how beautiful it would be to camp one night under the trees, alone with the stars twinkling through a dark canopy of branches.

Along the cliff top we peer through ferns and shrubs to the blue below, where boats drift dreamily. Small sandy steps lead us enticingly down to the beach, to which we descend, full of delicious anticipation. Every twist and turn on the sandy path shows a new vista. Cosy enclaves beneath trees stand dappled and still, the strongly sunlit path brushed with shadows from pine and fern, the air redolent with them. Wood ants scurry feverishly about. Insects buzz. The beach curves around like a protective arm, cradling delicious calm. Forests fringe the sand and two young girls, about eight or nine years old, walk together hand in hand, bare feet in the shallows, epitomizing the timeless, innocent freedom and nostalgia which this island possesses.

(2010)

*

Back on the boat to Poole, I watch the Brownsea dream recede as we cream through thick, swirling waters. Their motion stirs memories and takes me back to when I was a teenager, returning from the island on a moonlit night after taking part in a concert. There was something magical about playing classical music there in a clearing with only the natural sounds of the night and silhouettes surrounding us. Buzzing with the wonder of such an experience, I looked back sadly as our boat pulled through the obsidian sea, a white trail of spume leaving a passage though the water like a passage through time, for stepping onto the island was like stepping back, and leaving its paradise made it a wrench to return to the modern world. I feel the same now as I ride gentle waves of nostalgia, watching the blue, foamy pathway of the boat rise on the surface of the sea.

And so emotions move like the ebb and flow of the tides, the lilt of water. Sailing boats gracefully glide past us, temporarily ruffled by the wake of puttering motor boats. Throughout history this nostalgic harbour has seen many a ship: smuggler's ships, pirate's ships, merchant ships, pleasure cruisers, luxury yachts, power-boats as well as wind and kite surfers. It has witnessed a succession of ship wrecks; the oldest perhaps being a three-thousand -year- old log boat which was preserved in the marine silts just off Brownsea Island. The most exciting and perhaps beguiling wreck is the Swash Channel wreck of the seventeenth- century Dutch trading vessel. Carved baroque woodwork of fanciful, seemingly mythological heads, and decorative, flowing designs, almost capturing the motion of the sea, allude to the ship's status of wealth and serve to add to the intrigue of this ill-fated vessel.

(2010)

Maiden Castle

A contrast of bronze light and black shadow; so intense is the sunlight as it flows over ramparts and down steep slopes at Maiden Castle where we are running a race. This is an ancient place with four thousand years of history now steeped in the silence of reminiscence. The footsteps of all who lived within the embrace of its protective 'circle' have long since faded, their voices muted by time, only the hollow pounding of our running feet on the ridges and the ricocheting bleats of sheep expel the silence. A flock of them, backlit, graze the golden slopes, more align themselves on top of a distant ridge, their four-legged forms comical as they stand silhouetted against the glare of the sky. As we pass the sheep on the slope, they look confused, wondering perhaps what this invasion of lycra-clad, crazy runners is. Their heads turn this way and that, totally disorientated and then, in true sheepy fashion, they all decide to join us; a sudden scrambling of stick legs and bleating bodies follow the flow of people around a lower ridge. They can keep up with us quite well for a short distance, running, as I imagine the fictitious haggis would, since they are still mostly stationed on the slope. But then they soon tire and drop behind to eat the grass again.

Coming out into quiet lanes adjacent to the hillfort, birdsong is sweet under a blazing blue sky on this warm July evening. Cow parsley grows in lush green hedgerows and golden light illuminates the deep shadowy furrows, like laughter lines, on characterful ivy -clad tree trunks. Despite the heat and the crowd of runners, the atmosphere of peace has permeated all joviality so that what we are doing seems superficial, temporal, a mere diversion to pass just a drop in the ocean of time; but then I have never been a serious or competitive runner and normally go along just for the chance to be immersed in the countryside.

The atmosphere of antiquity, the soft inner strength of the land and its natural beauty in which I am able to run freely has so engrossed and compelled me to run on, that I have not noticed the passing time, the struggle of the slopes, nor any pain. And as dusk draws in, we wend our way homewards; a lively group once more united, after being stretched out in a long contorted line, completing our own race in our own time and in silent endurance. Lost in our own thoughts we took on the challenge of this softly fortified world, sharing its stories, its ups and downs. Now we share our own stories while the sheep still stand on the ramparts like regimented outposts, silently silhouetted against a deepening sky.

Sherborne

Sherborne meaning 'the bright stream' [52], where the streets may not be paved with gold but which is nevertheless warmed by the melted – honey tones of its soft Hamstone, comprises an eclectic combination of architectural styles stretching from medieval times. It feels as if the town, with its feet teetering on the edge of the Blackmore Vale, is falling off and over the threshold of something distinct from Dorset; the rosy-red-apple lanes and equally honey hues of Somerset, dripping with a delicious, lazy light like a heavy sleeper's dream. Yet in Somerset it is a stifling sleep, one from which you might awake as if you have slept away a century, wandering dazed, in a beautiful nostalgic dream world, spiced with a soporific unreality. This world embraces you to its bosom so that contented country lanes and small villages seem to yield everything in abundance. It can be overwhelming. The Dorset dream is gentler, more softly tuned with the senses so that we feel refreshed, elated, rejuvenated when we awake to its reality.

In addition, the collegiate, ecclesiastical atmosphere of Sherborne, with its abbey and prestigious private schools, makes the town feel slightly self-contained and reclusive. It stands with an endearing, academic loftiness, far from unfriendly, perhaps just more reserved. However, once understood, it becomes an old friend and I feel totally at home here and love catching glimpses down intriguing side-streets, no wider than little alleys, tumbled with ivy where small plants peer from the cracks in rough stone walls.

The abbey, founded in AD 705 by St Aldhelm, stands in the heart of the town, exuding warmth and benevolence in its golden tones. Inside, one is transcended to an elevated world of dreamy dimensions and airy loftiness. The eye travels ever higher, marvelling at the intricacy of the fan-tracery spreading like the branches of a beech tree, shadows stealing across surfaces, light illuminating delicate gilding.

A piano is being tuned, repeated single notes echoing into the transepts. There is to be a concert here tonight. As well as being an obvious inspiration for painters, Sherborne has always struck me as being strong on the musical scene. I remember there was a music shop where my grandfather once purchased a piano duet for me to play with him. He was a wonderful pianist and very patient, encouraging me in my faltering, playing. He and my grandmother, both having a passion for afternoon tea, surely took us to one of the tearooms on that day, but I only remember indulging in a picnic (another of their passions) on the abbey green and consuming copious amounts of chocolate ice-cream that very same hot July day over thirty years ago.

My memories seem shut in, trapped in time like the town. It is a place of cosy somnolence, with its warm stone and ancient streets giving it a feeling of comfort like a thick blanket. In its environs stand two castles. The old, a ruin, picturesque against the skyline, the 'new', with its pale grey battlements and fortified façade, occupied in Elizabethan times by Sir Walter Raleigh. Although, he fell out with the Queen and was banished there, he must have derived much comfort from the town of Sherborne nestled in the snug, velvety folds of the surrounding fields. Indeed it was here that he wished to be buried after his execution in 1618, although this wish was not granted [20].

(2014)

Place Names

Many of our Dorset place names conjure images of places past; pastoral idylls sustaining fauna and flora which perhaps no longer dwell or flourish in those areas today. These names therefore provide an archive of natural history, of what once was. In addition to the place names already mentioned in this book, there are others worth mentioning here. Stinsford, for example, takes its name from its ford where sandpipers or dunlins came, while Cranborne is named after its stream frequented by herons or cranes. Wimborne means 'meadow stream', Verwood 'fair wood', Hazlebury Bryan was once a hazel wood and West Parley was a place where pear trees grew [52]. It seems that the Saxons, from whom most of these names originated, might have derived a significant pleasure from nature just as we do today.

Skyflights

The ever- changing canvas of the sky, framed by the skylight of my attic flat, was crossed by jets at the end of every August. Scouring engines sliced the silent blue, their rumbling force ricocheting through the expanses of the sky, instilling wonder into the inhabitants of Bournemouth and leaving contrails in their wake. The Bournemouth air show was in full swing and one year, while my husband tried to sleep off the hours of his night shift, I sailed on my father's boat from which we watched throngs of people gathering on Bournemouth beach, a microcosm of humanity watching the spectacle on land while we moored up with many others out at sea.

There was something of a dichotomy between the peerless day with its cloudless sky reflected in the lapping idle blue of the summer sea and the frenetic force of the jets searing the skies above us. Energy, enthusiasm and excitement soared in the air of expectation and spectators. The atmosphere was electric, charged with positive adrenaline yet the jet engine's power also unleashed an edge of tension, as if walking on a narrow mountain path in a beautiful landscape. Red-arrows dived so low that we thought they might clip our mast and we momentarily cringed in the hull, hoping they would not do damage, relief surging through us like a wave as they climbed up again. The invasive roar of engine sound travelled down the mast, through the hull and through us ourselves before descending down into the all -engulfing depths of blue to be swallowed by the silent sea.

As we all eulogized over the highly merited, acrobatic skills of the pilots, enjoying the contrails of red, white and blue which spewed out so cleanly before dissipating into a purple, lingering haze above the beach, I realized that, caught up in the clamour, we were perhaps inadvertently celebrating man's technical prowess, his obtrusive dominance and his insidious destruction of what is natural, peaceful and pure. This was pollution disguised as 'beauty' by lurid, chemical colours. This 'beauty' lasted minutes but its pernicious presence could ironically help to contribute to longer lasting, ill effects on our surroundings.

Landscape

Flowers

Seascapes

Wildlife

Other aspects of Dorset

AUTUMN

I view the evening bonfires of the sun
On hills where morning rains have hissed;
The eyeless countenance of the mist
Pallidly rising when summer droughts are done.

(Thomas Hardy: *A sign-seeker*)

SEPTEMBER

Sandford Orcas

One day we plunge headlong into deep Dorset countryside just outside Sherborne by way of a narrow, high-banked single track. Green and lugubrious, the steep banks of this tarmacked holloway sprout with ferns and bracken, trees from each side touch to form a roof above our heads. Enticing, for want of a better word, sums up this place. For as we progress along the single track, I feel excited about what we might discover at its end. Unable to turn around, we are being drawn down into a compelling past time that exists in a cosy world of green seclusion; of rolling, forested hills, the trees tinged with autumn. We are being brought into the bosom of Sandford Orcas, a tiny village, where we leave the car and continue our exploration on foot.

Sandford Orcas lies sleepily silent, embraced by green pasture which seems to encircle its entirety. A few locals pass the time of day near the church and more congregate up at the Mitre inn; we hear the murmur of their voices; tangled threads of sound weaving through the silence. Leaving the village, we follow a footpath, climbing up into the pasture behind, pasture grazed by cows which stop and stare. Up we climb, looking back down over a chaotic collection of rooftops clustering below. Blackberries glint in hedgerows and melt in the mouth. The sunshine, which seems absent today, leaves its legacy in their savour. The day has taken on an autumnal twist. Someone has made a bonfire in the village and its insidious smoky drift still lingers in my hair.

Up above the village, we skirt around a field, peering through gaps in an old hedge. These are perhaps created by cows pushing through twisted knotted trunks in order to shelter from the wind and sun, for they are cow-sized clearings, and as we look out through them, we see the gabled east front of Sandford Orcas Manor nestled in its green surrounds. Built in the sixteenth century, this Tudor manor is said, in more than one source, to be the most unchanged and therefore original of its time [3, 20]. A true gem placed in a verdant setting and exuding a sense of mellow tranquillity from its Ham stone surfaces, it has rested here in quiet seclusion, perhaps unobservant of the many generations of people passing unobtrusively by, people hardly known, just like itself. So little fame has it gathered that it has indeed existed within forty miles of the place where I have lived most of my life and I had never heard of it until I began researching this book. On this, my first fleeting glance, my eyes drink in a delicious spectacle, delighted by the aesthetic encapsulated in the whole picture of an ancient manor, peeping through mullioned windows from its private green enclave and framed by a hole in the hedge.

The village of Sandford Orcas itself comprises a contained community which has existed through the centuries, dwelling in its collection of cottages which stretch a considerable length of the road. Inhabitants are immortalised in the churchyard, their names set in stone; neither remembered nor forgotten. Like the majority of us, their lives would have been important to those they loved, but not well-known beyond. As I look at the old font in the church, I wonder how many babies were christened here, infants presented to God in acts of humble belief, while their names and identities were presented to man. They were christened in the shadow of the manor, which, hidden from the village, seems lost in the past as it looks out across the fields behind. And so as time seems to have travelled backwards, we also seemingly step back into its perceived memories, shared with those who sleep beneath the soil. Modern life breaks the illusion for an instant; a passing car, a man walking his dog, a cyclist shocked to see a delivery van blocking the road, but the past soon pervades, hidden, like the manor, yet tincturing the present.

(2015)

Abbotsbury

It is early September and the sky blazes a brilliant blue above honey-hued terraced cottages as we wander down Abbotsbury's streets, savouring the warm echoes of pigeons and enjoying every angle as small side streets reveal cosy cottages with flower-filled gardens. Pink valerian still peers from cracks in golden walls and virginia creeper begins to blush. Here is the epitome of the picturesque (in the modern sense of the word), bombarding the senses with excitement and delight. Terraced cottages are burnished while cool, white- washed art galleries are flooded with streams of sunlight. Bright hanging baskets leave a legacy of summer as do tearooms which entice us into their secret gardens where we can laze in dappled shade and indulge in delicious homemade cake.

We take a small path out of the village and climb up to St Catherine's Chapel, the landscape rolling away in soft green, gently moulded contours. Looking back we see the village nestled in its cusp, a warm cluster of sixteenth and seventeenth -century cottages, the tower of St Nicholas Church, built in the fifteenth century, and the ancient tithe barn, a legacy of the abbey of St Peter. Sheep graze all around us, greedily ripping the grass. In the distance the histrionic call of swans carries across the fields from the swannery. Established by the Benedictine monks of the abbey in order to provide them with banqueting fare, it was therefore in existence well before 1539, the year of the Dissolution of the Monasteries, and was not destroyed, making it unique in the world, not only for its age but for the fact that it is the only place globally where a colony of nesting mute swans is managed [1].

The stoic form of St Catherine's Chapel, built in the fourteenth century by the monks, stands solitary, deserted. Its strong, buttressed exterior walls create an interior haven of peace. The sun sends down dusty shafts through windows, creating blocks of brilliant light across the floor and a white dove nests on a stone ledge, high up on the wall. I find this somehow symbolic. A small vase of wild flowers stands in a recess where people have placed prayers on pieces of paper. One can only imagine that this chapel would have been built as a place of retreat and reflection, contrasting the brutal torture that Saint Catherine herself was supposed to have experienced, tied to a wheel, giving name to the spinning Catherine wheels which have brightened bonfire nights throughout the centuries.

The Chesil can be easily seen from the top of the hill on which the chapel stands, making the latter, to my mind, a suitable lookout for smuggling ships for which the Chesil was notorious. From here we watch the reflective expanse of the Fleet Lagoon languishing down below; a flat, full-length- mirror of virtually landlocked sea crossed by the long ridge of shingle. Hundreds of swans collect in its shallows and a gaggle of geese, which have been waddling in the pastures near the lagoon, suddenly rise altogether and form a perfect line, flying out over glassy waters, calling. Crossing more fields of sheep, we descend towards the Chesil, wandering down green slopes and eventually onto a path flanked with tall bushes which toss pink fronds like manes in the wind. To our left the delicious babble of a stream rushes its way down to the Fleet; cool, refreshing. Behind a hedge to our right, cows congregate in a field where swallows dart backwards and forwards across its summer-scorched surface and the air resonates with the drone of bees which feast on flowers beneath the hedge. The path seems nostalgic, as if it has ever been there, leading the way, for countless generations of excited village children with bucket and spade, to the beach.

We reach the Chesil, sinking into its smooth stones, finding it hard to pull our feet from their grip. Again this place is unique in all the world; an eighteen- mile shingle bank which links the Isle of Portland to the mainland and runs parallel to the coast, thus creating the lagoon. It is not known exactly when or how it was formed, for it is not a typical spit, which, created by a combination of erosion and longshore drift, normally protrudes outwards, away from the coast.

After ten minutes of trudging across the moving surface while stones scuffle and tear at each other with a chinking rasp, we are slightly out of breath, the muscles in our legs well worked-out. We collapse on the shingle, casually picking up odd stones to examine. Smoothed by the sea, their slightly salty texture feels waxy and powdery on the fingers. There are pebbles of many colours from shiny black, to charcoal, pale grey, hard beige, orange, russet, muted green, pale pink and deep purple. All perfectly polished and so sun- warmed that they almost feel alive, elemental, an integral part of this place as is the constant calm breath of the sea, its steady deep echo coupled with the rasp of sea-sucked, bone-clattering pebbles and harmonised with the distant mew of a buzzard hovering above the fields beyond. Time has stood still here and I savour the unchanged soundscape while watching the coast curving away in both directions, the sea slowly unfurling and retracting. A heat haze hovers above the Chesil like the buzzard, its mirage distorting definition so that the horizon wavers in between dream and reality. Lying on the pebbles in the full force of sun, slipping in and out of sleep intensifies the sense of dreaminess.

I have a picture of Abbotsbury taken in 1936 showing a cow grazing sunny, terraced pastoral slopes under the protective eye of St Catherine's chapel. It is a sublime scene, and because it is black and white, it makes one slightly nostalgic, imagining those days to have been the trouble-free, halcyon days of past generations. It is easy to forget, looking at that picture, that those were the interim times between two world wars and the storm-clouds were in fact brewing. Time continues, people pass away, some places stay the same for future generations, others change, each generation leaving its legacy like layers of an archaeological dig. Here, I imagine, remains more or less unchanged and it is comforting to know that such quiet places of sublime beauty and reflective solitude can always be, despite what terrible things are going on in the world. They are a sanctuary, a safe-haven, an escape from humanity's wrongs, places where animals can innocently and gently graze green pastures before the flat calm of the lagoon and we can watch them without a care. Into my mind comes Howard Goodall's setting of Psalm twenty three, used as the theme tune for *The Vicar of Dibley* and as I walk, I think back to the solitary white dove nesting in the chapel and how she looked distrustful of us as we entered, an innate fear of human beings. Yet she remained steadfast and peaceful in her white purity, a gentle symbol of reassurance within the heart of a tiny chapel which has also remained solitary and steadfast since the time it was built and dedicated to God.

As we go home, storm-clouds are really brewing, bubbling up on the eastern horizon. I realise that what we are experiencing now is a halcyon day and we have made the most of it before the rain comes. We should make the most of every day, for no one knows the future. It is as indistinct as the mirage wavering across the horizon. We might need to be stoic, strong, as the white dove in the chapel, but as this whole place testifies, peace can always conquer.

(2015)

Badbury Rings

My earliest memories of Badbury Rings are of summer picnics as a child with my grandparents. It was here that they taught me to recognize and name the wild flowers of chalk grassland, areas of which have diminished by around eighty per cent in the British Isles since the Second World War [68]. I remember seeing beautiful orchids here, harebells, ox-eye daisies, cowslips and milkwort. As there can be anything up to or beyond forty species of flora per square meter in this densely populated microcosm, and not all the plants mentioned flower simultaneously, there were obviously many others that I missed. I also remember bumblebees and butterflies, perhaps in more profusion than there are today. On windy days, we would fly kites with my father, delighting in the vibrant shaking thump of the kite material as we tried to elevate it and bring it back down, amazed by its ability to weave and soar freely through the blue sky.

On this September day, as the month draws to a close, we are up on the rings wandering through flocks of grazing sheep, naturally inquisitive creatures, which stop ripping grass to stare at us as we pass. As a four year old, the hillfort had seemed overwhelmingly large with the walk around the periphery, holding an adult's hand, long and arduous. Now it only takes twenty minutes at a gentle pace to complete one circuit. Today, however, we walk across the rings, heading straight for their centre and summit where the crowning clump of trees barely whisper on this still day, their leaves turning with a tinge of autumn so that they are crowned with gold. Sunlight and shadows daub the ground. From this hilltop place we can see far and wide, the countryside sweeps down to Kingston Lacy and as the eye travels further beyond, Bournemouth's balloon, 'the Bournemouth Eye', a tiny ball ascending and descending, climbs high into the blue expanse of sky. Beyond that, the ethereal image of the Isle of Wight can be just discerned. Skirting the horizon in the direction of Blandford, the eye catches sight of Charborough Tower, the setting for Hardy's *Two on a Tower*, an elegant landmark in the distance.

Walking over the back of the rings, the ramparts, despite erosion, still look impressive and tall; an amazing feat of Iron Age construction, which has endured more than two thousand years. I wonder how many lives were lost, and the vast amount of human labour required to dig these massive ditches. They record a history of turbulent times past, an inhabited arena of defence softened by time. The entire landscape is once again summed up in the words of H.J Massingham who wrote of this place,

> Nature has pressed all these ages of man, those of peace and war, into one harmonious masterpiece where contemporary man, slipping for a moment out of the clutch of his own age, more menacing than any in the past, may drink deep of a unity and repose transcending time itself [49].

Sunlight sweeps down the slopes of the ramparts with a soft wash of amber, melting into shadows at the base of the dip. This is an autumnal light which tones deliciously with the bright berries of rosehips and hawthorn. I still find the seasons miraculous, that these berries will provide food for wildlife against the cold. Perhaps they are a little premature as it is far from cold today; summer lingers in the warm, still air yet the vista is suave and softer than summer, with the warm intensity of autumn colours creeping into the palette. The blackberries have virtually gone now. We have been feasting on them during every excursion into the countryside during the last weeks. Now we find a tree laden with crab apples, the majority of which have tumbled into a large puddle where they ferment richly, infusing the air with a cider smell. I wonder how many animals could become intoxicated on eating the fruit.

Out in the fields, numerous opportunistic gulls have collected, following a tractor which slowly trawls up and down an empty field, turning the rich earth. I am amazed that they have flown in all this way from the sea, probably about ten miles as the crow flies, and know that the earth is being ploughed. The bright blue, clear sky of earlier is now veiled with a thin film of cloud through which sunlight filters, illuminating dust churned up behind the tractor. I remember harvest festivals at primary school when we were reminded of where our food came from and how hard the farmers worked. We all brought in vegetables for the display table. Now, as then, I can sense the comfort and satisfaction of bringing in the harvest and preparing for winter, yet the warmth in the air still evokes the soft indulgence of carefree summer.

A large male pheasant stands in a cut cornfield, his rich, exotic colours blended with the autumn backdrop of golden fields and rolls of hay. His wife, by contrast, is quite camouflaged in brown. But the long tail feathers of a pheasant are far from drab when examined closely. There is so much intricacy in design and detail, the patterning of black, brown and white stripes and stipples; subtle and elegant, just like the birds they belong to.

(2011)

Kingston Lacy

On a pale autumn morning Kingston Lacy stands serenely, bathed in a misty veil, grey façades rose-tinged with an early, watery sun. Red Devon cows graze the adjacent land, flanks gilded, as they chew dewy, gold-tinted grass, the faint wisps of their breath dispersing in glowing curls on the fresh morning air.

I volunteered at this place as a sixth-former. I had chosen an environment that would inspire me, with my passions for history, art, architecture, interior design and nature all being satisfied simultaneously, regardless of what practical experience and skills I acquired. My family has also always been an avid supporter of the National Trust, taking me, to my delight, to many stately homes around Great Britain from a very early age. When Kingston Lacy was acquired by the National Trust in 1981 my grandparents, who probably visited most of Britain's National Trust properties during their lifetimes, were overjoyed that a stately home had been opened in Dorset, for there are no others in the county which belong to the trust. Perhaps they were even more excited when they learned that I would be doing some work-experience there, but not as excited as myself.

Every morning for two weeks my mother would drive me to Kingston Lacy. By the second week as we travelled up the same sweep of long drive, catching the familiar sight of the house, foregrounded by the Devon cows, we felt as if we were coming home. I arrived early, before the house had opened its doors to welcome visitors, and was given the privilege, on several occasions, of opening up the rooms and preparing them for visitor's arrival. Feeling like a maid, or sometimes Lady of the house depending on my mood, I relished the wonder of walking down vast creaking empty corridors and around rooms alone. The sweet, spicy smell of polished wood was comforting. Rooms stood shuttered and dark awaiting the new day in silent anticipation, each slumbering quietly, locked in dreams of the past so that I almost felt as if I were intruding, eavesdropping on unspoken secrets. When I clicked on a light switch or opened blinds, I revealed all, chasing away dreams or suddenly bringing them into vivid reality. The dark forms of furniture which had loomed in a dim dusky half-light, gradually took on real forms in their woken state. Shadows ebbed and colours advanced, drawing out substance and giving life to inanimate objects.

I do not have a favourite room as each possesses its own distinct character and ambience. There is the intimacy of the library with its floor to ceiling shelves of thick, leather-bound tomes, scuffed at the edges, faded gold imprinted in the spines. I was and still am enthralled at the wealth of fascinating literature and imagined members of the household reading in front of the fire on cold winter afternoons, watching the frost or snow forming white rinds over the lawns. On the wall above the fireplace there is a curious selection of keys, unlocking more secrets. I remember they were the keys to the many doors and gates of Corfe Castle before it was destroyed in the Civil War.

The house, as I learnt from the guides during my time working there, was built between 1663 and 1665 by Sir Roger Pratt, sustained additions and alterations in the nineteenth century and is modelled on an Italian palace, with interiors by Indigo Jones and John Webb. It carries a tasteful elegance without ostentation. Even the dark Spanish room with its walls of gilded leather, large Murillo paintings and a ceiling imported from a Venetian palace is beautifully aesthetic in its richness, a faded flamboyancy, an exoticism which now only lingers, pervading the shadows, leaving a legacy of sunnier places now stifled by shadows of time and the frigid hostility on the faces of many of the portraits that hang there.

The Saloon, with daintily frescoed light ceilings, is an antithesis to the Spanish room. I love the miniature detail in the four paintings by Jan Breughel the younger of the four elements; the deeper I look into them, the more detail is revealed. For an art historian, Kingston Lacy offers an impressive collection, not including the frescoed ceilings in some of the rooms and the painted details in the door-panels of others. There are also many old family photos in black and white taken at the turn of the last century which provide an intimate feel and draw the visitor closer, inviting them to step into the family's world.

The nursery is perhaps the room where I can feel the family the closest and I marvel at the tent design, whereby the sloping ceilings have been painted with the stripes of a tent, tied with ribbons. It looks quite contemporary and original, certainly novel for its time. There is something about sloping ceilings, being hidden away at the top of the house away from the world to think your own thoughts while other members of the family go about their business downstairs and I remember doing likewise as a child in our own attic playroom.

I imagine the children sitting on the faded and worn, yet beautiful rugs, eating tea at the small table in front of the fire with scruffy teddies and china dolls; waking up to an exciting day of discovery around the beautiful gardens, perhaps to go riding or to take the trap along the long driveway of stately beech trees to Badbury Rings or east to Wimborne.

There is so much to comment on about the house that I cannot do it justice in a cameo of writing. However, there is one area which I cannot overlook and this is the fascinating basement collection of Egyptology which gives one a deep impression of ancient Egyptian civilization, lifestyle and belief. I find the delicate paintings of Egyptian musicians particularly evocative but can only imagine at what their music would have sounded like, very possibly modal and quite raw. The scope of this exhibition, which extends to two large obelisks transported from Egypt and erected in the garden, shows the degree to which William John Bankes went to complete his eclectic collection of cultural trophies. Works of art and architecture, craftsmanship and archaeology can all be seen here and all blend into the background of the house, helping to give it a heart and make it a home.

*

In autumn, the gardens of Kingston Lacy display different moods. Today, in late September, still clinging to the remnants of summer, the ornamental, Italianate flower gardens at the front of the house are bright and blooming with red, white and purple between clipped round bushes. Despite the sun, there is an autumn chill on the air; creeper is turning a delicious deep red, while the trees have not yet shaken off their green leaves. In the fernery, undulating shafts of sunlight filter down through them and finger the fringes of ferns in ripples when the wind touches the trees. Ferns are like foxgloves in that they are ancient, oppressive, dark, yet seductive in their beauty.

The weather of this day is reminiscent of a day in late summer several years ago when, after visiting a point to point at Badbury Rings with all its energy, enthusiasm, cheering crowds, colourful picnics and English eccentricities, I with my friends, one of whom worked at Kingston Lacy, returned to the refuge of peace that the empty garden offered in the evening. Without visitors, it seemed to exude a sense of self, softly breathing secrets from the growing shadows, revealing new vistas and aspects perhaps missed amongst the crowds. The soothing croon of pigeons hung in the evening air while the trees stood still, motionless.

The friend from Kingston Lacy talked of the ways in which the estate was carefully and faithfully managed by his team at the National Trust. He showed us examples of this; pruning, clearing, tree-surgery, and revealed the identity of many of the tallest trees towering above us, some of them quite rare species. But it is the peacefulness of place that lingers most in my memory; the gentle winding down of day, the echoing harmony of tall tree trunks bronzed with burning amber evening light, the satisfying calls of birds settling to roost, the evening sun sifting down through branches casting long, lethargic shadows fused with even longer fingers of lazy light which stretched across the grass.

The English have always loved their gardens. This can not only be seen in the numerous landscaped grounds of stately homes with their laid out, manicured lawns, clipped hedges, symmetrical flowerbeds, herbaceous borders and shrubberies, but also in the small suburban front gardens of East Dorset and the cottage gardens of the rural Dorset villages beyond. It shows, despite the fact that nature is giving way to building, as has sadly happened over so much of East Dorset, people still desperately want to be in tune with it and own their small square of green. It could be argued that in such a setting, flowers invariably come into their own, displayed in serried ranks rather than growing in a natural, haphazard setting where they would be choked by contenders. I think this very much depends on whether or not the flower is able to grow naturally in the wild or whether it is a hybrid. The point is, in a garden, while man wishes to control nature and make it look orderly, he nevertheless wishes to experience; even possess a part of it. We are taught that his spiritual roots began in a garden so perhaps it is the subconscious call to take root again.

Walks Near Wimborne

An evening stroll by the Stour on a Sunday evening in late September reveals a hub of activity as wildlife, stimulated by the encroaching gloom, prepares to sleep. It has been a warm, non-descript day swathed in grey through which the sun has at times tried to penetrate. Now the grey sweeps a wash across the blank canvas of the placid river, which slowly drifts, an occasional hint of sunlight breaking its still surface. Despite recent rain, it runs low so that the riverbanks tower steeply. Mud has created small islands in the centre of the river and on each of these perches a motionless, solitary heron, each huddled into itself, appearing to be asleep. Disturbed by us, one of them opens its wings and lazily flaps a few meters onto the far side of the river, letting out a single squawk. It then assembles itself on the opposite riverbank and assumes its somnolent pose.

We wander on along the banks of the calm river, meeting hardly a passer-by; Only a runner fast disappearing into the grey stillness, and a man with his dog who ambles at some distance behind us. It is so still that I can only catch faint waves of the evensong bells at Wimborne Minster as they come in snatches of almost indiscernible sound, faded threads of joyful bell song weaving across the water meadows.

Under the foliage of the nearest riverbanks, coots and moorhens float in the shadows of the shallows. Some of them still half-heartedly fish, a few breaking the silence by giving out little cries or splashing the surface of the water, but the majority quietly sit under the trees that sweep the riverbank, offering cover and protection for the night.

In a nearby field, the white cotton -tails of rabbits busily bob about. Only ears and tails can be discerned in the glooming light. A few magpies join them to hop on the grass, the white flecks of their feathers more prominent than the black. Perhaps the rabbits feel safer under the camouflage of evening or perhaps they are having one last graze before bed, for when we retrace our steps past the field half an hour later, most of them have gone.

We turn past a farm. Cows idly graze in dim fields, sheep both black and white. There is also a frisky black goat with floppy ears and so much pent up energy that it tries to climb a pole. Suddenly it senses something and darts away towards the farmhouse, through a gate to the yard. The sheep, which were calmly grazing, all look up simultaneously bleating and follow the goat. They are surprisingly agile and have quickly pushed through the gate into the yard where a man can be seen with a big bucket. It must be feeding time. As the evening glides in, I imagine that the animals will be taken inside to spend the night sheltered in barns. Perhaps later it will rain.

(2013)

Hambledon Hill

Once again we feel as if we were on top of the world! After the steep ascent up Hambledon Hill, we arrive slightly short of breath and fully exhilarated, looking down across the spread of Dorset landscape which stretches like an unruffled patchwork quilt to horizon's edge. Trees are on the turn, small pockets of forest copse transformed into hues of copper, gold and red. Cows wander the hill's highest point, a line of black silhouettes stretched out along the ridge like jet beads on a string.

Below us in the Blackmore Vale nestles the village of Child Okeford, a warm vibrancy beneath a sleepy exterior. When we arrived there, locals were laughing outside the creeper-clad pub, others were queuing for a jumble sale, chatting, more laughing, exuding a warm sense of community spirit. We spoke to several. A man on a bike told us that St

Nicholas Church was built with flints from the fields which the farmers had ploughed. Apparently it was much restored in the late Victorian times but its tower dates from the fifteenth century. Inside the church, a woman was arranging flowers for the harvest festival; a mixture of old man's beard with yellow and red flowers, fruits and vegetables. I could tell from the number of locals passing by and dropping into the church that this, with its central location, was indeed the hub.

Up on Hambledon Hill, all is still, so still, a peace which comes with permanence. This place has remained the same through centuries and although the surrounding landscape will have changed from forest to pasture to intensively farmed field, its essential contours will be similar to those which the ancients looked out upon. Over to the east, the land has changed more dramatically. A field of modern solar panels shimmers ominously in the sun. It strikes me as ironic that in order to preserve the natural environment, we choose to cover it in something so ugly, obtrusive and totally alien to the beauty of the surrounding landscape. Windfarms are equally an eyesore, yet looking over the spread of green countryside, which is such a delight to the eyes, and such a comforting reassurance, I am only grateful that it has so far escaped the onslaught of urbanisation and that a solar field is a small price to pay by comparison.

And so the landscape languishes through another day in time, a radiant, cloudless day with a nostalgic atmosphere as if clinging onto the edge of summer, not wishing to mature and so staying scintillating and vibrant with its blazes of bright leaves and blue sky. Children do mature though, growing up to pursue their dreams, and far below I see the windows and chimneys of Claysmore school, one of three private schools in the immediate vicinity, which has no doubt nurtured some of them, enabling them to begin their life journeys and reach great heights. Hang-gliders are also achieving great heights and pursuing dreams. We watch them take running jumps, lifting off into the air where they float freely, suspended on the currents. The line of cows has now formed a huddle of spectators. They stand and stare, a group of curious faces all looking the same way, seemingly watching for hours, entertained by this strange form of air acrobatics and I wonder what goes through their minds.

Tomorrow night they will witness another aerial spectacle as the harvest moon will totally eclipse. I would love to be here then, watching the silver spread of moonlight washing across the fluid ridges and contours of the hillfort which are now defined by golden sun. I'd love to see the forests darken, huddling beneath the hill, spilling their shadows into the silver spread. I'd love to see the curdling face of the moon- a permanent, unchanging serenity striding above the landscape, yet eclipsed by the shadow of the earth. I imagine the placid stillness of this place being intensified on such a moonlit night. Mystery magnified.

Now we lounge in the sun while the cows chew round about us, the grass rasping under their abrasive tongues. It is hard to leave this place, to come back down from these elevated heights. Yet we do, like children, taking the steep, helter-skelter descent. Below are paths where blackberries abound, where hazelnuts fall from bushes and are the freshest I have ever tasted, and where conkers gleam like perfectly polished wood. Wandering past a blaze of hawthorn berries and the black bryony which drapes itself in pretty loops, languorously twisting around trees, adorning hedgerows, we sense autumn. Back in the village, we are once again aware of the close community; secure, enclosed within their own little world and protected by the Iron Age fort, which stands guard, as it has done for centuries.

*

The eclipse is beautiful but I am only able to see it from a forest clearing- not the best place. A wash of silent silver embraces the ground and plays wavering, soft shadow patterns across the backs of my hands and face as the intense harvest moonlight floods through oak trees. After a few hours, deep dark moon shadows slowly subside, a waning wash of silver light becoming ever more insipid as everything slowly turns dark and I see a reddened moon peering between the branches of the trees.

(2015)

OCTOBER

Chettle

The church at Chettle snuggles attractively in a nest of golden green leaves, framed in an arched stone gateway. Leaves whisper and stir, scintillated in an air still redolent of summer. On the edge of the grounds of Chettle House a man saunters with his springer spaniel. He is a local, having known this village since he was a child when, apparently, he used to climb the large trees in the grounds. Chettle is a unique village in that it has been owned by one family since the nineteenth century. Everyone who lives in the village is employed by them, some even residing in flats inside the house itself.

We become so engrossed in a conversation with the man that the air becomes laced with a lazy sense of sweet nostalgia. Nothing much seems to have changed in this quaint village where long-fringed ponies are stabled in the main street, meek-looking cows with large, limpid eyes are herded across the road to the dairy, chickens poke around the grass verges and 'free-range children', according to a sign, play. The atmosphere is so quiet it is as if time holds its breath. As the man tells us about the Blandford brewery and its wonderful ales, the springer lies down at our feet, head between paws. His master tells us that if you brew your own beer, it is important to use water which comes from the same area as where the barley is grown or else the beer will not taste as good. Tap water is not good to drink anyway according to him, rainwater is far superior.

By the time we finally leave him, a thin veil of cloud has begun to spin itself out across the sky, leaving it a watercolour-washed blue. Lawns lie so feebly under thinning rays of sun that we decide to visit the garden before entering the house. At the back we wander in a garden of full-blown white roses; subtly- scented dowagers revelling in the last breath of summer, remembering their prime of life, before the fast fading sunlight steals their beauty. My eye travels beyond them, along the lawn and up the steps, following the curves of the cornerless Queen Anne house, serene in its paling elegance, its symmetry aesthetically pleasing, graceful and feminine.

The house, built in around 1710, is welcoming yet bare. Tantalising interiors hint at what was once even ostentatious but now lie like comfortable, well-worn leather shoes too tired to walk. The impressive staircase lined with portraits is out of bounds so we descend down narrow stone steps, which open out into dank basement rooms. These are the lungs of the house without which, it would have ceased to operate, for with no life below stairs there would have perhaps been little life above, in the sense which a landlord and his family would have been accustomed. A small museum of memorabilia laid out on tables in one of the rooms is fascinating, but my attention is captivated more by a doll's house (Chettle house in miniature) which serves to frustrate and tantalize me even more, for as I eagerly peer through the shadowy windows I see the dark, intriguing shapes and forms of four poster beds and chandeliers.

Many adults love doll's houses. They satisfy a childlike imagination. Not only because of the wonder of their lifelike interiors with an amazing attention to detail, but also because they represent a world of order and perfection where everything appears calm and collected without stress and strife. My roving eyes devour delightful glimpses of frescoed ceilings, panelled walls and framed paintings so that I wonder at the marvel of miniature intricacy, and the talent that it requires. I also imagine what this house must have been like, excited at what aesthetic secrets may be hidden within its interior. No doubt this is a model of a past Chettle and I long to pull open the front and reveal all, and yet there is a delicious feeling of not quite knowing, of always wondering, imagining and being left in suspense. Sometimes this is better than knowing every reality.

As we wander in the cool gloom of the basement I notice that the sun is no longer shining and on re-entering the garden, the basement cool clings to us so that I wish I had brought a jacket. Air leaden with the earthy-metallic, elemental smell of rain on dry ground witnesses to impressions of drops, left like tears on the path. The church has become two dimensional; snug grey stone receding into itself and the dense, glooming green of surrounding foliage. An insipid sky hangs motionless, drained of vitality and threatening to descend in more drops upon us - the last shreds of summer seeming to have slipped away even in the two hours that we have spent here. The defiant dowagers, now defeated, will have collected raindrops like tears welling in the tender cusps of their open petals. The man and his dog have gone.

(2012)

Blackberrying

Early October and we are out to glean the last of the late blackberries. Armed with bag and bucket we balance on sloping banks at the roadside stretching up for the tantalizing, gleaming fruits which hang just above our reach. Silence surrounds us like a comfortable, warm blanket folded under the leaden calm of a grey sky. We could be here in any century. The only sound which brings us into our own is the occasional car, or the purr of a cyclist zipping past, the voices of the cyclists carrying on the still air. A cockerel calls across the silence from somewhere, a horse whinnies from a field, a cow grows restless, flies buzz about the hedgerows.

The simple way of approximately dating a hedge, I have been told, is to multiply the number of species growing in a thirty-metre stretch by one hundred, but this hedgerow is a tangle of so many species of plant, that it is hard to identify each and every one, let alone count them: elm and oak intertwined with ivy, hawthorn, and dog rose, whose hips blend a beautiful, autumnal red against the backdrop of changing leaves and the black gleam of the berries, which we pick. They are also interspersed with some snowberries. Amidst all this foliage, spiders hang suspended at the centre of large orb webs, patiently waiting. Other, long-legged arachnids appear out of nowhere and scamper away through the leaves. Striped snails cling to twigs and we continue to forage.

The beauty of the English hedgerow with its unique eco-system is something to be cherished. Although we have lost many miles of them, the ones which remain provide a valuable habitat to our wildlife. As wan shreds of sunlight penetrate the cloud canopy the hedgerow is transformed into new and deeper dimensions; colours contrast shadows, and blended textures disentangle themselves and take on new forms. The trunks of old oak trees, growing up through the hedge are smudged with sunlight, impressions of their turning leaves brushing soft shadowy forms which whisper and rustle. Wasps, their bodies now burnished by the sun, poke around ivy flowers which the red admirals enjoyed a month earlier. The flowers must be sweet, for the wasps are neither interested in the blackberries nor in us.

After picking over a kilo, our sticky hands stained black and mottled purple, we decide to go. We will infuse most of the blackberries in gin for Christmas and some of them will be mixed with the dropped apples which a friend gave me from her orchard. I will make blackberry and apple pie tonight.

(2013)

Wimborne Model Town

I am alone in Wimborne Model Town, peering through the windows of individual shops. When I stand straight, towering above these small buildings, I feel like Alice and crouching down, it is as if I have drunk her potion, shrunk and travelled back in time to one which is uncomplicated. The model town is a replica of what was here in the fifties. A thriving town where you would purchase what you needed from a specific shop, passing the time of day with people you knew while life went at a leisurely pace. Although it is still like that in Wimborne to a great extent, modern life with faster cars and increased technology has meant that people have upped the pace, move about more, have less time for each other, have formed higher expectations of what they need to achieve in a typical day and have developed more sophisticated tastes.

Modern Wimborne has maintained a distinct individuality in the variety and creativity of its small, bespoke shops, restaurants and gastropubs and most of the simpler shops of the model town no longer exist. Some were still there when I was a child, a couple still remain today; family businesses, whose children I went to school with. In this Wimborne of nearly seventy years ago, I notice there were no supermarkets or chain stores, with the exception of Boots the chemist, Woolworths and Barclay's bank.

I am strangely lost in a familiar world, for I recognise everything after a fashion and yet the differences make me feel as if I am a visitor here, on the outside looking into the lives once lived. I am so lost in it that I become part of it. It is literally as I imagine travelling back in time would be. The streets are silent. I am the only one walking in this surreal ghost town, fascinated, not wishing to leave and return to the real world. For this reality evokes fantasy and I love anything miniature.

Coming out into the real Wimborne as the cars flash past on King Street, I feel disorientated, as if I have stepped out of a time capsule and an all-embracing experience. For an hour I have been totally engrossed in that miniature world, a world which once was. To me it seems a relaxed and slow-paced world, a world without materialism where people lived in a closer community and trusted each other, the world in which my parents would have grown up. Still recovering from the impact of world war, people perhaps valued things more highly and learned to live with less. It might not really have been the halcyon world which everybody imagines it to be, and it might not have been better than the world we live in today, but it possessed certain qualities which have perhaps now been lost forever.

(2016)

Remedy Oak

We are trying to find Remedy Oak, purportedly a tree under which, in 1552, fifteen- year-old Edward the VI (1537-1553) sat and 'touched for King's evil' [70]. According to The Woodland Trust, the touching for King's evil was a medieval superstition, practised up until the time of Charles II. It was thought that if the king of England or France touched someone who had skin disease, they would be cured, thus receiving a perfect remedy.

We follow signs to the prestigious golf club where we assume the tree to be located, passing through imposing gates and on through the spreading parkland of Woodlands Manor, where the same King apparently stayed to hunt during the sixteenth century. I wander, welly-clad, into the swanky lobby and up to the reception desk. We are the only people not carrying golf clubs. 'I am looking for a tree,' I begin, as passing golfers fail to hide their curiosity. The staff look amused, but are very friendly and helpful. They even go to the internet for assistance, for although they have obviously heard of it, they are not sure of its exact location. After trawling the net, they assure me that it does exist somewhere, in the world outside the exclusive golf club, somewhere in a field off the main road but they can't be more exact than that. So, off we go on our mission like children on a treasure hunt. The day is sullen, leaves turning golden on the trees languidly twisting down. I feel as if this place is alien, that the town has come to the countryside, which is the atmosphere I generally feel about this whole area from Horton eastwards, perhaps associated with my trips in the vicinity as a child.

The tree, we find, stands just off the road from which it appears just like any other oak tree. Yet from behind, its hollowed-out trunk indicates extreme age, half fallen away to reveal a cavern, damp and dark. Standing inside this curved recess is comfortable and protective. The presence of epiphytic ferns, saprophytic fungi and beetle holes dotting the rough layers of rotting wood show that this tree provides a rich eco-system and is home to many flora and fauna. Although still strong, there is almost something vulnerable about it, a degenerating form, becoming ever frailer as it clings onto eight hundred years of life supported by metal wires. Its age is incredible nevertheless, and even if it didn't see the boy King of England sitting beneath its boughs and remedying people with his touch, it must have seen so many other people passing along this road (which probably didn't even exist when the tree took root.) If only it could see and talk, and yet it can only continue to stand silently, exuding age and wisdom while I am hopelessly inspired by fairy stories and Arthur Rackham's illustrations from childhood books when trees not only took on real lined faces and twiggy limbs but communicated. Perhaps it is a remnant of the child left in us, our imaginations unable to conceive that anything would simultaneously experience a different world outside our own, or perhaps it is simply that in order to relate to and identify with all things within the context of our own world, we have a tendency to humanise everything- animals, cars, and even other inanimate objects. Because a tree is a living thing, we seem even more likely to endow it with human attributes, perhaps covering for an inability within ourselves to imagine something simply being; to be alive without consciousness or feeling.

Not far from this tree, apparently stands another, accessed through private ground so that we cannot see it. The Monmouth Ash is not the original but is apparently growing on the site of an older ash under which the Duke of Monmouth hid as he escaped royal troops. Monmouth was the illegitimate son of Charles II and sought claims to the throne by stirring up a rebellion in 1685 against King James II. The rebellion began at Lyme Regis and was quickly repressed at Sedgemoor in Somerset. Monmouth tried to escape to London disguised as a shepherd but was pursued across the county of Dorset and eventually captured near Woodlands, hiding in a ditch under this ash tree, where he was found weak and exhausted [57]. He was taken by Magistrate Ettrick* and was later executed at the Tower of London for treason.

---

* Ettrick's coffin stands in the wall of Wimborne Minster- not having wanted to be buried inside the church or outside it- and having falsely predicted his date of death as 1691, it had to be altered to 1703 on the coffin after his death.

Although mud from recent rains is not conducive to walking, on the way home we stop off in Holt Forest, an historic hunting forest also containing veteran trees. Before we have had a chance to get out and walk, however, our car becomes stuck in the layby where we have parked it, alongside two other cars. We try to push it out but the wheels spin hopelessly, flinging mud in all directions, digging deeper furrows while the engine wails in agonised protest. I get out and push to no avail, my feet slithering in flailing mud. We try putting sticks and leaves behind the wheels- still nothing. Feeling bleak and isolated on this rather dismal day, we wander up to a nearby farm only to be greeted by a dog's ferocious barking. Discouraged as there appear to be no vehicles at the farm anyway, we decide not to approach any further and wander back the way we came. 'Well this is fun!' I say sarcastically, trying to steal a smile from my husband. I actually think it is rather funny. It could be worse, at least it is not pouring with rain or freezing cold, and it will make a good tale in my book!

Passers-by do not help, but stare, a bit like the golfers at the club. I refer particularly to one woman walking her dog, watching us with an air of indiscrete suspicion (the woman, not the dog!) as my husband, driven to the last resort, calls a friend in Bournemouth on his mobile. Cars pass us on the road through the forest. No one stops; it is not their problem. Wandering back to our abandoned car, we finally see a merry party of people approaching, presumably the owners of the other two cars. They are clad in smart suits and short skirts, obviously having attended some function, perhaps a wedding, and blissfully unaware of the fact that their cars might also be grounded. As they enthusiastically begin piling into their Renault Clio, I warn them that they might not be moving very far. On realisation, some of them get out in order to lighten the load and we help to push, wheels spinning frantically, more mud flying in all directions. Once free, they then help us- men in DJs and women in high heels- there are at least three of them helping me push our car out as my husband steers. Luckily none of them become too bespattered, and we all see the funny side; relieved that they were there to help us.

(2014)

Tyneham

Wan shafts of October sunlight steal across tree trunks and the forlorn façades of buildings at Tyneham. Houses, whose hearts have been ripped from inside themselves, now stand empty, open, abandoned. The faint laughter of children and the bustling of a vibrant, contented community is all but a rustle in the dry leaves that skitter across paths and fall from trees when wind disturbs the branches. Sunlight is as wan as fading footsteps in this beautiful ghost village lost to fate.

Time heals wounds and nature does its best to beautify man's mistakes. If left abandoned, a place will revert to the wild. I remember coming here as a child and it had seemed very overgrown, melancholy, lonely, haunted by a sense of loss. Now, still completely natural yet maintained as an open-air museum, happy memories pervade this place along with the sense of a close-knit community. One can identify the houses and put a family name and occupation to their empty shells, one can learn how people lived and contributed to the community whether they were the baker, the postmaster, farm labourers or domestics to Tyneham house.

Although there is no doubt that life in the country would have been hard; sizeable families crammed into tiny cottages, and none of the modern conveniences which we today could not live without, I imagine that growing up here would also have been a wonderful experience, with the surrounding fields and lanes serving as a vast playground. The village children must have formed strong friendships with each other as they grew up together and would have known and trusted all the adults, being like a large extended family. In fact, many of the families would have perhaps lived alongside each other for generations and therefore intermarried.

This life ended abruptly when in 1943, the Ministry of Defence chose to extend their Lulworth firing ranges to incorporate this area. The population of two hundred and fifty two was ordered to leave temporarily for the remainder of World War II. However, in 1948 it was decided that a compulsory order would be put on the land for training purposes and the exiled inhabitants of Tyneham never returned. Their cottages remain abandoned; empty, roofless shells covered with creeping plants. Cast-iron fireplaces high up on interior walls confirm the presence of upstairs rooms. These were humble abodes with few rooms, each serving a purpose- a post office, a laundry, a bakery perhaps; each contributing in its way to the overall community.

The rectory, also reduced to one storey, still stands squarely, giving an impression of its former comfort and homeliness. Looking at the gaping holes which were once windows, I imagine that in such an exposed spot the wind could ride off the sea and whistle, like a phantom, through this empty shell. I also imagine in former, untroubled times a kind and caring family once living within; heavy curtains tied back at the windows revealing glimpses of books and ticking clocks. Life here would have revolved around the church and pastoral care. I imagine a hot summer sun baking the sweep of drive at the front of the house and afternoon teas on the lawn with perhaps even views of the sea. As a rectory, and from the dimensions of its outer walls, it was obviously once a respected and seemingly wealthy establishment; Tyneham House, the Elizabethen manor, which can only be seen from photographs, being wealthier still. Yet even wealth doesn't save; houses, rich and poor, have met the same demise. Only St Mary's Church, dating from the thirteenth to nineteenth centuries, remains beautifully intact, as one of the stipulations was for the military to maintain it. Now a museum, it reflects the faith of the people and evokes many impressions of the halcyon world which existed before the evacuation.

Inside the village school, the only other building which remains intact, all is 'left' as it would have been in the 1920s. Low wooden desks stand in rows with recreated displays of children's work. It is all about nature; drawings of flowers and insects for the younger children and with the older pupils, accounts of what they observed in the natural world. Many of the children would have been those of farm labourers, sometimes helping on the land, and others would have come to the school from surrounding villages and hamlets, such as Warbarrow or Kimmeridge, walking several miles across the fields. Thus they would be very in tune with nature, knowing the names of a wealth of flora and fauna, being observant of what they encountered. One girl writes in a piece of schoolwork, of seeing 'dozens of butterflies coming in off the sea from France'. She identifies the types of butterflies and which species she saw the previous year. Another girl talks about a walk which she made with her two friends one August, and the types of birds they saw. She seemed to not only be able to recognize the birds but also their songs.

We seem to have lost that now. Children are no longer so aware of nature. They have other distractions. Robert MacFarlane in his book *Landmarks* highlights the fact that a new edition of the *Oxford Junior Dictionary* has even deleted many words associated with nature which it considers to be of low-surrender value to the modern child and instead has added those which it thinks would be used more frequently, many associated with technology. It is true that much of the wildlife which was prevalent then is now endangered and elusive, perhaps offering today's children less of an enriching experience than their grandparents would have had. It is also true that language is forever evolving and adapting to reflect changes in lifestyles and, more importantly, changes in mind-set. The culling of words associated with nature would therefore suggest an acceptance within society that modern children tend to be much more sedentary, sitting indoors with their computers, unaware of and uninterested in the still abundant wildlife which occurs (even in cities) around them [50].

Times and attitudes have changed, as is inevitable, and although this rural area would still be regarded by most as being relatively safe today, because of advances in transport and technology and because of health and safety, I doubt if many modern parents would allow their primary-school- aged daughters to walk alone together across the fields. Perhaps it was no safer before the war and parents allowed it because they had no choice as few families had cars, but I think it was perhaps allowed because those might have been more trusting times, certainly they are perceived as such, with people living in larger, more permanent communities, local families knowing each other for centuries and thus forging strong neighbourly ties.

Accounts of life in Tyneham, such as those by Lilian Bond of Tyneham Manor, emphasise this. They suggest a happy, lively community which worked together in harmony. Here one finds an example of a model English village, each strata of society knitted tightly together for the good of one another. There is the dependable, honest working class, providing for the needs of all, the rector, with his responsibility over the whole community and the village church, the gentry, accessible, and far from lofty, caring for the wellbeing of their tenants, often working with them, repairing properties, assisting at the school, attending village plays and pantomimes and visiting houses. The farm with its beautiful big barns and brick outhouses must have been a hub of activity beyond which, the rolling countryside stretching on and on in every direction, sustained livestock. Across these fields probably came people from neighbouring villages such as doctors, schoolchildren and postmen. Although abandoned and empty, this place is a beating heart; a memory of a pulsing, thriving microcosm that has remained in a time capsule, never modernized to accommodate cars or technology. One can walk the streets and feel that one has stepped back to a time before the war, when life was slow and people lived for each other and in harmony with their natural environment. Not only did they live for the immediate community, but also for the more extended, for when the time came, every member of this village, both rich and poor, were prepared to sacrifice themselves for the sake of their country; evacuated, victims of a war which divided people, changed lives and broke hearts.

(2007)

Finding Fossils at Kimmeridge

A non-descript day without sunshine. The sky, devoid of colour, is reflected in the blank expression of the sea which broods, surly and pensive, gently scouring the edges of the rock ledge, which reaches out like a stage into its shallow depths. The ledge, deeply incised and imprinted in places with the circular impressions of ammonites, reminds us that we are on the Jurassic Coast and that this place is primeval. Not so far away along the coast, the remains of a fossil forest perch on the cliff face; doughnut -shaped tree stumps, called 'burrs', caused by fossilized swamp algae growing over them; their soft smooth textures turned to stone as if Medusa had cast her eye across the whole area. I imagine what it was like when forests spread down to the shore, forests full of now extinct creatures, strange and wonderful. It is something that used to fascinate me even more as a child. The sea too, would have been teeming with prehistoric sea -life. Today it is one of the best areas to observe modern marine wildlife and from the fossils it would seem as if it has always been an area where one could find it in abundance.

I have found fossils at Kimmeridge before, the sharp pointed imprints of pieces of ammonite piercing into rock. Today we find no fossils until a friend of mine, in desperation, picks up an unassuming lump of shale, its delicate, paper- thin layers, packed tightly together remind me of making baklava. My friend hits it against the stones on the shore where it splits open easily and cleanly along one of its weaker fissures. The rock is opened like a book to reveal, where it has split, the frail imprint of an ammonite etched in orangey-red; a renaissance red-ochre sketch before the paint is applied. Its print is mirrored on both pages of the book, as if a phantom form of the ammonite had previously occupied the almost non-existent space between them. How did my friend know that this secret picture existed inside? How did it open at exactly the right place? This print has lain hidden and silent for millennia. Amazed, I stare at the exposed surfaces of the open rock, each perched, a perfect fit on my palms. A square of orange is smudged around the ammonite prints as if they were both naturally framed as pictures. I carefully take them home, hoping that the tenuous impression of the fossil will not be lost. It looks so delicate. I still have both halves on a shelf but dare not dust them too much in case I brush away the image of what once was; the phantom creature which left its memory as a pale imprint, a last breath lingering between layers of stone.

(2006)

*

On the coast path from Swyre's Head to Kimmeridge I watch the ever changing colours across the Purbeck ridge behind Corfe Castle; shadows chased by sunshine; a frown turning into a big beaming smile. It is a day of sunshine and showers, the latter coming in squalls off the sea; a turquoise and lapis-striped sea which suddenly becomes silver, slicked with an oily shadow where the clouds course above. Portland Bill, which was bathed in dreamy sunshine, suddenly fades into a drizzled watercolour. A downpour soaks us and it is fun; heavy, wind-blown raindrops pelting a cosy patter on our hoods. The warm sunshine soon dries us out and I feel the freedom of walking the coast path, as if I were being carried along by the wind as it races through my hair, grasses seeming to hiss and shimmy in protest as they are tossed about. Sheep graze in a field, the wind tousling their thick fleece so that it blows backwards, and a happy group of teenagers lug tents up the hill. We had passed them enjoying a picnic before the rain came, but now in the sun again, they talk excitedly together. This wild, fickle, change-of-season weather is atmospheric, animating. It tantalises us with memories of summer and promises adventures to come.

(2016)

Stapehill

A warm wind surges through oak trees at Stapehill under a dark, brewing sky, threatening rain. Horses near the old abbey seem to sense the gathering gloom and huddle under tall trees that line the perimeter of their field, watching the bluster of windswept leaves as they fall. Mottled, jaundiced chlorophyll; leaves in clusters still attached to twigs, they litter the acorn-strewn ground. Decay can become soothing, satisfying when the seasonal change for autumn activates the instinct to gather, to shelter, to stow away the harvest and sit by a roaring fire. Now rain begins to patter through the trees; wildly tossed, more leaves are sent scattering. In thick waterproofs with hoods, we feel snug and smug beneath them, while watching a soaked cyclist battling against the elements as he pedals into the wind. Hiding beneath this cosy, childlike canopy, the branches above our heads weaving a protective, yet porous roof above us, I wonder if the horses feel the same. The weather energizes the imagination and as rain becomes heavier, pelting down, we excitedly brave the elements, inhaling the moist, mulchy odours of earthy damp, wet wood, moss and mould, wellies wading through drifts of fallen oak leaves, crunching acorns, while waterproof jackets stop us from soaking.

(2013)

Upton Country Park

Scuffing up beech mast along the paths that skirt the circumference of Upton Country Park is wonderfully satisfying. Towering layers of leaves sweep against grey skies in burnished orange, copper and gold, crowning the tree tops with final moments of glory. If the sun were shining, these colours would take on their true metallic hues against a brilliant blue, but today they remain subdued, as muted as the leafy downfall drift from glory, and the almost imperceptible rustlings of birds picking through leaf litter at the edge of the path. The air feels warm as if it were a shroud containing us in this secret wonder-world beneath the trees.

Along the path we wander, continuing around the perimeter of the park and eventually come to the silent, flat, grey fringes of Holes Bay, where the chattering of migrating geese drifts across the blank expanse, resounding against a strong, steely sky. We walk carefully, our feet falling softly on the decking which crosses the reed beds, reeds which seem to hold their breath, tentatively whispering into the stillness. Likewise we walk with care, not wanting to disturb any of the wildlife here, for this is like a hide, a secluded spot from which to watch the world.

(2009)

Bird Watching, Arne

Sitting in a hide silently watching birds through binoculars is such an absorbing, exhilarating and enjoyable activity that I can think of few things I would rather do on an autumn morning, observing nature in context while surrounded by its sounds; wind-stirred trees, the flick and flutter of falling leaves and the forlorn, enigmatic cries of birds out on the salt marsh. Today, I am delighted to watch a curlew picking its way through the grasses with its long beak while a teal busily scoops around in the mud with its bill. I could sit here all day, catching clandestine glimpses of birds going about their business; nature's never-ending cycle continuing, oblivious of what goes on in the human world, as it has done for centuries.

(2015)

NOVEMBER

Wonder Webs

Yesterday was Halloween, which I never bother to acknowledge, but this morning we wake to fog and the outside world draped in creepy cobwebs, as if remnants from the night before still hung in the air. As soon as I feel the draw of the outside world, I am instantly compelled to throw off the duvet, dress quickly, grab my camera and go out. The early morning is completely still; silent except for the hollow, regular dripping from saturated trees and the flutter of falling leaves. Any vestiges of the night have already been obliterated by the wonder of the morning and anticipation hangs as heavily as the fog which fingers my face, sealing the way in front of me so that I cannot even properly make out the rich display of autumn colours.

Up close, a secret, unseen world has been revealed, transforming the mundane into one of dreamy decoration. Festoons of filigree orb-webs lavishly embellish bushes and trees, seeming to float, phantom- like between branches. They shimmy silently in the gentle breeze, a ripple flowing through their diaphanous forms like the rise and fall of a tiny wave. Dew drops cling to each delicate silken strand, revealing a frail ethereality and in their short moment of glory, these webs indeed beautify; each a small- spun miracle, a wonder to behold, yet as soon as the sun burns through the misty veil, they will fade away back into their secret, unseen realm.

A runner passes wearing headphones, a young man plays with his phone as he walks, head down, engrossed, unseeing. They both disappear into the gloom; grey shapeless forms enclosed in their own private worlds. Then a woman walking her dog comes slowly into view. Emerging out of the mist, I can see from her face as she stops to talk to me that she shares my same enthusiasm.

'What an amazing morning! So beautiful, there are so many spider's webs. I bet most people have hardly noticed them but to me they are truly wonderful!' she eulogizes.

'That is why I have my camera,' I exclaim! The excitement in her voice strikes a chord with my own feelings; a kindred spirit! I warmly indulge in the delicious satisfaction of having shared something of this special, subtle beauty with a complete stranger.

(Ferndown, 2015)

Buckland Newton

I have come to Buckland Newton to do some research. This unassuming village is hidden in the heart of the countryside and we drive cautiously down winding single- track lanes passing hedgerows draped with old man's beard and adorned with berries. It is a bright November afternoon, the lowlight gilding everything. We climb out of the car and stand shivering in the churchyard, peering at the epitaphs of forgotten graves. Some are so lichen encrusted and weather worn that they represent memories fast fading and time slipping away beyond our grasp, yet the past is always present in the atmosphere of historic places. As the sun sinks down further, it shafts through yew trees reaching to touch tombs with long licking fingers of gold. Illuminated, words stand out as crisp shadows, suddenly easier to decipher. Mission accomplished, we take a stroll around the village. Holly berries are bright in the sunlight and delicious wisps of wood smoke rise like genies, promising to combat chill. It is indeed a roaring fire which does the trick. This one crackles heartily at *The Gaggle of Geese* with its friendly, jovial atmosphere. We stop there awhile imbibing tea and homely warmth, chatting to the locals with their dogs and children, before heading off homeward down windy, dusk- drawn lanes once more.

(2011)

Comfort

Drenched, we are heading for the tearoom in Corfe Castle to warm up. As I took a run this morning, the early sunshine had been misleading, shafting in misty streaks through the autumn trees, tinting the most mundane leaves and the horses' wispy breath with gold. As I ran, I planned to go out later and do some autumn photography, to capture the sunlight on leaves and perhaps find rutting sika deer, so an hour later, my husband and I headed out for Arne. Even as we left, the sky began to pale with a thin layer of cloud and by the time we arrived, a wind had picked up, rushing through the trees, wild, exhilarating, chasing away the wan sun.

The heathland displayed an impressive palette of muted, mottled autumnal tones: russets, browns, mauves, coppers and greens with golden fountains of silver birch leaves, all foregrounding the misted mirror of the sea. In fairy tale forests, browsing between moss-hung oaks whose ivy- twisted trunks glared emerald green, were deer grazing. A stag sighted me pointing the camera in his direction and called out with a rasping, rusty-metal wail; that ancient sound which seeps in reverberating echoes through forests, steeping them in wonder and legend. The heathland was dotted with other stags, one of whom had been left behind while his hinds skipped across the path to find another place to graze, their white tails bobbing and bounding through the gathering gloom. The stag eventually followed, looking uneasy as he walked alone so close to us, disheartened perhaps, but determined to find them.

It was when we wandered down a thin path to the shore that the wind picked up so that brown bracken, which framed the enticing tunnel entrance to the beach, stirred heavily, stretching itself as if awoken by the force of the wind. We stepped out onto the sand and our feet immediately plunged into the riding spill of grisly sea, which sucked and sighed its relentless, restless rhythm. We walked through the high tide, trying to stick to a thin strip of sand, barely a foot's width, where the roots of contorted, cliff-clinging trees, reached out to touch us. Then sharp spikes of rain drove through the heavily salted air; bitter, spiteful, and the place felt wild and ancient. Islands became smudges in the sea; waves now seemed to spit stinging words at the shore. We felt our jeans clinging cold to our legs. Saturated.

As soon as we reached the car, the sun came out again of course, so that the drive down the single track road to Corfe Castle was dappled with glistening and sparkling autumn colours, the rugged, romantic ruin of the castle looming out of misty, sickly, bronzed layers of moist, sun-stained atmosphere. Now we are walking along the path by the river which skirts around the base of the castle, wind chasing through the trees with a playful surge, sending sunlight scampering in front of our feet and all around us. The river's constant chatter is soothing, and special breed sheep with innocent faces graze the sunny slopes beneath the protective eyes of the ruined castle. Despite the sun and blue sky, the wind remains cold and my jeans still clinging wet.

The National Trust tearoom is decorated beautifully for autumn with ornamental pumpkins, teasels, berries, strings of rosehips, corn on the cob, smyrnium, dried everlasting flowers and the delicate orange and papery fruit coverings of the *Physalis alkekengi*, which have become what is known familiarly as Chinese lanterns. All these plants have been grown in and donated from local gardens and so beautifully and aesthetically displayed so as to present, for me, the epitome of autumn and its bounty. It leaves me feeling deliciously satisfied inside as we huddle in this small, old cottage tearoom, looking out through tiny, steamy window panes at the historic street outside, appreciating the effort that people take using their gifts of aesthetic and creativity to bring joy and inspiration to others. I myself am certainly inspired. Instead of tea we enjoy delicious bowls of homemade soup spiced with ginger. The root vegetables and apples, from which the soup is made, have been grown in National Trust gardens.

Now we feel warmer and drier and can look forward to tonight's bonfire party, anticipating the glowing satisfaction and excitement of seeing shadows flicking across faces in amber firelight, playing patterns on tree trunks and tossing silent shadows across illuminated lawns. Shadows shape these familiar faces and surroundings so that they become almost grotesque; distorted, disfigured, redesigning themselves then fusing with the firelight in a sudden warm recognition. The wind tugs branches, surging against the bangs, booms and crackles that resonate through every dimension of the night air so that light is constantly changing, lifting and falling below and about us in this new, ethereal world of illusions and dichotomies. And when we watch with captivated, childlike delight as glittering 'stars' burst and stretch across the sky, evoking more wonder, a new dimension is revealed above us as our attention and senses are transported to higher hemispheres

(2013)

Rainbarrows

Three Bronze Age bowl barrows called the Rainbarrows stand lonely and pensive on Duddle Heath, not far from Thorncombe Woods and Hardy's birthplace. Reached part way along a disused Roman road, which once ran from Dorchester to Badbury Rings and beyond, the place exudes mystery and antiquity. Tall pine trees rise above the bare brown heath, each seeming solitary and lonely while the day promises only a brooding silence, a dull weariness of being at the year's end. Visibility is not good in this lugubrious light. It is almost as if we are standing in our own microcosm, wrapped by the enervating atmosphere and looking out onto a remote and intangible world beyond. There is something slightly surreal today. In this setting, I think how well Hardy moulded the character of Eustacia Vye; the lonely, melancholy and impulsive heroine of my favourite of his novels, *The Return of the Native*. As was the custom in the nineteenth century, she lit a bonfire near one of the Rainbarrows. To her it was a diversion from monotony, a warm glow in the lengthening, caliginous evenings drawing up to winter, perhaps a reminder of sunny childhood days by the sea, a wilful signal to her lover and a reflection of her true rebellious spirit.

The idea of burning bonfires on the heath evoke feelings of comfort and good cheer in the face of impending winter, they were supposedly to mark Guy Fawkes, although they also were perhaps rooted in the ancient, pre-Christian idea funeral pyres, the ashes of which 'lay fresh and undisturbed in the barrow beneath' (40) . Bonfire night was perhaps therefore a mixture of tradition and celebration, but to my mind also seems to symbolise a significant act of wilful rebellion, as Guy Fawkes showed in the past and as heath fires do today. At least in the nineteenth century it seems, according to Hardy that the people who built fires, while not being wantonly destructive, were showing 'an instinctive and resistant act…when, at the winter ingress, the curfew is sounded throughout nature. It indicates a Promethean rebelliousness against the fiat that this recurrent season shall bring foul times, cold darkness, misery and death' (40). Such was the vulnerability of the nineteenth- century farm labourer who with little money to feed his family and keep warm would perhaps experience death amongst one of his loved ones more readily than someone with means and wealth.

As I stand on this open, elevated spot beside the Rainbarrows, I imagine the valley filled with many winking fires, 'the bonfires of other parishes and hamlets that were engaged in the same sort of commemoration' (40). One by one the fires would inevitably become extinguished; many burning brightly for only a short time because of the poor quality of material being burnt as the poor labourers could only provide turf to burn. These fires one by one dying out, thus also seem to symbolise the transience of life.

But while the fire gives off heat and light, the fire-makers can enjoy some of its comfort, wonder and mystery, 'standing in some radiant world, detached from and independent of the dark stretches below' [40]. There is no bonfire today, but even in the gloom it seems, as I said before, that we too inhabit a microcosm from which we look beyond. The surreal feeling remains and I think of the bonfires, making things more surreal, grotesque even, for surreality takes on a new dimension with Hardy, when delusions and tricks of the eye caused by the fire caused 'the countenances of the group (to change) shape and position endlessly. All was unstable; quivering as leaves, evanescent as lightning.' [40]. Age and death are exaggerated for an instant in the fire's fickle light, creating uncertainty before falling back into the shadows. Life is fleeting as the seasons pass, and full of deception. Here on this heath, as the day remains sombre, and the youthful, radiant exuberance of carefree, invincible summer cavorts far away on the other side of the world, I can almost imagine in this microcosm of the present, an uneasiness of rebellion spreading.

(2013)

Dusk Return

A clear crepuscular sky, softly muted with the ascending sweeps of brush-stroked, horsetail clouds provides the perfect sinking backdrop for the comfortable chuck chuck of an a-bedding blackbird settling to roost in silhouette trees. Its voice jabs at the evening, causing a contained sense of excitement and cosy mystery as dusk draws its curtains on the day, bringing in the creeping contentment of night with its many shapes, sounds, shadows and surprises.

(Ferndown, 2013)

Evening Walks

Wandering down half-lit lanes flanked by the silhouettes of ancient trees and filled with the comforting patter of raindrops on fallen leaves. Glooming light subdues autumn colours while this small world, wrapped up in itself, hunkers down for night. The night will be mild. Rain subsides, leaving the earthy-deep smell of damp leaves and wood as the scowling sky is slowly teased open; cloud pulled apart like a sulky child being coaxed out of a tantrum. Along by the river, silence hangs heavily, dragging the weight of descending dusk. Pairs of ducks sit below the riverbank, already settling to sleep. The only sound breaking the stillness is the erratic, electric tick of a wren in a bush, soon followed by the sudden sharp splash of a leaping trout. Another leaps, then another, leaving concentric circles which radiate softly outwards to slowly disband and ebb away as the evening.

The clouds have now split like torn silk to reveal a slice of setting sun. Blushing light marbles the water, mingling with the mottled sky. Then in the sun's soft glow the water turns nacreous. The trombone-call of a cow, a cackling duck. Dark trees from the water's edge leave reflections stark against a watery backlight. Soon they will recede into themselves, into the black banks of the river where moorhens pick the mud while mist rises stealthily over the water-meadows, a mysterious hovering layer which draws in the darkness beneath a rising moon; large, pale and equally ethereal.

(Eyebridge, 2016)

*

A colossal moon slowly emerges where sea meets sky. Its swollen, fragile disc appears as a pearly mirage, trembling, tantalising. As it climbs behind the Isle of Wight its colour deepens to a blushing bronze, a face watching sunset- streamers streaked across the western sky. We are captivated by its allure, its magnetic pull of wonder and mystery just as it pulls the tides. The spring tides are strong today, the water dragged back leaving seaweed stranded on exposed sand. Perhaps the pull of the moon is stronger than usual. Tomorrow it will be the closest it has been to the Earth since 1948.

A few photographers have gathered on Old Harry Rocks, placing cameras on tripods to capture this weird and wonderful orb as it climbs silently higher. Anticipation hangs suspended above the chalk stacks, suspense holding its breath like the motionless sea, not a wave riding its calm, opalescent surface. Birds fly to roost, silhouettes before an enigmatic sphere, but the swallows which swooped and soared off these cliffs only last month have now all departed for Africa.

Back in Studland village, the moon has climbed higher still, blazing a trail across the surface of the sea. A romantic couple stand silhouetted. Rocks have receded into shadows as dregs of light drain away to dusk. Dorset Horn sheep graze in a twilit pasture, ripping grass. They seem not to notice the splendour of this evening, its deep mystery and wonder, the heavens declaring 'the glory of God' [60] as the moon rises higher into the illimitable sky.

(Studland, 2016)

Nightscape

I wake to a three-quarter moon pointing its bright beams between the silent branches of the oak trees, silhouetting their lattice-work as does a lantern through ornate iron tracery, and casting complex, elongated shadows across the ground. So bright is the silvery spill of moonlight between the trees, that the ground has taken on an ethereal, snow-like transformation and I am left awe- struck by its silent wonder and beauty as if I had woken into a dream, stepped into another world, a secret garden, a different place or time.

As I peep from my window, half covered with a curtain so as to be concealed, my wish is to steal outside, out into the serene stillness of the night and become immersed in it. I will have to step carefully, for so quiet is it, as to be without breath, just waiting in all its loveliness like the silent metamorphosis in an upside down fairy tale which finds the frog becoming a princess at night and resuming its original appearance at the first blush of dawn. Captivated, I am the only one to behold its secret charms and breath-taking beauty. It is indeed like a living fantasy and I feel an intruder, breaking its spell.

This is the type of night whose wonder perhaps inspired some of the most renowned literature, often in the form of romantic poetry and prose, and which only becomes a reality when we encounter it. Perhaps it is the type of night which inspired the writing of some of my favourite childhood books, *Tom's Midnight Garden,* the title saying it all, and also J Meade Falkner's *Moonfleet*, in which he writes '…When the moon is bright, a great hush falls always upon nature, as though she were taken up in wondering at her own beauty' [37]. Other children's books also describe walking into secret worlds; more of my favourites were the famous *Narnia Chronicles* of C.S.Lewis, Lewis Caroll's *Alice in Wonderland* and *The Secret Garden* of Frances Hodgesdon- Burnett. So I step outside now, to write in the sun's reflected light which spills its fluid streams of silver across my page beneath the trees.

(Ferndown, 2013)

Autumn Colours

Driving down the A31 to Dorchester past the Drax wall that surrounds the enticing estate of Charborough Park, I am impressed by the stately sweep of trees richly clad in autumn colours cascading over the wall in indulgent layers of copper and bronze. The five-legged stag struts regally upon his gateway, his fifth leg comprising a tree stump which I imagine was added as support. A proud lion adorns another gateway, also surrounded by vibrant copper -tinted tones from the adjacent beech trees. The wall must be about three miles long. Behind it is a compelling, private world, a legacy of lost time. An old deer park and a stately home are both privately owned and have been so by the same family for centuries. I stare at the great cedars which majestically sweep like bowing valets and wonder what their world behind the wall is like. Trapped in time, the deer perhaps still browse as they have always done, the house still standing, elusive in its extensive grounds. I imagine its rich interiors, ticking away imperceptible time, rooms as presumably as tranquil and timeless as the glimpses of these magnificent grounds, which I catch at intervals as we pass. I imagine that the deer must have felt quite at home roaming and rutting here at this time in the season, concealed in their own private paradise away from the world.

Another place which strikes me in autumn is the avenue of beech trees along the B3082 Blandford road. Later as we approach it, we are greeted with a blaze of bronze, which causes me to gasp as the sun bathes beech leaves in gold. Burnished tree trunks are stroked with deep, crisscross shadows beneath the bright leaves. Again these trees are associated with a stately home, having been planted in 1835, I understand as an anniversary gift for Lady Bankes of Kingston Lacy and leading as the main driveway to the house. I imagine horse-drawn carts passing these same but younger trees in times past, and if the trees could talk, what stories they would tell. From Badbury Rings, grazed by contented sheep, one can see the line of their copper-coloured crowns rolling out along the 'driveway' and taking in the soft, undulating contours of the landscape, beyond which rises the thin, elegant, silhouetted column of Charborough Tower standing straight against the skyline and allowing us to catch yet another tantalizing glimpse of this intriguing place from beyond its boundaries.

(2013)

*

On the same day, so radiant and clear, we have just discovered a new Dorset drove, where deep within its hushed interior, the sunshine illuminates everything to its very best. The hedgerows, which protectively flank this silent pathway, are bejewelled with berries from the black bryony, fatally attractive as long, alluring bines drape themselves in languorous sweet seduction through tangles of ivy and blackthorn, flaunting festoons of forbidden fruit. Some of them appear as natural, early Christmas wreaths, looping and swirling, adorning the hedgerows in decorative ring-like forms. Others fall in cascading chains like strings of bright beads. They trail and tumble vertically through the foliage with such profusion, that there are undulating waves and pockets of red, woven into the hedgerow at frequent intervals all along the path. Spindle berries also add to the rouge effect and rosehips, standing out against a cloudless sky, blaze like beads of red coral, while old-man's beard, fluffy and creamy-grey, curls itself in smoke-like wisps, about them, adding texture and embellishment to the medley of yellowing leaves in which these hedgerows are attired.

At the end of the drove we encounter new beauty as strong sunlight shafts through bright beech trees sporting rich, flame-like leaves. Following a path streaked with long, strong shadows, scuffling layers of leaf litter, in the calm brilliance of this photographer's- paradise-day, I compose my pictures. Sunlight flows through the downy plumes of old-man's-beard, also known as traveller's joy, which is indeed a joy to behold, almost surreal in its floating, feathery effulgence.

In the adjacent wood all is hushed and calm. Coppiced hazel; wands still silvery- scintillated are all that remain as a reminiscence of spring; the bluebell's breath beneath and the blaze of birdsong above now silenced. It is as if the forest is ageing, winding down, waiting in resigned anticipation for something inevitable, a silent beauty settling to sleep. The brush of falling leaves slightly disturbs the silence: a squirrel scampers through the fall, odd insects burr and the whimsical, legendary call of a raptor circles seemingly endlessly in another world above the tree-canopy. Orb webs tremble in a dreamy clearing. Stretching down through the canopy, misty shafts of sunlight shatter on their suspended, broken-mirror -like surfaces to create a subtle spectrum of colour woven through each silk strand. The forest is full of illusion, dimension; pigments mingling in exquisite shades and tones, as enchanting as in springtime but more understated, sharpening the senses and creating a cosy intimacy which floods us with joy as we share in its secrets, for apart from us, there is nobody here.

Outside the wood, we meet a middle-aged woman who shares with us her excitement. She has just been watching a sparrow-hawk, its poised body quivering against the blue sky, until it plummeted like a falling stone and vanished into the grass. I wish I could have seen it, for the woman's face is full of rapture at such a spectacle, reflecting the same intense joy and wonder that I also feel on such an exuberant day when the whole of nature is putting on a performance and everything is so amazingly aesthetic and vibrant.

(2013)

Fungi

We are back at the copse again, this time looking for fungi, not for comestible purposes, but to photograph some realia. My husband is to lecture on fungi later this week and needs the photos for his presentation. It is a perfect autumn day of blue sky and sunshine so that everywhere the leaves look their best. Anticipation seems suspended on the breeze like laughter and the weather is mild and almost buoyant. Poking around in leaf litter and the moss-covered base of a stately old beech tree, I photograph delicate fungi from the *Mycena* family, angel's bonnet, each grooved white head a miniature porcelain lampshade, growing whimsically, ethereally. They almost look as if they have come from another world, perhaps one of make-believe inhabited by nymphs and fairies.

More down-to-earth, in a piece of hollowed-out, rotting trunk we find the saprophyte *Mycena haematopus* snuggled into the base of the hollow in a purple-brown cluster. At the end of a rotten appendage to an ancient oak, a group of *Mycena inclinata* or cluster (oak) bonnet cling precariously and inconspicuously. I have to zoom in with my telephoto to reveal their true identity. All these fungi do good, breaking down rotting matter and recycling them back into the forest's eco-system. They are therefore imperative to its cycle of life, death and decay. Other fungi that we see are less endearing; a parasitic beefsteak bracket fungus, *Fistulina hepatica*, has latched onto a wound high up on the same oak, quietly feasting on the wood of its victim. The insidious honey fungus, *Armillaria mellea* clusters around the bases of other oak trees in the vicinity, killing their roots. Other fungi have established a symbiotic relationship with the trees which they colonise, each providing the other with nutrients. As we continue through the sunlit forest, watching strips of light slant through dying leaves, I am inspired by the weird and wonderful; shapes, textures, and colours all combine, adding their individual dimensions to the creeping transformation of the forest as it quietly dies down for winter while at the same time being subtly and silently colonised by out-of-this world invaders. And yet despite being in a world of their own, these 'invaders', ubiquitous and vital, comprise an integral part of our world.

On the surface, some fungi seem innocent and innocuous, others grotesque and ugly, all seem alien, especially those which look like saucers wedged onto the sides of tree-trunks, and those which take on spectral, waxy hues. Some fungi apparently also have a nocturnal bioluminescence, almost imperceptible to the naked eye, which makes them alluring, attractive and mysterious. With many species of fungi attributed to being poisonous as well as others having hallucinogenic properties, it is small wonder that they became the inspiration for noxious brews in children's stories and that they are treated with a degree of trepidation and respect. Yet entering their world close up allows one to see how fascinating they are and how amazingly interdependent a small, thriving forest eco-system is. Its world impacts on our world and I also realise how lucky we are to have such rich variety in one small space of Dorset woodland and how important it is to preserve and treasure it.

(2014)

Shipstal Beach

On a wet day in late November Arne sustains a damp contentment. Out on the beach where a sharp salt wind blows off the sea and the rain bites, the sky is stained as if watercolour or black ink had been dripped onto a wet pad. The searing cry of oystercatchers carries across the mud. Usually an egret steps through the sea when the tide is right out, pointing its long beak delicately into the shallow water but there are no egrets today.

(2012)

Sunrise

Sunrise over frosty fields; a livid, glowing ball takes possession of the sky, staining it with pastel pinks and pearly orange and causing the horizon to meld into misty, violet- rose-tinted layers of hill and tree. More mist hovers over the water meadows in a diaphanous, lingering layer, rising in vaporous clouds above the river Stour. In the foreground, where tree branches encircle the scene, framing the sun's bronze ball, like a perfect picture, golden light glows through the last leaves, turning them to a soft amber.

Lightly frosted ferns; their once drab, desiccated fronds are now delicately beautified with the crisp white rim of tiny sparkling ice crystals. The icy air bites cold; nibbling nose, finger tips and toes so that they throb simultaneously in the growing light and from a bush, an agitated wren clicks its morse- code alarm call in my direction when I rub my hands together. As the sun climbs higher, what leaves are left will once more be illuminated to brilliant intensity. This is a medley of autumn and winter with autumn still indulging in its blaze of beauty while winter waits in the wings, testing its teeth and promising to bite back with bitter cold and chill.

(West Parley, 2013)

WINTER

Awhile in the dead of the winter
The wind hurries keen through the sunshine,
But finds no more leaves that may linger
On tree-boughs to strew on the ground.

William Barnes, *Seasons and Times*

DECEMBER

Wimborne Minster

It is the beginning of Advent, and a good friend and I decide to go to the carol service in Wimborne Minster. Tonight it is floodlit; its two towers looking down benevolently and protectively over the town which has been transformed with a filigree of white Christmas lights, resembling spiky ice formations strung across the streets. As soon as we leave the car, I can hear the bells- the call of centuries past pervading the present; that joyful ring which excites and delights me. The friendly old porch glows warmly as we enter the Minster and are equally warmly welcomed. We take a seat on an old wooden pew, the perfume of polished wood and unyielding strength as familiar as sitting on a chair at home.

After several pieces on the organ, Bach's sublimely ethereal chorale *Nun komm de heiden heiland*, generates an atmosphere of wonder and anticipation, cocooning us in its unfolding melody as one by one the lights begin to go out. I watch the familiar Norman architecture sink into shadows as it has done every night throughout the centuries; the strong and permanent becoming seemingly intangible as vast forms of solid stone slip into silhouettes- faintly discernible shapes in the near darkness. Yet the music remains the very antithesis, for its tune, emerging from the initial recesses of a sonorous single line, is a lone voice seeking hope and light, making sense of mystery and suggesting a gradual revelation. This slow awakening is a like a light which intensifies in contrast to the ever growing darkness of the nave.

With the shadows, we sink into silent contemplation, and I feel the breath of the past pulsating through the darkness like a beating heart as I think of all those who have worshipped here through the centuries and have moved on to a different dimension of life. This is a tenuous connection, and after the organ stops and anguished plainsong, laid pure and open in its simplicity, begins to throb out of the shadows like a soul seeking in earnest. People too are perhaps searching their souls in the darkness, calling out in their hearts to better know the truth that their predecessors have already found. As the choir processes up the nave, ethereal voices grow stronger, more certain, candlelight flickers across stone surfaces with a warm, wavering glow, casting a glimmer of hope and I watch shadows mysteriously recede and stretch with the guttering flames.

Soon we are all carrying candles, each individual face illuminated with a glowing pool of light as we sing hymns lustily and receive the word gladly. Ancient antiphons, wrapped in bygone mystery, sink into old stone, which was fashioned even before these tunes were written. Those were a God-fearing people who expressed their faith in sincere and awesome ways. It humbles me. The choir stand by the altar in their rich red cassocks looking traditional and carrying winking candles. Christmas has begun and I feel a flame dancing inside me. The service ends with the lights back on, the columns resuming stature and the rousing strength of the organ playing more Bach. For me, this is another of his most compelling and moving organ compositions- *Fantasia and fugue in G minor*. The evening is wonderfully complete.

Outside, as we walk into the real world. We are not brought down to Earth with a bump or snatched painfully into reality, for Wimborne, with its winking lights and glowing windows, seems to sustain that flame which I guard like a treasure in my heart. The Square, decorated with a tall, elegant Christmas tree covered in white lights seems almost ethereal and the tiny white lights, which are strung everywhere, enhance the unearthly, winter wonderland feel. In the coming weeks, the lights of Christmas trees will begin to peep round the heavy swags of curtains at the windows of the big Georgian houses in West Borough, and large, designer wreaths will appear on their front doors. Fires will roar in the grates of many eating places and pubs and I cannot wait to come and browse around the small boutiques and the gift shops one weekend before Christmas. Perhaps I will meet with a friend in one of the pubs or cafes to sit in front of a roaring fire and indulge in some Christmas cheer before embarking on some serious shopping and if I tire of shopping, I can continue down West Borough and out of Wimborne over the bridge to where the town becomes the countryside once more.

(2013)

Dawn Rise

It was dusk when I went out this morning, the sky only just drawing back its curtains on the day. In the barely quarter light, only the sharp tickings-off of a blackbird picked at my presence while scolding the softness of dawn. A drowsy dream- world was awakening, stirring from sleep, being chiselled, fashioned by sound. Some windows blinked back the light of early-rising while others stayed shrouded in slumber.

(6.45am Ferndown, 2013)

*

The morning sky resembles shot silk, a three-toned pink-orange with pale blue dissolving into tints of yellow. As the sun climbs higher, the colours become bolder behind silhouetted, skeletal trees, capturing a timeless scene of enchanting mystique, reminiscent of that which is captured in the illustrations of Jan Pienkowski. Outside, the air is woven with thin strands of sound as wintering birds awaken. Light infiltrates the house, the interior of which becomes infused in a surreal, blushing glow which lasts for a few minutes before the sky dissolves, clouds chasing away colours, and everything becomes insipid and uniform once more.

(Ferndown, 7.30 am 2013)

Evening Descent

Cushions of cloud absorb the inky, dusky dye of twilight as it seeps into them. A swollen silence is chipped for an instant by the echoing cries of birds settling to roost. Within the woodland walkway, houses nestle snugly beneath the oak trees' black embrace. Christmas-tree- lit windows seem to sparkle as I step through swathes of crinkly, fallen leaves and I am home.

(Ferndown, 4.30pm 2013)

*

The sky an open veil; diaphanous, silk-spun, spreads out into the night while the moon melts within its misty aureole behind stark silhouetted trees. A robin still sings, despite the evening; the shrill, piping notes of his passerine nocturne fusing with the freshness of the winter air. The incandescence of these notes will continue, bright and hopeful in the darkness as they do most nights until gone eleven o'clock and even when they cease, they leave impressions lasting on the mind like light images on the retina. Somehow the misplaced nature of this melody intensifies the sense of wonder. There is something unreal, incongruous, as exists in dreams when juxtaposed events blend beautifully together. So because he refuses to sleep, the robin's song evokes a sweet sense of escape into that dream world and the joy of unexpected discovery.

(Ferndown, 2015)

Horton

Horton Tower, an old eighteenth- century folly, stands melancholy and solitary on the top of its hill on this dank, bleak December morning. It was built in 1726 by Humphrey Sturt, Lord of Horton Manor as well as MP for Dorset, as a flight of fancy, a 'folly' as was the fashion for the wealthy of his time. The looming austerity of the folly is enhanced by forty- three meters of height, and serves as a landmark for miles around [43]. On this dreary day it stands in all its gothic- looking splendour as heavily as the petulant clouds that encapsulate the whole area. Yet it is a familiar face now, almost friendly, and causes my mind to jump back a quarter of a century to when, as a child, my brother and I often came to the village of Horton to spend the weekend with school friends. Leaving our Edwardian house in the suburbs for their eighteenth- century cottage in the depths of the Dorset countryside was a wonderful adventure. I was transfixed by the cottage's historic atmosphere where time seemed to tread eternally on creaky floorboards. I could never sleep for excitement, wondering who had walked and lived there before, and in that quiescent state of hovering in a grey twilight between dream and the conscious waking world, my mind would fantasize on the supernatural, so that I fancied someone was watching, and I would tremble with a delicious fear.

During one of those stays it snowed. It had started at night so that we had gone to bed full of an extra sense of excitement, peering through dark windows, mesmerized by the constant falling of silent snowflakes drifting endlessly down in front of the streetlight outside. We had not been totally prepared for the transformation of the landscape when we jumped out of bed, four young children, full of the delights of the white wonderland which greeted us. A pristine patchwork quilt of fields, a 'pleasant land of counterpane'[64], unblemished and smooth had been spread out silently over this new dream world; thin lines of hedgerows defining black borders, skeletal trees standing strongly against the snow.

After breakfast we wrapped up warmly and raced outside, feet sinking into a dull, muffled crunch, our mittens soggy over throbbing fingers, our cheeks snow-slapped as we wildly pelted each other. Up the slope behind the village we ran, through the field to Horton Tower. The old folly seemed more sinister, black against the achromatic backdrop, the pinnacled roofs which crowned the sections of its lower tier wearing hats of snow. Our parents had told us never to enter the tower, never to try to climb it as it was abandoned and pieces could fall. If they had not succeeded in instilling a sense of fear in us, at least the tower commanded our respect. But that snowy day we didn't care; our friends' father was with us, accompanied by the farmer from next door and his young children. We were quite a party, starting at the top of the hill to roll a ball of snow, which squeaked and cracked, protesting at our every nudge as it became more compressed. At last it became so large and heavy that even combined effort could heave it no further. We began again, fingers still throbbing through sodden mittens, this time making a head, which we struggled to set on top of the body and after much pushing, slipping and sliding about, two men and six tired children, rosy and exhilarated, had built a worthy snowman. We gave him a face and then excitedly scampered back down to the village, proud of our exertions. From below we could see the green track in the snow down the side of the slope from where the great ball had been rolled and we could admire our new large friend standing robustly upon the hillside, counteracting our foe- the cold, forbidding folly looking on.

(2011)

Alum Chine

Although snow was quite common as a child, it has become more of a rare occurrence in recent years. Sometimes, however, cold snaps return and today Alum Chine has been transformed into a winter wonderland with trees taking on delicate filigree forms as every twig is royally iced. The silence of snow, falling softly, gracefully, layer upon layer, cushioning sound so that the air becomes muffled as if through a thick scarf. Having slithered down the slope of the chine, made glassy by the endless trails of toboggans, we step out onto a white beach, which stands silently like a blank open book, waiting for an exciting story to be written across its snowy surface as it blends with stippled cliffs, and sweeps into a grey monochrome of sea and sky. Snow sits in sickly leaden clouds waiting to fall afresh. I feel as if we have stepped into an old black and white photograph and am amazed at this white sand stretching on and on as far as visibility allows. It is something so unexpected. Usually salt and warmer coastal 'microclimates' do not allow snow to settle but then, two years ago, at Sandbanks, we witnessed a frozen sea. We wander almost alone on the beach, knowing that we might not witness such a sight again, and wondering why no one else has come to see it, then as the sky seems to sink, enclosing in on itself, dusk draining it of any form, we wander, back through the magical chine, now strangely, and alluringly tinted with orange streetlamps, and home to the warm.

(2011)

*

At thaw, the chine echoes with pattering drips. As the snow melts, morning sunlight sparkles on bare branches catching the forming drops and lighting up the trees with a glistening array of natural fairy lights.

(2011)

St Aldelm's Church

It is still early December and we walk from Worth Matravers to St Aldelm's Head along the coast path. The foliage in the lush valley which runs alongside the path to Winspit is festooned abundantly with old-man's beard, draping itself along and around every bush and tree, almost giving the appearance of snow. It is certainly a natural Christmas decoration and subdues the dull feeling that the gradual wind- down to the end of the year creates, as the last leaves fall and the promised sun has hidden itself away. A strong, cold wind off the sea buffets and blusters at the coast path as we walk up above the caves at Winspit. It tugs at teasels whose dry, empty scratch scores against the extensive sighing swathes of beige, buffeted grasses.

It is not long before a reclusive sun creeps out of hiding to shine brilliantly for fifteen minutes or so before the wind calls the clouds back in; sullen and grey, they scurry across the sky until they are blown beyond its boundaries, giving way to another bout of blue. And so the afternoon continues unsettled, as one of sunlight and shadow, and where whipped -cream clouds gather in towering, silver-lined mounds on the clear horizon, the sun sinks long spears of trident-like light, plunging through them into the languid looking-glass of a deceptive sea. Away from the cosy cottages of Worth Matravers with their sparkling, decorated windows and wreaths on doors, this place is bleak, untamed and enigmatic.

We are heading for the tiny Norman chapel of St Aldelm's, in itself an enigma. Situated one hundred and eight metres above sea level on the cliff top at St Aldelm's Head and built within an ancient Christian enclosure, it is named after its seventh-century association with St Aldelm, the first bishop of Sherborne. I always assumed it to have been built as a place of worship, comfort and refuge for sailors in peril on the sea, washed up in squalls on the shore below. However, it is thought that it might have actually served as a beacon to light them or a chantry to pray for them, and as chantries fell into disuse in the mid sixteenth century, this might account for the fact that the chapel was abandoned from around that time until the 19th century [68].

During the time of abandonment the chapel might have been exploited by smugglers, who could have used it as a watchtower over Chapman's pool and Winspit, where in the deep quarries hewn into the cliffs, contraband would have almost certainly been stored [71]. The current coastguard cottages, built in 1834, perhaps stand as the legacy to control the smuggling which had been so rife in the area and was apparently supported by many of the inhabitants at nearby Worth Matravers, which stood as a 'control centre' for smuggling [71]. There is therefore nothing new in tax-evasion, or the smuggling of illegal produce. Man has essentially not changed.

In this wild and windswept spot, so exposed that the gusting wind constantly tugs and tousles, we are glad to find shelter in this silent, reflective chapel, standing alone beside a field of sea cabbage, and looking out speculatively across the sea. A cruciferous smell mixes with salt. Out over the horizon, the clouds continue to collect, their towering peaks still sun-touched. We enter through a Norman doorway into a comforting haven of peace. The echoing swell of a deceptively calm-looking sea accompanies the roar of the racing wind outside, its chill unable to penetrate the thick walls of Portland stone. I wonder how many have taken welcome refuge here. The elemental sound of sea with wind is both strong and eternal, alluding in my mind to the Refuge of peace whom humbled, shipwrecked men might have sought within this sanctuary, thankful for physical and spiritual salvation.

Peering through the gloom, I turn to the intriguing interior walls; so lined and pitted with scrapings and scratchings, as to be almost ornamental in their design. There is nothing new in graffiti, as the numerous examples in this place testify, and it is therefore safe to assume once more that people haven't really changed, always wishing to make their mark, to be remembered in some small way. Never did they perhaps imagine that they would be still making their mark over three hundred years later, when people like us would be puzzling over their etchings and scratchings. Several initials are dated 1665, just twenty years after Corfe Castle was destroyed, Could they allude to the presence of smugglers gathering together in secret or perhaps sailors; hopeless and abandoned, seeking refuge? They might have been the doodles of prisoners, idling away hours in dark dank solitude, or maybe even passers-by who wanted to tell the world that they were here, as they do today. These people from the past will always remain a mystery and we can only speculate as to who they were or what they were doing here. What is clear is that we blame current generations for annotating walls, when actually it would seem that our predecessors did exactly the same.

 I am suddenly struck by an attractive piece of graffiti high up on the wall, a woman's name, which I have never noticed before, despite having been here often. It lingers, taking on length and form in the dim light, a name without date, and judging by the meticulously executed copperplate handwriting, quite difficult to achieve in stone, I would imagine the writer to be well- educated and eloquent. Another carving by someone with the same surname is written further down the wall, below hers in bolder, more masculine block-capitals. This second person, by use of their initials, perhaps wishes to remain anonymous. There is no date, but since this chapel remained in disuse until the nineteenth century, I imagine that people would have felt quite at liberty to carve their names during the time when it was abandoned, although for a woman to do this was perhaps considered outrageous. Why would she want to risk her reputation and her name?

 It seems that for whatever reason, she had painstakingly and carefully added her name to the collage of others, its altitude on the wall suggesting that she wanted the elusive signature to appear subtly, half masked in darkness. Perhaps wishing to make her presence more strongly known once discovered, she had carefully etched her full name, not just her initials; thus revealing her entire identity, whereas her companion preferred to partially conceal theirs.

The surname of these two 'graffitists' appears in local church records in Swanage and also in nearby Kingston, perhaps not bearing any relation. If the woman was local, I imagine her walking out across the fields here one carefree summer's afternoon, with her husband, brother or cousin to accompany her. They were perhaps young, rich, hedonistic, and perhaps a little egocentric, endowed with the ever -conjoined feelings of invincibility and delicious rebellion which most young people possess when visiting somewhere secretive and abandoned: 'It might be forbidden, but who cares? Nothing bad can possibly happen, despite the fact that it might be falling down.' The same can be seen at the Winspit quarries, where despite the warning signs not to enter, generations of people from past to present have defiantly chiselled their names within.

The woman and her companion perhaps entered the abandoned chapel as a dare, or out of curiosity. Perhaps she came alone, attracted to a smuggler or pirate, meeting him secretly, as did Dona with the latter in Daphne Du Maurier's *Frenchman's Creek* or there could have been direct involvement with smuggling as was the young widow in Thomas Hardy's *Distracted Preacher* for there is something distinctly clandestine about the positioning of the carved name. It might have been a man who chiselled it; carving the name of the one he loved and longed for, a secret admirer, a jilted lover; although the writing style appears to me as feminine, and the existence of the other name would suggest that she was not alone.

I am of course only speculating, allowing my imagination to run wild, for this place is in itself wild and intriguing and holds the key to so many secrets which cannot be unlocked. It is apparent, from all the graffiti that many people spent time at this spot, leaving only their initials to prove that they were once here. The walls, which have indeed witnessed all, only share the secrets in tantalizing 'riddles', which are almost impossible, with the passing of time, to understand. However, we do know that much of this graffiti has survived, remaining understated and subdued in the silence of this sanctuary for three hundred and fifty years, waiting for someone to take interest in it. Today, the idea of defacing an ancient, consecrated building with graffiti is sacrilegious, no short of criminal (the abandoned chapel would have already been about five hundred years old when they did this). Yet the tangible presence of names set in stone speaks history in itself, more compelling than simply seeing old handwriting on a piece of paper, for we know that those people, whoever they were, were once standing in this very spot, experiencing something of the same. Now the only tenuous connection we have with them is that they stared up at the shadowy vaulted ceiling, saw the same stones, looked out at the sea, listening to its surge, the gusting of the wind, feeling small and protected or defiant and empowered, they left a lasting legacy to their long lost presence, distanced through time but brought closer to us by place and the realization that we are indeed not that different.

(2012)

The Priest's Way

We turn from Langton House down to the Priest's Way, a three-mile, medieval path which connects Worth Matravers with Swanage and was used until 1506 by the local priest of the former to visit his sister church at the latter [66]. Perhaps some of the early vicars and rectors listed in the porch of St Nicholas Church in Worth also made this journey. Knowing the origins and purpose of a path makes it so much more exciting to follow. The low winter sunlight is sharp, bright and clear, flooding the fields as they gently roll down to the sea. Red cows graze peacefully on green slopes, behind them Swanage nestles under a high chalky cliff looking out onto a basking blue sea, the stark white needles of the Isle of Wight almost ethereal in the crystalline light.

The Priest's Way branches in two directions and we take the way towards Worth Matravers. Peaceful and radiant in the sunlight; twiggy, skeletal trees are twined into hedgerows and covered with ivy and frilly yellow lichen- evidence of pure, clear air. There is indeed a purity and clarity about the whole atmosphere and place today- the peaceful, innocent grazing of livestock in the meadows, the soft green undulations of the fields, the lazy spread of sea and the path which gently winds through the countryside. I almost feel like a pilgrim on a journey, following this path to a sacred shrine and imagine the priest on such days as this, full of the joys of life, feeling at one with God and creation, tranquil and reflective in this beautiful timeless place, which has probably changed little, feeling the air sink into his soul, perhaps thinking about his spiritual path as he walked the physical.

From the path, there are views across the fields to the small, stoic chapel of St Aldelm's and the chimneyed coast guard cottages, characteristic, shadowy silhouettes on the horizon, the former of which, the priest would also have seen along his way. Both landscape and path therefore serve to link past with present because these things have remained. Although landscapes can subtly or even dramatically change through the centuries, the excitement of old paths is that they remain etched in the earth as they were first dug, and therefore tangibly re-enforce that link through time and place.

Along the path stands an old seventeenth- century farmhouse called Eastlington, owned by the National Trust, and used to practice organic farming and nature conservation. Further on is an active quarry, but today being Sunday, it has been abandoned by workers. The sun continues to shine as we walk, gilding the softly sweeping slopes of the dreamy landscape. Shadows fall into and shape their soft folds and the ridges of land once tilled or extensively grazed. The flat plain of sea takes on a mottled iridescence like fresh watermarks on satin. Gulls shriek over it, a cockerel crows somewhere and the air is picked at by a scurry of sparrow voices.

With this beautiful calm it is hard to imagine the plight of the Halsewell, a British ship from the English East India Company, which was wrecked in a stormy sea below Worth Matravers in 1786 on its way from London to Bengal. Although just over twice as many died, eighty two men were saved through their own endeavours combined with the bravery of locals and quarrymen. In his story, *The Long Voyage*, inspired by the shipwreck, Charles Dickens writes,

> See the Halsewell, East Indiaman outward bound, driving madly on a January night towards the rocks near Seacombe on the island of Purbeck! The captain's two dear daughters are aboard and five other ladies. The ship has been driving many hours, has seven feet of water in her hold, and her mainmast has been cut away. The description of her loss, familiar to me from early boyhood, seems to be read aloud as she rushes to her destiny. [28]

Today the sea is suave and placid, yet when its mood changes, it can become dangerously hostile, a notorious place for shipwrecks, and although it is not responsible for plane crashes, perhaps something of an association made it a suitable location for scientists to develop the British radar system for the RAF between 1940-1942. The research was carried out at nearby Renscombe farm by a team of scientists, whose ensuing developments played a crucial part in the Second World War [68].

This is not the only scientific success that can be contributed to Worth. As we wander through the field of grazing cows on our entrance to the village, I think also of Benjamin Jetsy, an unsung Dorset hero who apparently was 'the first person (known) that introduced the cowpox by inoculation, and who from his great strength of mind made the experiment (from the cow) on his wife and two sons in the year 1774', so reads his gravestone in the churchyard [57]. Edward Jenner, his contemporary, conducted his first, similar experiment on eight-year-old James Phipps in 1796, twenty two years later, yet Jenner's is the name which takes all the credit.

Putting facts from the past behind us, we stop for refreshment. People sit outside the Square and Compass even on a winter's day. According to their website, it has been an inn since about 1776 and owned by the same family since 1907. I remember one of the first times I came here on a clear and starry summer's night over ten years ago, my friends and I using the backlights of our mobile phones to help guide us from the carpark down the road to the pub. The black silence of the still sea was melting into a sky of glittering constellations, vast and full of wonder, distant, elevated. We were brought back down to earth by the steady rise and fall of mirthful voices from the pub and I was delighted to walk around the small fossil museum while having my drink; the fascinating array of local fossils is the private collection of one of the family owners and an amazing testimony to the prehistoric life which existed along this Jurassic coast.

Retracing our steps later, it is already early evening. Behind us, the sun is sinking delicately behind St Aldelm's Chapel, which continues to stand like a stoic beacon with its unique square and robust stature. The sky has become opalescent, as if a front is forming, and as we walk, shreds of purple cloud curdle into the opaque mother-of-pearl, as if oil had been dripped onto water and was slowly curling across its meniscus. The fields are flooded with a stronger, richer gold, swept with long shadows. We pass a drystone wall built beautifully on the diagonal, the top crowned with triangular stones whose points catch the golden evening sunlight on their angled surfaces. Ivy wraps many of the walls, as it does the wind-warped trees; stunted skeletal, bent inwards by the frequent gales coming in off the sea. Today the slight wind is chilly, unwarmed by the long, fingering light of evening. Runners pass on the path, people with dogs.

Soon we have lost the sunlight and the path becomes duller and darker. Textures are taken from trees and twiggy hedgerows when light and its contrasting shadows both ebb away, as does the feeling of time, so that we are left with blank pages in a drab history book.

We return to the red cows. Sheep have been introduced to a field in the foreground and they sit, woolly and rotund, looking completely content in their evening environment as are the cows, peacefully grazing in the fields behind. In fields further on, down towards Swanage and the sea, where the sun still reaches out to touch the soft slopes with warm, amber radiance, the sheep have golden fleece!

In bare, twiggy bushes, covered in lichen, a group of yellowhammers sit for a few seconds before flitting together to the next, blissfully unaware of the world outside this silent enclave. The sky has become powdery; clouds rise in the west like plumes of thin grey smoke through which sickly sunlight tries to penetrate, emphasizing the black, stark nakedness of the trees. A storm is brewing in the natural, yet despite the fact that there are so many 'storms' unleashed in the world at present, here is a haven of peace, a purity of place which allows one to see the world as perhaps it should be.

(2013)

Awakening

I leave early, the half-light hanging, suspended in slow-moving time, which waits for the day to dawn. Like a Christmas rose emerging, softly unfurling its petals, so, the day unfolds with the stirring of sound- the comfortable chuck chucking of a blackbird pitting the calm, a smooth, sweet, almost imperceptible backdrop of other birds blending into the blissful, dreamlike state of the morning and revealing the fact that not all the birds have deserted us for winter. In a split second, a cat darts across my path, a swift apparition disappearing silently through the lifting veil of darkness.

This particular cat usually sits framed in the window of my neighbour's house, warm and indolent, looking out with calm complacence at the wintry world outside. The day continues to open up like a fresh chapter in a book about life, the fleeting journey of the spirit passing swiftly through it to something brighter beyond, summarized in the cat's passing presence. This is then followed by a more detailed description of birth as senses stir from slumber, and the dream of blue dawn-light drains away, leaving a marbled sky of pearly grey.

Freezing mist drapes itself in a thick cloak, which hovers several metres above the fields; trees- skeletal spectres cloaked in mist, horses dressed in coats, seemingly surreal and legless within the misty shroud. It is as if one were still clinging onto sleep, locked in a bizarre dream, yet a pale impression of the sun is trying to burn through it with tentative, beckoning fingers, coaxing consciousness and reality. It touches the languid dawn river, causing it to blush subtly; light against the inky reflections of foliage which blacken its banks. As the mist hangs, covering the clandestine, shrouding secrets of a new morning, so anticipation waits in breathless time-suspended, excited, anxious to make the most of whatever the awakening day will bring.

(Ferndown, 2013)

Silton

The sleepy village of Silton basks in the amber light of early evening; the sun sinking with such intensity that the fifteenth- century tower of St Nicholas' Church blushes a deep bronze. Despite the completely clear skies and constant sunshine of the day, the temperature has barely crept above freezing and pockets of frost have remained untouched by the sun all day. A meadow, full of spindly trees and their windblown leaves, skirts around the edge of the frosty churchyard. We follow a flattened path of footprints through damp leaves and muddy grass, which leads us over a stile and out into a larger meadow. Beyond this, roll Dorset hills, stained with the setting sun; a landscape interjected with solitary trees, hedges and small copses, each casting their long shadows over amber green.

Judge Wyndham's Oak stands alone in this meadow watching out across the sweeping vistas as it has done for centuries, perhaps even a millennia, although no one is quite sure. What is known is that the tree takes its name from a Judge Hugh Wyndham, resident of Silton Manor, who was, according to an information board, 'judge for Charles I, II and Oliver Cromwell.' His high profile career required him to travel extensively, and returning to his home at Silton, he found relaxation while sitting under his favourite tree, admiring the wonderful view and perhaps pontificating. Wyndham was knighted by Charles II in 1670, and his tree appears on the Ordnance Survey map.

The calm, serene atmosphere hangs pensively; silent except for the chuckle of ducks in the Stour. Because of the calm, it is almost impossible to believe that this tree might have once been at the hub of a now lost village [44] and was once perhaps used as a gibbet to hang two of the Duke of Monmouth's conspirators in the seventeenth century [65]. This fact is not mentioned on the information board by the tree and I prefer to consider it as having always served as an innocent boundary marker for Gillingham Royal Deer Park, which is what it is generally purported to be.

Whatever its history, its antiquity nevertheless cannot be disputed; it stands crooked, leaning on a wooden prop with various wires and other contraptions holding it together. Its mighty girth, at around ten and a half metres, is completely hollowed-out in several places so that when I peer into the dark cavernous inner chambers, I can look up and see the sky. The textured, interior walls of these large hollows reveal different patterns of wood grain. Soft shapes and shades blend in muted, wooded colours defined with white rot, blackened with damp and greened with silky moss; a beautiful blend of natural colours and textures running together as if woven. Standing inside the hollowed out trunk, we feel cocooned from the world, standing at the heart of the ancient tree as if we were in a secret cave. Outside, the mighty, lop-sided bole, knotted and gnarled, provides a microcosm for an array of life-forms. Oak bonnet fungi (*Mycena inclinata*) cluster in little hollows in the huge swirls of haggard bark- a cosy fairyland of more colours and textures. Higher up, holes in the bark suggest an invasion of beetles. Other insects and, of course birds all also find homes here.

If this tree is one thousand years old, then at six hundred, it would have been well into its prime at the time of Judge Wyndham. Now its angular, naked branches, exposed by the stripping of winter, seem to be reaching higher and higher, almost stretching from the sleep of age and trying to touch their former youthful glory as they jut into a still blue sky, catching the last spill of amber sunlight. As the sun sets, cold begins to gnaw at our fingers, but it is hard to leave this peaceful idyll. We wait as this stourside meadow sinks deeper into slumber under the watch of a tree which has seemed to stand guard so serenely through so many centuries.

As we head back across the meadow, we see its offspring, deliberately planted from an acorn, growing proudly within the confines of a wooden frame. Nothing stirs in the village. The sun sends long, sweeping shadows across grass and floods the facades of cottages. The only sign of life is a very old woman, slowly walking her dog along the edge of the single-track road, her crinkled face spelling anxiety as, in our car, we carefully creep past her.

As we drive homeward, taking the road from Milton-on Stour to Fontmell Magna, the landscape is breathtaking; hills rise and fall away in steep, frosty escarpments, climbing and dipping in a never-ending panorama. These are timeless hills where sheep graze and on which intriguing patches of forest remind us of a landscape which once existed before sheep and dairy farming became so important for this county. Tonight everything is touched with the nacreous peachy tones of winter, fields tinged with a frosty film as the sun sets and an elusive sheet of mist begins to hover in the valleys. Away to the south, just spilling over the horizon are the mauve shadows of bubbling clouds. The bright ball of the setting sun has met them just above horizon's boundary so that their whipped peaked tops are edged in flaming orange, and as the sun sifts through, sending strident shafts heavenwards as well as earthwards, the scene is not only breathtaking, but also apocalyptic.

As the hills plunge down into sleepy, misty valleys and the sun sinks further, so peach-tinged hues turn to purple and the dream of dusk takes its hold. It is half past four and the day is done. The chill creeps colder and small cottages with Christmas lights winking from windows and curls of wood-smoke rising from chimneys, look inviting. My mind returns to that peaceful meadow, settling down to sleep while the oak stands, a silhouette, unmoving, unseeing, every century the same and any notion of time unknown. Its long life, which could have even begun around the Norman conquest and remains something tangible and alive from that time, seemingly stands still as other lives are born and end like passing seasons; small circles within its long lifecycle through centuries of time.

(2014)

Weymouth

I once read a letter written in 1834, sent from Weymouth by the daughter of a baronet to her father. Just as young people do today, she was asking him to send her money to pay for bills and expenses required for living away from home. From the tone of the letter, it was evident that she was only temporarily staying in Weymouth, spending the summer months with her maid and perhaps a brother in a house on the Esplanade.

The Esplanade, gracefully stretching for over a mile and overlooking the sea, consists of fifteen terraced blocks mostly constructed in the Georgian and Regency periods (1770-1855). Much of it was designed by a local architect, James Hamilton and was let or sold to wealthy and fashionable clientele, with the purpose of providing summer retreats in a popular location frequented by King George III himself between 1789 and 1805 [41]. Considering the length of the Esplanade, which still retains its elegance and charm, it would seem that the wealthy must have flocked here to stay in these fashionable abodes and that the area was expanded to accommodate them. Indeed, according to Historic England, Belvidere, which is the terrace from which the young lady wrote, was begun in 1818 but was still under construction until the 1850s and Weymouth continued in its expansion as a fashionable tourist resort, becoming more easily accessible with the advent of the railway in 1857 [41].

I decide that I should like to find the house where Catherine, the aristocratic young woman of the letter, spent her summers. The day hangs half asleep; a heavy, drowsy sky, like lazy eyelids. Places out of season are compelling, taking on a new character, and Weymouth is no exception. I am enchanted by its maze of little lattice streets, each leading onto another and eventually coming out on the Esplanade itself. Looking at the architecture, it seems that a significant part of the town centre, namely the back streets of the Esplanade, all appear to have been built around the same time, although the history of the town as a major trading port goes back much earlier to the twelfth century. Small shops decorated with strings of lights and selling beautiful artisan bakery, arts, crafts, and boutique clothes vie alongside high street stores. Teashops compete with cosy pubs situated in the small streets behind the waterfront. I imagine these might have once been drunken alleyways, their watering holes the frequent haunt of smugglers and sailors, a world away from the refined clientele who resided on the waterfront, and certainly not as aesthetically pleasing as they are today.

Today Weymouth's main streets are bustling, vibrant, crowded with Christmas shoppers. Overhead the sky rings with the searing cries of seagulls, their laughter-like cackles filling us with nostalgia for summer and the feeling that we are walking in a large, jolly fishing village. In the chuckles of the gulls I can 'hear' the drawl of sailors telling nautical tales laced with excitement and adventure. They are an echo from the past breathing into the present, for the gull's cries, being a sound familiar throughout the centuries, are so evocative that they stimulate my imagination to make these bizarre connections.

Despite it being still a week before Christmas, many of the hotels along and near the Esplanade are already full. Glittering Christmas trees languish in bay windows, yet the buildings of the Esplanade reflect a former affluence and have taken on a quietly nostalgic air of shabby, elegant repose. It is as if they have served the summer and are now putting their feet up in front of the fire for winter. Their quiet windows watch out across the sea, not a movement breathes from within as they exude the silent memories of brighter days. I wonder what they have seen; modern families with excited children, buckets, spades and dogs, further back in time, aristocratic ladies of leisure mincing elegantly on the arms of top-hatted gentlemen, the colourful comings and goings of sailors, captains and their crews, drunkards, prostitutes, merchants and their ships, the illicit landings of smugglers. They would have watched King George the III, his bathing hut, and no doubt others like it, wheeled out to sea, and in 1805, they would have perhaps even witnessed the wreck of the Earl of Abergavenny which sank two miles off the shore, its masts sticking out of the water. The Captain of the ship, John Wordsworth, younger brother of the poet William, lost his life at the age of thirty nine along with about two hundred and fifty others.

Behind the far end of the Esplanade lies the old harbour, perfectly picturesque and tranquil today, yet the hostile breath of the chill wind gently reminds one that it has not always been so amenable and comfortable and that in 1348 it was host to the Black Death, which rampantly spread across the surrounding area. Later the port held association with the Spanish Armada and Civil War. It is generally known that in the eighteenth and nineteenth centuries Weymouth was teaming with smugglers, who due to the incompetence of the local customs house, could easily pass their illicit wares through a trail of tunnels leading from under the Esplanade and sell much in the maze of small streets up in the town, the presence of the gentry providing them with a ready market for luxury goods [53]. In contrast to this history of deception and lawlessness, Daniel Defoe, writing at the beginning of the eighteenth century, perhaps before smuggling had really taken a hold, describes it much as

> A sweet, clean, agreeable town, considering its low situation…'tis well-built and has a great many good substantial merchants in it; who drive

a considerable trade and have a good number of ships belonging to the town. (27)

He also mentions witnessing a ship full of cargo bound from Porto to London, which fell victim to a storm off Weymouth and sent its guns firing as a distress signal. Apparently the 'venturous Weymouth-men' hurried to assist, lending the desperate vessel an anchor and cable, its own having been lost at sea, in order for it to stabilize itself and not run aground and crash. However, they expected 'a good price' for the help they had given, and a return of the anchor and cable when the ship set sail again four days later (27).

Today in the harbour, bright fishing boats moor in front of the colourful façades of old houses with their feeling of timelessness, watching the world go by as the boats come in and out and people pass by across the bridge as they have done throughout the centuries. Thinking of the letter, I make tenuous connections in my mind. No doubt Catherine would have looked across this same harbour and passed in front of these colourful facades. She would have admired the beautiful, majestic curve of ultra-modern, terraced housing sweeping away as far as the eye can see, not as complete in her time. Across the water, scurried cliffs; chalk swirled in cloud, rise ominously out of a grey sea, from which comes the wind, biting at our fingers and faces. Catherine would have surely seen a similar view as she took her promenades here in summer and although the sea and cliffs might still have been sullen sometimes, the wind could not have been so bitter.

The road out of Weymouth back towards Dorchester passes through some beautiful countryside, the landscape smudged into a watercolour sky of pale peachy blue and liquid grey, the latter of which runs into the green folds of the fields. On the way home, we pass a dead badger at the side of the road, probably hit by a car. Death can come so swiftly to all, without time to fear or prepare, but for an animal dying slowly it seems as if it might be easier than it is for us to give up on such a beautiful world as this landscape portrays.

(2013)

Hardy's Cottage

In the depths of Thorncombe Woods stands the hamlet of Higher Bockhampton. As the day drags like heavy sleep, yawning through frail, chill gusts of wind, we amble in this woodland of bare beech trees, its floor thickly strewn with damp, matted copper leaves and mast, which sink and stick softly underfoot. Although it is only two o'clock, it easily feels like five, so dismal and enervating is the light and the dank, cold air, the latter hanging like lethargic limbs, heavy with humidity, smelling slightly earthy. Somewhere through this wood winds a Roman road, a legacy of time's tread ever marching onwards.

Coming out into a clearing, we see a memorial to the writer, Thomas Hardy and on our left his cottage nestling in the grey pout of the listless, lifeless day, which seemingly reflects the hopeless moods of many of Hardy's characters. The picture-perfect cottage could be even more perfect if a wispy trail of wood-smoke were rising above its thatch, spicing the air with singed sap. However, it is empty, vacant; seemingly hibernating for the winter, its windows dark and blank as if it has shut its eyes to dream of distant halcyon memories.

By the summer it will be open again; its windows flung wide and its simple, snug interior aired and flooded with fresh sunlight reflected in crisp starched whites and polished wood. The garden will be full of flowers attracting pollinators (and tourists!) and the summer air will be filled with the warm memories of happy days. This is the place where Hardy was born in 1840. This cottage, built by his great-grandfather thirty-nine years earlier, would have witnessed the birth within its very walls amongst many other happy times. It was also evidently once a place of inspiration, for Hardy wrote two of his novels here.

But now it is winter and, like a child on a chill wet day, the cottage stands with its bored, blank face waiting for nothing. With nothing more to do ourselves, as the cottage is closed, we follow a woman with dog trailing themselves slowly up the main path through the hamlet as if killing time. The path, potholed and puddled, passes a silent row of terraced cottages whose blank expressions give away no glimmer of life, no smile through the muffled dusk. And so we leave this pensive place, a place which was once so remote that, according to an information board, the Hardy family's only friends in the vicinity on arrival were the lonely *heathcroppers* (the ponies that grazed the heath) while back at home, they tolerated snakes, insects and the bats which invaded their bedrooms at night! This cottage was, therefore, perhaps not as cosy after all, despite its situation as a snug retreat and its purpose as a loving family home.

(2013)

December

Wimborne St Giles

In Wimborne St Giles I am disappointed to see no garlands, wreaths nor twinkling lights on the Sunday just before Christmas; no smoky chimneys. The air feels cold and a vapour of thin mist hovers, phantom-like, just above the grass in the village centre, its quiet, understated presence a distinct contrast from the persistent cacophony of rooks which nest in the tops of tall skeletal trees, silhouetted against a tissue sky. Pigeons offset them with their fluid call of calm reassurance and we begin walking towards the river where, for a glorious moment, the sun shines strongly into glistening, chattering waters and we watch a heron, its inquisitive head sticking above tall grasses on the river bank. Suddenly, with a single flap of huge wings, it takes off in graceful flight and disappears.

Clouds collect ominously as we return from our walk. Skirting around some fields and re-entering the village past the old school, the atmosphere intensifies, sky suddenly darkening mysteriously and with a crack of its whip, thunder unleashes a lightning flash, which makes us jump. The atmosphere continues brooding and throbbing. We pass the old stocks in the village and think of those poor victims of the past who would have been pelted there. But now the first heavy drops begin to pelt us and we dash for the car where inside, we enjoy the comforting metallic ring of hailstones hammering on the roof as they cascade down with powerful velocity. In a minute the ground is transformed to an icy white while more hailstones bounce off the bonnet of our car with astounding energy. All this entertainment provides a cosier, wintrier feeling than Christmas trees and open fires. Now the hail is here, their absence does not matter.

(2012)

*

The inhabitants of some Dorset villages still get together to sing carols in the days leading up to Christmas. In the past, such singers would have gone to the village manor house where they would have been given some Christmas cheer in the form of food and drink in return for their efforts. Others who visited the manor would have been the mummers. Today they tour local pubs with their colourful costumes; the atmosphere cordial, jovial, spiced with alcohol and mirth as a community comes together in the flickering log- firelight beneath trails of fairy-lights.

The tradition of merry-making, so often the way in an age without technology, to pass time in entertainment and company, is evocative in the firelight and as we watch the mummers, imaginations run away into the grotesque, the make-believe, the larger than life. This is perhaps also the attraction of pantomimes, when children and adults enter that fairy-tale realm of laughter and banter. These activities, I believe, are not presenting an alternative, secular side of Christmas but merely coincide, for they are perhaps rooted in an ancient longing, a connection with the deep past, when communities sought distraction and diversion from the long, dark winter nights.

*

One of my favourite pieces of choral music amongst many beautiful carols sung by cathedral choirs around Christmas time is Sir John Tavener's *The Lamb*. Its hauntingly beautiful use of homophony creates an aura of mystery, ethereality and wonder, so characteristic of many of Tavener's works. In the latter part of his life, Sir John Tavener lived in Dorset.

(2013)

Christmas Past

Kingston Lacy has been decorated for Christmas, Victorian style. Two huge, traditional wreaths adorn the front doors. At least half a meter across, a medley of pine, holly, a trailing wisp of ivy, mistletoe sprigs, red ribbons, dried orange slices and sticks of cinnamon. Through the large doors we are drawn inside the wonder of the house, dark and flickering with candles. A magnificently tall Christmas tree towers in the main hall, festooned with ribbons and handmade, traditional decorations. We sip sherry in the glowing study and enter the dining room where the table is set for dinner. I imagine the excitement of Christmas in such a big house, the scampering of tiny footsteps about the passageways as children became completely overwhelmed with suspense and excitement, people coming and going; visitors, friends, maids about their business.

In her memoirs, Viola Bankes, who lived at the house in the early twentieth century, eludes to a more formal Christmas. She talks of church in the morning and a large Christmas meal of turkey and all the trimmings in the evening. This was invariably interrupted by local carol singers who would be invited into the kitchen for refreshment by the butler. The servants apparently had their own party with roast beef, handmade gifts from the children and more sober, practical gifts from the lady of the house, for which they lined up to receive. Despite the formality of festivities conveyed, there was also a certain amount of anticipation eluded to: the round of children's parties, where the smartly groomed children were given elaborate teas, the making of presents for the servants, stirring the pudding and wishing, decorating the house with garden greenery, lighting the candles on the tree and the feigned sleep of an excited child awaiting Father Christmas [5]. Christmas held magic, mystery and suspense and this is suggested at Kingston Lacy even in an era where children were seen and not heard.

In the parlour, the long oak table has been laid out with homemade biscuits and sweetmeats for us to try. Another Christmas tree, decorated with simple, childlike decorations adorns the doorway. On polished sideboards beside huge silver meat covers, stand magnificent poinsettias, as large, velvety and rich as those upstairs in the main hall. As I look at this array, I wonder whether Christmas held more religious significance then, whether it was an act of faith, or tradition, or possibly both, or whether, as now, people became so absorbed in the preparations and celebrations, that, after probably paying lip-service at midnight mass, they perhaps might have forgotten why they were really celebrating at all.

What I do sense though, is a soft austerity in such a Victorian Christmas, of things done well and properly; lavish without being frivolous, extravagant without being over indulgent. I sensed the same at the Russell-Cotes Museum where we went a few years before, with friends, to an Edwardian Christmas night. A similar tall tree stood in a candlelit hall, dark against the warm background glow and decorated with ribbons, candles, beautiful glass baubles and barley twists. These trees, so beloved of Prince Albert and his German culture, became a Christmas commodity in fashionable houses soon after the beginning of Victoria's reign.

At the Russell Cotes, light glowed everywhere, lowering the shadowy ceilings, normally high and resonant, embellished in frescoes and gold. In each of the intimate rooms, dark and glowing with candlelight, came traditional carols, beautifully rendered in four- part harmony by a small group of local singers dressed formally; the men in top hat and tails, the women in long evening gowns. Their exquisite voices; clear and mellifluous, radiated sincerity, warmth, joy and Christmas cheer, so that I felt embraced by the past, the lost legacy of simple, but quality entertainment, and the art of appreciating and using what talents we have. This is what I noticed at Kingston Lacy too; where all the decorations had been handmade, using foliage, fruits and berries. Food would have been local, quality produce, every appetizing morsel made by hand.

Without a doubt, it was the tireless work of the servants, which would have enabled the celebrations to go with such a swing. Accustomed to waking early, they must have woken even earlier on Christmas morning. Despite their own celebrations and small gifts, offered by the lady of the house, they would not have been able to spend Christmas with their families. I therefore see sacrifice, loyalty and devotion expressed in these Victorian and Edwardian Christmases.

Both houses have left me lost in a delicious reverie of Christmas past, more appreciative of the non-material offerings, given freely with love to bring pleasure to others. As I leave the warm, glowing interior of Kingston Lacy House to the bitter bite of the gaunt, grey chill outside which infuses itself in stone exteriors, I am still wrapped in the warmth which has kindled a delicious desire to do more creative things for others, to appreciate the aesthetic more deeply, and therefore create a Christmas to be more beautiful.

(2012)

*

Children chase each other through ferns in an enchanted garden. The fernery at Kingston Lacy has been festooned with threads of blue and white fairy lights which weave a web in and out between the trees and create a dazzling canopy above our heads. As dusk draws in, treetrunks illuminated with changing colours undergo metamorphosis as light-play shapes them. These surreal trees seem to have come to life, as if empathising with the children, for while shadows grow and fade, so scampering footsteps and delighted voices approach and die away again as their owners run backwards and forwards in an exhausting game of tag or hide and seek.

As I stare at the chameleon trees, I want to catch a colour and hold it there, just as parents cling to childhood. Yet these children running free in the fernery do not want to be caught; living in the present they are unaware that they will change and grow like the colours and shadows which sculpt the trees and sweep freely through the ferns. Time stands still for them and as we enter their world of illusion, hours become meaningless; by five o'clock it is 'night'. A wonderland of reverie is conjured in this twinkling, secret garden and with its touch of transformation we can all become children again, spinning a web of fantasy around the reality which lies at Christmas' heart.

(2016)

Arne

From Shipstal Hide we see the biggest colony of spoonbills in the UK. They cluster together out on the saltmarsh, a huddle of thirty- one individuals, about half the number that there were back in the autumn, according to an RSPB guide at the hut. These birds are rare in the UK, wintering here from northern European countries such as Holland, and have reached amber conservation status. It is relaxing to watch them, the saltmarsh stretching away into a blue reverie, birds going about their business a world away from every day. We could be in any century. I relish the elegiac call of a curlew floating like a lost soul across the flats, its shrill, anguished, pleading trill reflecting, in my mind, the sad case of the curlew becoming so endangered that it is now labelled with red conservation status. Sadly, although I scan the area thoroughly with my binoculars, I cannot view the elusive caller.

At a watery enclave we watch and wait, with a small expectant group of photographers, for a water vole. I feel as if we are paparazzi; large-lensed cameras all pointing towards the small unsuspecting animal's nest, listening at the door with rapt anticipation and bated breath as it voraciously munches. When the little creature eventually emerges, its streamlined, furry brown body cutting through ripples and reflections on the water, excitement spreads and shutters click. It is wonderful to see.

We are once again alone on Shipstal Beach. The sea exhales in a continuum of ripples which break with a sigh on the shore. Yet before we even set foot on the sand, the enticing path entrance with its window onto the strandline frames a couple of oystercatchers busily picking about. They lift the big flat shells with their beaks and drop them again, totally oblivious of our watching presence. We observe them for ten minutes before they scurry off to join their group further up the beach. A holly bush flames bright berries against amber cliffs, sandy, streaked. On the bush a robin sits and watches us, puffed up against the chill wind, both holly and robin, symbols associated with a Christmas which is shortly coming.

A silver birch forest resembles a Nordic painting, the simple, clean-cut, vertical lines of silver trees, drawing us into the heart of their wonderland. Although these trees barely live eighty years, they are some of the oldest species on Earth. A medley of ancient and modern seems to fuse in the silent forest, or perhaps it is timelessness. Other forest areas around the peninsular take on a more obviously ancient feel; twisted and contorted trees whose writhing roots are restrained by moss and whose branches blindly grope along the ground. There is something enigmatic about this other -worldly place where stories are conceived.

Arne in itself is a place of secrets, which is why I never tire of coming. Despite numerous cars in the carpark, we hardly ever pass more than half a dozen people. It is a place to escape, to dream, to remain secret oneself while watching the clandestine worlds of others; deer moving surreptitiously, their figment-like forms flicking between the trees, birds skulking in the shallows or flitting through bare branches. Once we even saw a literal stag party, the animals all sitting together in a secluded field, watching from beneath an array of antlers in the heathery gloom. It is a place where the light can be elusive, bringing beauty, harmony and form to even the most mundane pine tree. The most wonderful place to be is secluded in the hide at Shipstal Point, secretly watching the world away from anything manmade and as I sit there, surrounded by peace, the avian soundscape soaking into my soul, there is no place that I would rather be.

(2015)

Christmas

We were blessed with a white Christmas this year, even though the weather has been unseasonably mild. Returning from my brother's after midnight on Christmas Eve, and leaving the lights of Bournemouth behind us, we noticed on arrival home that everything was soaked in silver. This was moonlight from the 'full cold moon', the final full moon of the year, which was to peak on this special night.

Where we live, there are no streetlights at night and so in those chill, clear early hours of Christmas morning, the atmosphere was awash with a magical sense of anticipation and wonder, waiting for the big day as the moonlight spilled its silver shimmer across everything. The ground under the trees looked as if it were thinly sprinkled with snow or tinctured with thick frost, while usually dark paths were softly and strangely illuminated. The moon's luminosity striking through the bare branches of old oak trees caused a stirring, shadowy effect across the silver sheen of the ground. It touched the trees from behind, smoothing bare bark, and shone fully onto our front door, plating the berries on our wreath, the carved decorations and angles of the pediment above the fanlight.

Christmas Eve always felt a little unreal when I was a child, hovering between dreams and consciousness, trying desperately to sleep, unable to for excitement. While the calm serenity of this silver wonder-world spoke of an adult excitement contained, controlled, yet no less intense, it still seemed equally illusory so that if I were a child, I could think I had wandered into another world, like Lucy in *The Chronicles of Narnia*. As an adult I was enchanted to have stepped out of the car into this winter-wonderland, a special secret world created by the light of the 'full cold moon', its beams embracing us and bringing with them all the senses of excitement, mystery and awe which I used to experience as a child at Christmas. Standing in the deep, calm moon-shadows beneath the trees, silver light flowing through my fingers, I thought of the real Christmas, the wise men seeing the star in the east and how that must have stimulated similar senses and many more within them.

(2015)

Melbury Deer Park

We saunter through Melbury deer Park from Evershot to Melbury Osmund one morning just after Christmas. We have entered a secret, peaceful and self-contained world surrounded by wooded declivities, which descend gently into valleys, where open green spreads away beneath solitary trees. On this cold, clear day, sunlight flows across the trunks of these old trees while their long shadows stretch across the park's smooth spaces. I am reminded of the walk out to Alfred's Tower at Stourhead with its similar silence; a containment breathing in the stillness as if time had stopped so that beauty could never be broken, and a similar gilding of naked trees in winter sunlight which warms the misty, wooded slopes and sends golden streaks through twiggy branches. Maybe this is because both parklands were designed in the eighteenth century. Melbury was the work of 'Capability' Brown [63], and I admire his capability in creating something so natural and restful. Surely he must have incorporated much of the original landscape into his design, beyond which one catches a hazy blue glimpse of the real world; one of fields, trees and gentle hills rolling away to the horizon, yet perhaps less protected, less contained.

There was a heavy frost in the night so that we woke to a blanched world; each tiny twig of every tree delicately and intricately edged in ice, every blade of grass and brown fern made beautiful by a softly sparkling crystal coat. Even now at midday it remains, glittering thinly on the tarmac footpath, flecking the grass where sheep graze, backlit by the low spreading sunlight. Thicker frost collects in deep pockets on lower ground, which seems to plunge away below us. It is only three degrees and I can see the sheep's breath gently billowing on the air as they stand and watch us with blatant curiosity. We turn a corner and Melbury House comes into view, adjacent to a small church. The lawn before it is iced with thick frost so that it looks like a card depicting a white Christmas. As the church bell chimes twice; a high-pitched ting, indicating that it is two o'clock, I realise that the cold has got a grip and this will not thaw today. My fingers throb and the sheep's trough remains thickly iced over.

The seventeenth- century façade of Melbury House before us presents a graceful elegance with classical proportions; symmetrically placed windows and tall chimneys. Behind it rises a hexagonal Tudor tower, part of the original house and an unusual architectural feature for its time. This was the house where the pioneer of photography Henry Fox-Talbot was born in 1800 and spent most of his childhood [63]. From the clarity of light and the subtlety of shadows shown today (a photographer's paradise) I wonder if he derived his inspiration from this place. Later in life he lived at Lacock Abbey, now a beautiful National Trust property located in the most stunning Cotswold village of unspoiled timbered houses and cobbled streets. It was there that he took his first photograph.

We wander further; to our left the sun streaking down the slopes and through the trees, to our right a cloudless blue sky hanging above flat, sun-drenched grazing ground, a pale half- moon suspended above a periphery of dense pine forest. Suddenly the small village of Melbury Osmund can be seen clustering on the hillside between the trees ahead of us. The path leads straight into it and I am delighted by its old, grey, forest marble cottages, some dressed in Ham hill stone, which gives them extra warmth when soaked in sunset. A stream babbles deliciously under the small packhorse bridge and narrow, frosted lanes are silent although a few people are about. Simplicity is the charm of this village with the only vestige of Christmas being welcoming wreaths on cottage doors. A warm amber light floods the church exterior; the church where, in December 1839, Thomas Hardy's parents were married as his mother, Jemima, came from this village. Hardy obviously knew the area well and was inspired by it. Tess Cottage is situated in Evershot, supposedly one of the cottages where in fiction, Tess of the D'Urbervilles lived. It is also said that Melbury Sampford (the now lost hamlet which once surrounded Melbury Manor and church) was once called Melbury Turberville after owners of the manor [63].

As we return through the park an hour later, the light has changed; blanching frosted misty forests, contrasting crows which call and wing across the valley. More mist has risen around the house and long tree shadows stretch further, striping the slopes where deer also browse as well as sheep. In the golden, lowering light we see glistening, trembling corridors across the green pasture where the sheep still graze. Each one looks like a tunnel of gossamer, sparkling in the sun's sinking rays and catching the smallest breath of breeze. We realise that the entire pasture must be spun with spider silk, a fine blanket of gossamer spread subtly across its surface so that from whichever lower angle one looks, one sees the same silken pathway, catching the light along individual threads as they move. It is incredible, delicate, ethereal, made for tiny footsteps. I have never seen anything like it before and wonder how many spiders were involved in its creation and when they spun their secret silken charm, barely visible unless you just happen to see it in the oblique rays of sunset. The unseeing sheep graze on, oblivious.

Back at Evershot, the delicious fragrance of wood-smoke rises on the air, curling from chimneys in the village to creep into our nostrils and fill us with a sense of comfort and indolence. The setting sun casts its peachy golden glow across an undulating landscape on the way home, a landscape grazed by sheep and cows alongside their boisterous calves, which seems slightly premature, hinting that spring promises to be not so far away.

(2014)

Eggardon Hill

Sunlight moulds the contours of Eggardon Hill where ramparts rise from deep shadows. So many lines and textures: weaving, wave-like curves, stippled turf, deep ditches, soft slopes and golden grass, drawing the eye in all directions. We climb a gate and enter the fort. Below, the countryside falls away; snug pockets of forest plunged into the penumbra of the hill, contented cattle grazing lazy valleys, a patchwork of fields gently unfolding, brushed with the slanting shadows of skeletal trees. We feel free, on top of the world, and I can understand why the people of the Iron Age chose this for their habitation, erecting small circular huts. I also understand why Isaac Gulliver, the famous Dorset smuggler, chose this place as a lookout for smuggling ships, for from the summit one can see the sea stretching away, today a silver sheet laid out to meet a hazy horizon. Gulliver apparently planted pine trees to create a landmark [53]. They no longer exist. Instead sheep graze the summit, small brown sheep with delicate features and curly horns. They greedily rip the grass and seem un-phased by people passing by: an after- Christmas family enjoying spending precious time together, a young couple holding hands…. This is now a place for recreation and enjoyment, a place from which to marvel at the landscape unfolding like a beautiful dream beneath. Somewhere in that landscape snuggle other sweet escapes such as Powerstock, Kingcombe and Hooke, nestled within the patchwork eiderdown of forest and field.

From this elevated spot, all seems idyllic today but this place would have formerly been practical rather than romantic, the surrounding landscape dotted with the humps of Bronze Age tumuli suggest that this was used for burial long before it was inhabited as a fort. I cannot explain why I feel so elated here, perhaps it is the combination of bright sunshine and strong chill wind riding in off the sea, maybe the gentle trust of sheep which wander around us, or perhaps it is that from these heights we are looking down on the Dorset landscape; an area of outstanding natural beauty which stretches all around us, embracing us into its heart.

(2016)

*

Once again I feel as if a beautiful dream is unfolding beneath me, a story untold. This time in the form of a purely picturesque hamlet in the vicinity of Eggardon Hill, which may seem unremarkable to most, but to me, on this glorious evening surrounded by sheep, there is nothing more perfect. From a hill above the hamlet, we look down on an old seventeenth- century manor, an assortment of old barns, a collection of cottages, some sheep grazing near a small stream and a tiny chapel;

simple and complete in the strong sunlight. A stone eagle perches on top of the manor house's central gable, surely indicating from where the hamlet took part of its name. A family with two young children and two labradors climb the hill where we stand. The children run, chasing the dogs, revelling in fresh air and freedom. This would be the perfect place to grow up experiencing a carefree childhood and it is only the presence of parents which makes one realise that we are in the twenty-first century, for in the past these children might have more likely roamed unaccompanied.

(2016)

Kingfisher

The sun's gin-clear, winter light gilds tree trunks that dip and reflect into the mirror- like Stour as it calmly takes its course. The usually muddy path is hardened with frost, ice cracks under our feet as we walk on puddles, earlier we threw sticks, watching them skitter across a frozen pond.

Ducks appear in pairs today, sleeping by the riverbank, heads tucked under wings or sitting watching us, each time a drake with his mate. Suddenly the sunlight shining on a tangle of trees at the riverside illuminates something turquoise and iridescent on one of the golden branches and to our delight we realise that it is the hunched back of a kingfisher, the sunlight catching her beautiful feathers. Excitedly, yet quietly, I reach for my binoculars. They accompany me everywhere in the countryside especially for the odd time like this. I focus. Now I can see a beautiful bird, small, secretive, she turns her head in the typical kingfisher pose. I say she, because the orange lower beak shows her to be female. She sits and waits perhaps about a minute while we watch quietly, still full of disbelief, and then someone's dog scampers down to the water's edge and in a receding turquoise flash, she is gone. Kingfishers are described by the RSPB as 'a fairly rare, easily disturbed bird' [62] and I cannot count the amount of times this year, let alone in my whole life that I have walked by a river hoping to see one. I know that they live and breed here secretively in the river -banks. In fact, the RSPB states that they seldom move further than twelve kilometres from their original birthplace [42], so this female, as well as other kingfishers, has probably been living in her secretive world somewhere in this vicinity for quite some time, so near yet so far, for we have never noticed. That single minute made my day. It was a dream come true before the year was quite out. I cannot dare hope for another!

(2014)

JANUARY

New Year

I spent one New Year's eve with an old school friend, a writer and graphic designer, who at that time was living in Dorchester. Her mother had moved to an exquisite old town house there, with the intimate, homely atmosphere which comes from centuries of lives being lived. They had painted the entrance hall and kitchen a warm, welcoming yellow, which melded deliciously with terracotta and old brick and set a perfect backdrop for a glittering Christmas tree, which stood in the hall. A delicious dinner by the Aga, followed by rounds of cards in front of the fire set us up to go into the town where the festive, friendly, community atmosphere of a roisterous crowd swelled in the streets; the town-crier was there in his red coat ringing in the new year and talking jovially with members of the public. The atmosphere was even more exciting and intimate than it used to be in Wimborne Square where we usually went as teenagers to meet with friends from school. It is interesting that Daniel Defoe also described Dorchester as being

> ..a pleasant, agreeable town to live in……. and a man that coveted a retreat in this world might as agreeably spend his time, and as well in Dorchester, as in any town I know in England.

He perhaps attributed this agreeability to the warmth and community of the people who

> though there are divisions and the people are not all of one mind, either as to religion, or politics, yet they did not seem to separate with so much animosity as in other places. Here I saw the Church of England clergymen, and the Dissenting minister, or preacher drinking tea together, and conversing with civility and good neighbourhood, like catholic Christians, and men of a catholic, and extensive charity [27].

There was something special about that night in Dorchester; the majestic Georgian frontages of the buildings staring through the light cast by streetlights, the soft mizzle of cold rain falling in front of them, unfelt by the warmth of the people. This was a rural community atmosphere, which wouldn't be out of place in one of Thomas Hardy's novels. Even in the modern, individualistic society in which we live, people come together, restoring one's confidence and trust in humanity once more.

(2003)

Snow Day

The white Christmas never came, but after all the celebrations have died down and the term has once more begun, we get snow. Children (and teachers!) excitedly sit by the radio, hoping with bated breath and fingers crossed that there will be a snow day. I can hear some of them out in their gardens; excited shrieks accompanying the sound of soft, dull thuds. This euphoria is well-founded for two reasons; the fact that there is very probably a snow day and that this is an unusual event.

Everything has typically ground to a halt but we cautiously take the car, venturing up the slushy roads at ten miles an hour. We want to see the white fields spread like a sheet beyond the avenue of beech trees which leads up to Badbury Rings. In their skeletal state, these trees look particularly beautiful, wind-blown snow stippling their dark trunks and moulding each definition of branch and twig. Icy limbs are extended like slim, beautiful fingers as if reaching to touch with an exhilarating, bone-tingling chill. This is emphasized by the wondrous spectacle of the ground also coated so that the white silence stretches in a surreal slumber as far as the horizon. It is as if we have entered an imaginary world, yet my imagination can only focus on the farmers who still have to feed their livestock, facing reality despite the dream and wonder that most people are experiencing today. They must dread such wintery weather, the effort of going out into the cold, milking the cows, shivering in sheds and plodding out into frozen fields.

Silence falls on silence like a ringing in the ears. Uncanny. Badbury Rings stands subdued, ancient; the black clump of trees at its summit, snow-stained yet still relatively dark against white rings that blend comfortably into the surrounding wash of white fields. Whenever there is an extreme, this place evokes a sense of ancient awe, wonder and mystery. Sustained by itself, it seems to absorb everything and reflect it back, so that vast atmospheres are magnified, compelling. I remember a lunar eclipse that happened here once, the eternity of silent space breathing beyond the boundaries of understanding, the atmosphere seemed to hold its breath in brewing suspense as the moon's brilliance slowly slipped into the violet penumbra of the earth.

Rosy-cheeked children and adults alike use the slopes of the rings to practice tobogganing and energetically pelt each other with cakes of snow. It begins falling again. I watch a tiny flake, which has landed on my black coat. Even with the naked eye, I can see that this one is shaped like a tiny star, a transient beauty which lasts for a few seconds before melting away. I have seen images on the internet of snowflakes under microscopes, marvelling at the intricacy of their design, their symmetrical precision, each unique and varied as if someone had been especially commissioned to fashion them individually. Formed in the clouds, and shaped by temperature and electrical charges, they are more beautiful and imaginative than some of the most ornate geometric shapes that are found in many manmade decorations, and have been constantly fashioned through time, undiscovered until the microscope. For unless there is a creature with eyes which are able to see with vast magnification along with a brain to comprehend and appreciate such intricacy and symmetry, the minute secrets of snowflakes can only be enjoyed by the Artist Himself.

The snow's compressed crunch yields underfoot as we walk, feet pinched with cold and ears throbbing with the silence. It is the silence beyond the immediate which is so overwhelming; again the delicious suspense as if waiting for something and nothing, the expanse of snow stretching on and on as a sweet, eternal sleep or a never ending dream.

(2013)

Mudeford

We walk along an avenue of pine trees to Mudeford Quay. In the glooming light, its old houses are closed, hatches battened down for winter, their blank windows looking out with unseeing eyes across the sea where heavy, rolling clouds accumulate, turning slowly from deep violet- inky-blue to Payne's grey as the dusk-light is wrung out of them. Feeble shreds of sunlight briefly try to reach through the cloud's clenched fists, leaving a last pink streak in the darkening sea, and a wavering ribbon in the indigo panes of sleeping houses. This final flicker of daylight will soon snuff out like a spent candle. A weak wind maintains a continual flow, sharp and cold. Across the water rises the dark hump of Hengitsbury Head, mysterious, historic, its secrets stilled in the shadows of impending night. There are no little lights glimmering on it, and soon its form will be engulfed in darkness, a slumbering black hulk which will not stir until dawn.

We peruse a pile of fishing nets, buoys and crab baskets upon the quay. They have been left in an untidy, tangled heap, waiting for another day. The dark and empty hulls of vacant, traditional fishing boats lie about idly, sea-slapped at the shore where the hard air smells of salt and fish and the wind whistles like a lost phantom finding no rest. Out of season, Mudeford seems to brood on its precarious past life of fishing and its cat and mouse legacy of smuggling. It seems to have forgotten the fun of families holidaying here, all its moods and memories being played out against the cycle of the seasons and the eternal wash of the sea.

Wandering up behind the old houses guarding the quay, we slip into narrow side-streets past small, terraced cottages. Although many are summer lets, a few are inhabited, their interiors glowing with winter warmth, while the wind casually and callously tosses at a tattered Christmas wreath on a small front door. Soon it will be twelfth night, and without any vestige of decoration, this place will become even more nostalgic for summer, at the same time deriving a curious comfort from its winter wistfulness.

(2011)

Hengitsbury Head

The wild sweeps of Hengitsbury Head seem almost primeval in the winter light. We crunch along the pebble beach, wind in our ears, the sea swirling in with a hissing froth, the winter light clear, sunshine catching the water as it washes onto the shore in foamy layers. The breath of centuries stalks this beach. Originally an Iron Age trading port, it was one of the largest to be importing and exporting overseas and continued in this way until the fall of the Roman Empire. Later on, the area became a haven for smugglers who were supported and assisted by the locals, as was common practice all along the Dorset coast. The locals here built boats which were faster than those of the custom's men, although they were caught out at the battle of Mudeford in 1784 [53]. One of the locals in particular, the landlady of The Ship in Distress at nearby Stanpit, regularly kept contraband on her premises. Hannah Siller, known as 'the angel of the marsh,' even has the Mother Siller's channel named after her (53).

The wind continues to whisper of wild past as it tugs at the long grasses crowning the plateau of Warren Hill, which we have now ascended. Here one travels to the prehistoric past once again. I have been told that Paleolithic tools have been unearthed here, and it is also the site of Bronze Age burial. There is something elemental, the wind full in my face, salt stinging my nose, and I imagine what a barren, harsh existence these people might have lived here and yet what wonderful nature and beautiful views they had to reflect on. Views change through time as a result of erosion and settlement, but the fundamental rock structures must be essentially the same. Although the coast would have receded significantly since those ancient times, these prehistoric people must have looked at a similar undulating shoreline with towering cliffs plunging down to a strip of sand, smudged today by high tide and the swirl of the sea.

Now Bournemouth blights the cliffs to a certain extent in that its high-rise buildings have made alien incursions into the natural backdrop. Christchurch Harbour has developed through time with an eclectic blend of buildings. Pale golden sunlight lingers on the Norman tower of the priory which stands above a comfortable collection of boats and low-lying modern buildings nestling in the foreground. To the east we look towards Highcliffe and the low buildings that straddle its cliffs, out across the Solent, we can just make out the Isle of Wight.

Despite all this proximity to urbanization, I am reassured by the fact that Hengitsbury Head apparently lies in the vicinity of one of the oldest natural forests in the country, and along with its adjacent areas of Christchurch Harbour and Stanpit, has been designated an area of special scientific interest. Strangely, I always seem to come here in winter with dogs and children, and do not get time to pay close attention to the variety of fauna and flora to be found here, but today with the children, we stop to watch a bird of prey, my brother capturing it beautifully on camera, as it hovers above us in the cloudless sky.

As clouds cross the sun, the mood changes, shadows sweeping a frown across a flat land of browns and greens. A shadow also brushes across the sea's surface for a moment before the sun returns and the water resumes its wintry blue. Warmth is sustained in the sunshine, but when the clouds cross the sun and an icy wind rakes through the grasses, it reminds us that there is a wild side to this solitary place, which has perhaps been tamed through time. It is therefore as if Hengitsbury Head has now reached old age, content nowadays to provide people with pleasure and recreation. Under its earth are stored ancient secrets, the legacies of what once was, while on its surface, nature lives, reproduces and dies, giving it still a sense of an abundance of life.

(2011)

*

Since the Industrial Revolution, vast areas of English countryside have been tragically and sometimes senselessly engulfed in concrete through the ugly, pernicious onslaught of urbanization. As Bournemouth developed from a wild, empty heathland, locally known as Bourne Heath, to a thriving coastal resort, many of its once lonely tracks, traversed by solitary travellers and frequented in the eighteenth century by smugglers, became the main roads that now lead through and out of the conurbation. Hamlets and villages expanded to become areas of the town, as has occurred in many cities around the country.

Just as some places have become buried beneath concrete, others have reverted to nature. I have been looking at aerial photographs of Dorset, taken during the transition of day to dusk when low, strong sunlight sweeps across the Earth. This lowlight reveals ridges, shapes and lines, which have lain unseen beneath the soil for centuries, yet seem to be drawn out softly across the smooth surface of the fields, as if inscribed by an indelible, ultraviolet pen. These are the legacies of lost time, the manmade marks of past civilisations which once inhabited our present, for something of the landscape we still share with them.

The photographs reveal a landscape crisscrossed with the contours of small Iron Age or Roman fields which seem to strangely melt out of the Earth; prehistoric hut circles traced in the ground, the sunken shadowy hollows of pond barrows or the mounds of bell barrows, and roads, once the arteries of civilization, now more akin to veins peeping through skin. They draw their ethereal lines as vague impressions across fields, fingering the grass. One such road is Ackling Dyke, a Roman road whose phantom form marches straight across the countryside near Badbury Rings, brushing shoulders with the outer rings of the hillfort itself. From the photograph, its image is almost an illusion, a soft, straight scar in the surface of the Earth, which has healed over with grass-grown time so that it becomes almost a perception, a breath in the evening light.

On another aerial photo I catch soft, shadowy glimpses of the Dorset Cursus, the longest in England which, at just over six miles long, stretches across Cranborne Chase, and although hard to see from the ground, where only the odd ridge can be seen skirting a field, aerial photography clearly shows the four- thousand- year- old, parallel Neolithic tracks tiptoeing their course across the fields with the lightest brush, faint yet indelible on the landscape.

There are also the lost villages, most uninhabited since medieval times, in many cases due to dwindling populations perhaps as a result of plague, poverty or famine. Linda Viner, who writes extensively on this subject, maintains that the acquisition of land by wealthy landlords after the dissolution of the monasteries, much of which was then turned over to sheep farming, along with the enclosure of common land, also made it impossible for rural people to maintain themselves [67]. Evidence of their former settlements are again seen at their best from aerial photography where rectangular forms; ridges and gullies, lumps and bumps, often alongside the elusive tracks of disused pathways appear to rise from the fields; ethereal images which whisper of a past still present yet almost hushed, memories barely breathing beneath the soil. Bardolfeston near Puddletown is claimed to be one of the 'best-preserved' of these medieval village sites, according to Viner [67].

It is when the day drifts into evening that dreams unfold with the sinking sun as it illuminates what was once and unveils mysteries which have slumbered sweetly forgotten through the centuries. These are dreams come true, an awakening reality as history still strives to live through its own legacy, the soil forging a fascination with what was once occupied, thriving, thronging with humanity, yet is now by nature silenced and reclaimed.

(2014)

Woolsbarrow Hillfort

When it is windy I often think of the overhead electricity cables which were frequently brought down by tree branches as a child so that sparks and flashes of light arced with a resounding clap across the road. Such is the power of pylons, which I remember I used to hear simmering ominously up at Wareham Forest where we often walked as a family on winter afternoons after Christmas. It was nearly always muddy and horses waited impatiently and perhaps a little nervously in fields at the beginning of the walk, where the pylons started their strident ascent up the hill. The air seemed to be charged with static and I disliked walking beneath those austere constructions with their sinister electrical monotone buzz, just audible in the brewing air. I always thought if one of their cables were to break, what force would be unleashed and I almost felt the tension, the small hairs on the back of my hands rising. Everything seemed linear- the vertical, towering metal frames of the pylons, their straight march up the hillside carrying the lines of cables. Long lines of conifer plantations, straight slim trees in straight rows, looked equally dark and foreboding in the gloomy, leaden light of a winter's day and I was glad to pass both scowling trees and menacing pylons. I am sure I was not the only one who felt threatened by the pylons, for animals apparently not only hear the electricity but, with an ability to detect ultra violet light, can see it flashing from the powerlines. This inevitably impacts natural habitats and migration routes as animals and birds are scared away.

Past the powerlines the path became sandy, soft and light, trailing through the close, damp smell of the heath, almost oppressive in its earthy -bracken richness. I always consider bracken to be an ancient plant, its fronds giving away its membership of the fern family. Ferns have been found fossilized along the Jurassic Coast. At the summit of our ascent stood Woolsbarrow Hillfort, an Iron Age settlement- a few lonely tumuli perhaps testifying to an earlier Bronze Age. The lines had stopped, replaced by curves, and the windswept elevation of the spot provided extensive views across the surrounding heath. On one dismal day we stood for a while taking in the entire panorama sweeping away below us in swathes of sullen brown, deep green tinged russet and purple. It was clear from this easily defendable location why Iron Age man chose it for his habitation. The atmosphere clenched its brooding fists, wild and ancient, closing in upon itself, as the day also closed in upon itself, nimbostratus clouds collecting, threatening rain.

I always considered it an unwelcoming place to call home, and a complete contrast to other parts of the Purbeck, but perhaps the contours of the landscape would have become familiar, friendly faces in a wild, prehistoric world. There would certainly have been none of the frowning conifer plantations here, but the heath would have existed. Heathland is a result of extensive deforestation during the Bronze Age, the poor soil quality not allowing the forest to regenerate and thus inadvertently creating a new and important habitat for a diverse range of wildlife.

As human beings, perhaps it is fair to say that we only feel comfortable with nature to a point. We live simultaneously within it and outside it, living in fear of its power, trying to tame it, control it, subdue it, to make our mark on it and exploit it. This was as true of the past as it is of the present and the marks and characteristics of much of the present landscape, such as field, ancient mound, road, track and even the barrenness of the heath, are shaped by past human activity.

Prehistoric communities used land they had cleared to graze animals and grow crops, they also cut turf to make fires. The presence of a community with small huts and glowing fires would have softened the perceived threat of the outside world, drawing the people further inward to the heart of their community. There is no place for solitude here, for it can invite anxiety and tension into the heart, as each manmade pylon, a solitary figure striding up the hill, hissing its malicious taunt, would testify.

Floods

Flooded fields. A water-world stretches as far as the eye can see across the flood-plains. Stillness. Naked trees stand tall and proud of the wash; elegant, narcissus -like, casting their reflections into the mirror deep, relishing the novelty of their replicas branching beneath them. Swans are perhaps overwhelmed by a sudden expanse of territory. They swim across shimmering, silver fields, freedom knowing no bounds, for it is almost impossible to see where the river runs its course.

In the grey light, absent of sun, the wash spreads like slightly dirty snow, reflecting the grey white eternity of sky, there is something surreal in the stillness, something beautiful about the languid pallor of the flood. It is so extensive that we stand and stare, feeling almost marooned and wondering at this beautiful freak of nature. Yet I wonder if it is a freak or whether winters will become wetter with time and whether this is a pattern of things to come. Last year was also wet. I remember walking on New Year's day at Pimperne where water flowed off the fields and down the path in a refreshing, clear stream, sparkling where the sun shone on it. We waded through it, several centimetres deep, swirling around our ankles. The roads were breaking up last year because of the water and the cold. But this year has seen more rain, a succession of storms and flooding as I have never seen here. The floodplains are stretched to capacity and the wind and rains continue to come.

I fear for the farmers whose crops will once again be threatened, the food which we so often take for granted, forgetting the hard toil and labour required to grow it, as well as the necessity for congenial weather. If farmers are affected, the effect is knock-on. I imagine the food prices will rise like the water levels this year.

Man has always settled beside rivers, the arteries of the earth, carrying water, so necessary for life. Thus many of the major towns and tiny villages of Dorset are situated on or near these vital sources and are now feeling the floods. Water indeed provides life but also so easily threatens with danger. I watch it with respect; contained in the quiet water meadows, where it naturally belongs, as yet restraining itself from becoming a raging torrent. We play games with nature, taunting, coming too close perhaps in order to reap its resources, and yet when it retorts, coming too close to us, we are forced to eat humble pie and retreat, or experience its consequences.

(2014)

Beach Combing

Wild weather enables one to recall forgotten stories of shipwrecks of which there were many off the Dorset coast. When one sees spindrift billowing off the sea, a beach flecked with foam which flicks and skitters, crablike, across the surface of the sand or when one watches waves whipping up over rocks and sea-walls, showering down spray and roaring with thunderous velocity, it makes one understand once more the dangerously combined force of wind and water.

There is a lull in the storms. As we scrunch through the deep shingle on the Chesil one sullen afternoon, our calves pulling against a sinking weight, the continual clatter, as stones are displaced, spurring us on, I think about these stories. The tarnished, antique mirror of the sea stretches away- still, flat and indolent in the manner of a leopard-skin rug; lines of light occasionally cast through clouds as the sun's searchlight roves about above, perhaps trying to shed some light on what treasure lies below the idle surface.

On the beach itself, debris is left lingering- a legacy to the storm: pieces of plastic, wood, containers tangled in rope, glass washed smooth and opaque by the motion of the waves. Apparently there were carcasses of animals washed up here too- so violent were the storms. Man makes his mark carelessly, thinking the sea will swallow it up secretly so that no-one will know. Yet the sea has brought it all back, has spewed its indigestible contents, angrily, forcefully onto the shingle, thus uncovering man's clandestine goings-on. I am affected by this regurgitation. It is not the romantic message in a bottle which finds itself on remote and distant shores, this is a direct and blatant message in the here and the now which finds itself on shores probably not so far from where its 'bottles' were cast. Some of the animal corpses testify to this.

A throw-away society driven by consumerism. The latter is perhaps not such a novel concept. Although past societies tended to make-do and mend, re-use, and waste nothing, they still apparently had a love of money. They did not have the technology to make plastic and all the other throw-away, non-biodegradable materials which poison our seas and landscapes, nevertheless, the actions of many were still motivated by material acquisition which could render them more prosperous.

On this very strip of shingle which stretches parallel to the coast and is thus susceptible to shipwrecks, normal people apparently demonstrated lawless and acquisitive behaviour time and again. When such shipwrecks occurred, the locals would set about to loot and pillage. These were not just a few hopeful villagers, but determined bands of men, women and children, hundreds strong, some of whom threatened the customs men with knives as they rifled through the flotsam and jetsam washed up on the shore [2]. No doubt the corpses of the unlucky crew would have been lying alongside. The locals, however, are purported to have been more interested in taking the plunder than saving the lives of those doomed to be lost at sea, but perhaps, to do them credit, they were too afraid of being swept away themselves. John Meade Falkner writing about the Chesil at Fleet in his book *Moonfleet* maintains that during such a storm:

> ....the sea has little mercy, for the water is deep right in, and the waves curl over full on the pebbles with a weight no timbers can withstand....
> There is a deadly under-tow or rush back of the water, which sucks

them [the sailors] off their legs, and carries them again under the thundering waves [37].

As I watch the sea's shimmering calm, silver sunlight contrasting petulant patches of darkness, I see it as perhaps symbolic of those turbulent memories softened by time. The legacy of a recent string of storms, leaving destruction and turmoil in their wake, as they did then, serves as a reminder of those wrecks. The debris, today worthless, is collected by conservationists rather than looted by violent scavengers. So as I reflect on the sea's calm and silver surface, I see that hearts are hard but can be softened, are tarnished but can be polished. I wonder at whether man in the past really was more godly than he is today, as we were always brought up to believe at school, or whether it was all a mask, a respectable surface hiding a treacherous heart, as smugglers buried their booty beneath churches and locals ignored the sailors being sucked under the sea as they stole from the shore. This lawless behaviour is perhaps innate in all of us in our raw, elemental, survival state, as rough and dull as the lump of precious stone extracted from the earth. Yet like the stone, the heart can be shaped and polished, genuinely showing peace towards its fellow men, a peace reflected in the soft, silvery patches which the often steely- hard sea has today set before us.

(2014)

*

The recent storms have caused landslides at Charmouth. At Black Ven, the near-complete fossil of a one- and- a- half- meter Ichthyosaur (a 'fish-lizard') has been exposed. The earth keeps on yielding, bringing back the dead. I do not know how many marine fossils have been discovered along the Jurassic Coast during the centuries and cannot imagine how many more still remain uncovered, having sustained their secrets for millennia. Yet as each is unearthed, we learn a little more about their prehistoric, pelagic past.

(2014)

Tree Talk

As the day draws down to dusk, we are enticed to enter through a small gate into a low-lying copse. From a distance it appears almost Hobbit –height but as we enter and walk along the main aisle of this complex cathedral of coppiced trees, their tall wands reach high above, tapering, smooth and silver-sheened to create the living line drawings of gothic arches. These are wands of naked wood, roused by the wind which moves through their vaulted canopy so that they seem to squeak and rub with a dry bony scratch in response. Then the copse goes quiet again but a palpable feeling of intimacy remains. This is perhaps enhanced by other life, for beyond the mysterious, muted conversations of the trees, the caw of a crow cuts the silence, the sharp tick of a wren, and the occasional rustlings of other unseen birdlife busying in the leaf litter between spears of green, which quietly push through the silent earth and promise a spring soon to come.

A prying sun pokes fast-fading fingers into one of the corridors of coppiced hazel- a small side aisle, of which there are many in this secluded labyrinth. The trees become tinged with wan gold for a few moments- pale, elusive, yet three-dimensional. We have become enclosed and engrossed in their secret world, waiting for sun-fall to complete.

Coming through the copse, maiden trees begin to occupy the space, their trunks twisting away from each other in different leaning directions as if repelled by each other's presence. They are escaping actors frozen on a stage and I sense an unexplained juxtaposition in this tiny woodland world where coppiced trees 'talk' and rub shoulders with each other, as if sharing secrets, crafting the wind's encrypted messages into whispered rumours, leading us down a choice of clandestine aisles to secret side chapels, while maiden trees turn their backs as if giving each other the cold shoulder. In this secret society, we are silent witnesses, outsiders observing from the inside and feeling like invisible intruders stumbling through a world which remains delectably enigmatic and intangible, one which will never be understood.

Through vertical boughs I glimpse the sea; pale, withdrawn, as if it existed in a dream or in another world or time. I remember on a summer's day how I stood in the cool of this copse, the atmosphere sun-splashed, radiant with light and life. Then I encountered a different sea; its brilliance breathing the stillness as I was drawn to it. These thoughts make it seem as if life in this present has temporarily ceased, become a mere memory, a shadow of summer, yet the copse is certainly alive today, speaking subtly; a squeaking, shifting murmur.

Out on the main path back to Studland, the sky has drained to a pallid opalescence against which the strong, skeletal crowns of trees stand silhouetted, black. There is a sheen on the sea which, despite the wind, washes calmly and imperceptibly into the beautiful curve of Studland Bay, a glass reflecting the last of the lingering sky. Shadows and mist start to stretch across the heathland which spreads beyond the bay, the landscape drifting into the dream of night. Now out in the open, away from the protective covert of the copse, my hands throb with the constant, icy stream of wind which flows in a hard, unabated current from the west.

Studland village is redolent with wood-smoke trailing from the chimneys of the Bankes Arms. Adorned with fairy lights outside, its interior also glows, enticing us like moths around a candle. But we cannot stop for a pint by the fire, as we have come without money. Instead we wander on towards our car. On a wooded slope, the first snowdrops of the season have tightly closed their nodding heads against the night as if, with eyes shut, they had dropped off to sleep.

Driving home, Corfe Castle stands silhouetted against the sky as the last dregs of daylight dissipate into dusk. It stands a ruined and iconic shape in time, history looming large in the echoing presence of night. Cosy Corfe village also glows with warm interiors yet we continue driving through the countryside, which sinks away to sleep, drawing into itself and the inky, indigo recesses of approaching night.

(2015)

Murmuration

At Shell Bay a murmuration of starlings sweeps and climbs like sinuous, swirling smoke. Dense at the core, the body of birds seems to ripple and flow in a fluid unity of action; another one of nature's wonders, compelling and humbling. It is as if each bird were either protons or neutrons, making up the centre of an atom, or orbiting electrons attracted to it. The combination creates a simultaneously gaseous and liquid substance, one without solid form, which perpetually twists and turns; spaces being drawn into the dark vacuum of an expanding nucleus, only to drift into diaphanous dimensions before being brought back into the main body with an almost magnetic force. It is this continuous exchange of energy which causes unceasing motion; renewable, sustained. The action, accompanied by the loud sweep of unanimous wing beats, serves to mesmerise like a screen-saver infinitely changing, and we watch, riveted with many others who have come to share the experience. Despite the crowds, there is a sense of escape and rapture; the flowing clouds of birds causing our attentions to be drawn away from humanity and be caught up in the free expanse of the sun-stained sky. I find it sad that these days such an event is so rare that it has become a tourist attraction. Surely in the past, such spectacle was encountered more frequently. But because of this, it was perhaps not regarded as so special.

(2017)

Lulworth Cove

A shimmering sea washes in and out again, pulling pebbles back in a rush of respiration accompanied by a hollow rattle. Blue blends with white, the pure white of sea-smoothed chalk pebbles which cover the beach and with which I cram my pockets in order to fill a glass vase on the windowsill at home. We are contained in the circle of the cove which reaches round like an eternal embrace, a ring and all its promises.

Above the cove, looking down, we have escaped the many tourists who come here even on a winter's day. St Aldelm's Head hangs on an intangible horizon; sky melding with sea in an infinite blue. I become suddenly excited by the zigzagged swash marks fluting the circular sweep of another still blue bay below; natural art so perfectly sculpted.

At Durdle Door a solstice-style sun hangs directly above the arch, propelling a pathway through it, and we watch waves riding onto the beach, each stirring a pattern in its foam, fusing with footprints on smooth-swept sand. My camera captures these unique movements. There is beauty in evanescence, in something seen only by those who watch. I felt the same this morning when out early with nobody about, I photographed frost formations on a bus-shelter, each small structure, a fascinating inflorescence of fernlike intricacy compounding a wonderful sense of mystery, for in the past, the legendary Jack Frost intrigued people with his secret bursts of nocturnal creativity. My sense of wonder was brought on by the beauty of art in nature, enhancing even the mundane; marbling patterns in puddles and glazing blades of grass. It was my own secret spectacle with no one to share it that made it more special.

Now in West Lulworth it feels like spring. Despite the frosty start and a colder forecast later, we peel off our jackets, too warm to be worn. Wandering past the mellowed faces of sun-blushed thatched cottages, the air rings brightly with birdsong. This is a day almost too good to be true, a day for which one dare not hope, for it seems to hold a promise; echoing the embracing ring of the cove.

(2017)

Kingcombe Meadows

At Kingcombe Meadows we have stepped back in time, drawn down narrow, single-track lanes into the heart of deepest Dorset. Without evidence of mechanisation and ploughed fields, this is the unadulterated landscape of our ancestors which rolls away before our eyes; a landscape of grazed meadows, mature hedgerows, intriguing ancient paths and wonderful views, once we have sunk and sucked our wellies in and out of thick, sticky mud and climbed to higher ground. The Meadows are one of the Dorset Wildlife Trust's many nature reserves and according to the trust, have remained virtually unchanged since the time of Queen Victoria. In spring and summer they are alive with flowers, insects and butterflies; a common sight to those people back then.

We wander by the river Hooke which meanders through this valley and no doubt gives its name to the small village no more than three miles off, with its captivating springtime bluebell woods, its elegant fourteenth-century manor and fifteenth -century church. Today the river sparkles in low winter sunlight, water chattering as it spirals across pebbles, blending into the background of complete silence. It is the silence which really speaks to me, for at the top of the hill, looking down into the valley of the Hooke within an area of outstanding natural beauty, I hear no traffic, not even a bird or a breath of wind. Golden winter sunlight embraces the flowing contours of the landscape and the village of Toller Porcorum a mile to the South, its cluster of cottages huddling around the comfortable fourteenth- century tower of St Andrew and St Peter's Church, which rises between the trees. There is nobody about today, perhaps because it is winter, and no animals graze. Their frozen troughs stand abandoned and are the only evidence of this morning's cutting temperatures when we slithered about on black ice.

We leave the pasture by a small gate out onto a green lane. The path, an enticing tunnel of coppiced trees, shimmers in the sunlight and I want to discover its ancient trail. There is something compelling, exciting. The path's sunken sides support ferns and ivy, beyond their boundaries lies an adjacent field where sheep graze peacefully in a glorious pastoral setting. The only sound is the gentle trickle of water which courses as a stream flowing over stones which line the most deeply eroded parts of the path. Everything delights the heart, firing inspiration and I wonder why this way was so frequented that it remains deeply etched into the earth. Perhaps it was a main pathway from Hooke to Lower Kingcombe, where we began our walk and where the path indeed seems to terminate.

Today Lower Kingcombe is insignificant, a shrunken hamlet, yet there are many other ancient paths, including the Wessex Ridgeway and the Jubilee Way, leading into the hamlet itself, suggesting that it was once more significant in both size and place. Wandering down another green lane, which secretly weaves its sunken course through the countryside, we see evidence of ancient hedge-laying; the woven branches thickened and moss-covered with age while sunlight plays deep shadow patterns in the bark. My husband, who has been involved with such practice himself, informs me that the hedge-layers have to cut the wood carefully so that the interior part is not damaged and yet it can be bent and woven into the hedge and continue growing; a tradition which would be lost if it were not taught to students, as it is in my husband's workplace and other places such as the Kingcombe Centre itself and I believe also at nearby Hooke Court.

As the sun becomes wan behind a stealthy veil of cloud, sinking into the solace of evening, and the cold creeps in less stealthily, we head back towards the hamlet. Some sheep in an adjacent field come to the gate when they see us. They are beautiful animals; rotund, thickly-fleeced and bright-eyed, their curiosity having overcome shyness. I feel that sheep, which are perhaps my favourite animal, are much misunderstood. If anyone ever tells me again that they are unfriendly then they will be proved wrong by the actions of these animals who offer us their noses to stroke while others, less curious are more intent on eating, so that the only sound which scratches the silence is the regular ripping of grass as they hungrily graze.

(2015)

Ancient Yew

In the hamlet of Woolland, a mile or so from Bulbarrow, there stands an ancient yew. The circumference of its trunk, split into five, measures around nine and three-quarter meters or twenty three feet, and its age, according to information within the church, states that it is two thousand years old. I stand in complete awe, marvelling at this tree, which was here before anything else except, of course, the landscape and the earthworks. Woolland Church and manor house were built much later, the present church being mid nineteenth- century.

There is something about yew trees in winter. Perhaps it is the fact that they are bushy and evergreen, providing shelter and refuge in their copious branches to our resident birds, which stick the winter out and are perhaps more exposed perched on the naked branches of deciduous trees. On this biting winter day; cold, crisp and clear, the yew tree indeed appears dark, thick, and welcoming. Soft fingers of golden sunlight filter down through its dense branches, drawing the eye to deep furrows and vertical ridges on its trunk. If I were a child, I wouldn't be able to resist climbing it and I wonder about generations of children past. I also consider the many people who must have marvelled at it through the centuries, as we do today, gazing up into its heights, for it is completely impossible to comprehend how anything can stay alive so long. If it were indeed two thousand, this tree would have been seen by the Romans. It would certainly have been around with the Normans and if it had senses, would have no doubt witnessed a world changing through time. It would have experienced the natural soundscape now lost to our ears as species dwindled and declined, it would have heard long lost dialects, seen costumes and fleeting fashions passing through generations, felt the variations in climate. I wonder who planted it and why. As yew trees are prevalent in churchyards, I imagine it was planted, either by pre-Christian peoples, who revered the yew tree, and appropriated by Christians who saw it as a symbol of immortality, or planted by Christians themselves. Perhaps, though, it was self-seeded.

In the quiet churchyard, clumps of snowdrops, pure and fresh, have pushed up between graves of departed ones who would also have once stood here when alive, looking upon this yew perhaps with a similar fascination. Their names are left to us, forging a further connection of their past with our present. Golden sunlight washes the wall of the church where some of them probably once worshipped; a cockerel crows distantly somewhere, the mew of a bird of prey carries overhead and I see the hovering silhouette of the bird itself, high up above the church. We have seen many birds of prey up here today. On the road to Bulbarrow, we sighted a buzzard sitting on a post at the roadside, another hovering in the sky; slow-motion suspended, suspense in every tension of the wing and each poised talon before it suddenly swooped. For birds of prey, the whole world is mapped out beneath them in distinct clarity a little like the view from the top of Bulbarrow, which today spreads itself across the flat, sun-drenched patchwork of fields of the Blackmore Vale into a seeming eternity. Someone has erected a sign quoting Psalm 104: 24 'O Lord how manifold are Thy works! In wisdom Thou hast made them all: the earth is full of Thy riches'.

Here in the churchyard down in the valley, we exist as a separate world fitting into the vast expanse of the one seen from above. As evening approaches, the sun is doing its best to reach us now and the silence of a contained hamlet breathes a comfort and security within itself. Climbing back up to Bulbarrow, where a chill wind attempts to gnaw right through us, we can see the hamlet of Woolland down below us, an established place in the shadowing, vast expanse of Dorset landscape which stretches like an open map beyond. That is the buzzard's world, the one which hardly holds the horizon but spreads, uncontained, in a mirage of fields and forests which take on new dimensions when different angles are exposed by the shifting, sinking of the sun.

(2015)

FEBRUARY

Castleman Trailway

An evening in early February. After a gin-clear day, birdsong fills the evening air with warmth and hope. The shrill, piercing song of the great tit seems to swim above branches, sound waves ricocheting and revelling in a new-found freedom. Further along the forest path the acrobatic melodies of a song thrush, in conversation with another, cavort in soaring trills and whistles; such variety of texture and tone. Its sweet song creates a contained atmosphere, almost as if the place were wrapped in a blanket of sound, a cocoon of comfort, which we are privileged to enter, a hide from which to observe the avian world unnoticed.

We leave the song thrush and the hide of sound to walk back along the path where the sinking sun casts flames through catkin-festooned branches. As we walk we become obvious again, for we hear the familiar, flustered warning cry of an agitated blackbird shaking off the day. It is with a delicious joy that I return home, elated by the atmosphere, which has ignited a wonderful sense of spring approaching.

(2015)

Dorset Light

Somewhere near Lytchett Matravers I have found the end of the rainbow! The only gold to be found, however, is the strong light on naked trees, in front of which the spectrum falls in almost imperceptible translucency before it melts into the earth. It is but a breath, a figment in its frailty until I follow its bands of colour up above the treetops to where it arcs, a complete bow, bright across the steely sky. Strong sunlight stains the ground, licking long tongues of bronze across green pastures. As the rainbow dissolves and the sky becomes buffeted, black and blue, the clarity and intensity of a sunlight special to Dorset continues to flow across the fields and over trees. It is a penetrative light that enhances details and brightens the landscape's natural palette, awakening the artist's eye. It is a buoyant light, which enlivens the soul and quickens the heart. It is a golden, fluid light, which blends into blue, washing the landscape with its distilled clarity and it is a comforting light, which stirs the subconscious, and exudes a feeling of security from deep within the soil.

(2014)

Storm

An exciting surge of wind roars through forest trees- a drum roll, rising to a crescendo and dying away before the next heavy sigh escapes into the calm. Trees are tossed into a frenzy, their bare branches becoming acutely animated, gesticulating wildly, as if trying to convey an urgent message. Perhaps they protest against the incessant storms of the past three months, considered by some to be at least partially anthropogenic. Perhaps they give us a warning that it is dangerous to be out. However, we take no heed, enjoying the exhilaration, the power of the wind surging through us. And yet as debris of twigs and broken branches lie like severed limbs, littering the forest path, we do wonder for an instant that something might strike us unwittingly. Despite this debris, the trees show an extensive resilience. I marvel at the elasticity which gives them life, their ability to bend and bow but not break, allowing them their dynamic body-language, their powerful expressions.

In contrast, an ancient yew stands stoically in a forest clearing, neither bowing nor bending. So old and wise it seems, that the vast circumference of its twisted, furrowed trunk, rooted decisively in the earth, can hardly be guessed at. It will hopefully remain solid and strong despite all this weather, for it must have watched hundreds of years of such storms passing. Its dense, dark, mysterious, evergreen foliage surely provides a blanket of refuge for many birds, and although its branches beat about, it stands as a bastion and shelter, speaking a quiet reassurance with the wisdom of centuries, untroubled in the storm.

(2014)

*

High tide and the churning sea- swell wreak havoc. The camera captures images of incessant, towering waves; walls of water pounding the coast at Lyme Regis and Portland. With imagination, we find faces frozen in time, animal shapes, still lives caught in the act of living. As children we always looked for images in the clouds, pictures in the patterns of the wallpaper and it is the same with the waves. However, with waves you have to be quick, for if the shutter is not released at that split second of time, the right time, the image will be lost forever.

(2014)

Snowdrops

Snowdrops (*Galanthus*: 'milk flower') the harbingers of spring, always appear at their best in February on bright, wintry days. It is perhaps the simple, graceful humility of this flower that causes it to be so attractive, the submissive, bowed head; perfect buds bursting open to reveal an inner heart of pure white innocence. Their bashful unobtrusiveness, reflected in a natural tendency to clump together under hedge or tree has elevated them to being a flower which is adored so much so that *galanthophile,* a person who loves and collects snowdrops, has become an accepted word in the Oxford Dictionary.

Like the bluebells, I will let you seek the snowdrops, which can be found all across the county smothering secret enclaves. At Kingston Lacy, they put on a wonderful display each year. In the fernery, white clumps peep between the trees and rocks alongside small pink cyclamen. Streaks of golden sunlight finger their way through dense, dark foliage which encloses this secret winter garden. Robins flit around in the undergrowth stopping briefly on a branch to watch people, tilted heads full of curiosity, eyes beady and bright.

Down a long avenue of trees, the snowdrops have proliferated over grassy slopes on both sides of the path. From a distance it is easy to see why they were given this name, the serene spread, boosted with remnants of real snow, coats the slopes with a delicate white, striped with shadows. Sunlight filters through the trees in long golden tongues, shining through the snowdrops so that their pure petals become almost incandescent, fleshy leaves glowing. They have spread beyond the slopes and we can see swathes across an adjacent lawn, a snowy carpet stretching as far as the eye can see, bringing hope as winter retreats.

Even when the weather is grey, and cold wraps itself around everything with a sullen grip, there is hope when the snowdrops flower. On a sunny day, they seem to delight in soaking up the brightness and are seen radiating in their prime of sweet simplicity, growing wild and free. On a wet and windy day they toss their heads in silent submission, like slaves being whipped by a cruel master, yet delicately defiant, they stand strong against the storm, secure in the unity of their cosy clumps under trees, which take the full force of the wind's fury.

Every February we catch a glimpse of the secret snowdrop world, which for most of the year exists beneath the soil while bulbs prepare for this brief, but glorious spectacle of a few weeks or more. As a bride prepares for her wedding, coming forth in all her beauty for a day, so these single flowers come one by one for their special flowering time continuing for a few weeks through the honeymoon before the fairy tale fades and beauty dies down to the dust. Having marked an ethereal awakening of spring, these first, bold flowers have lead the way out of winter before silently slipping away almost as quickly and unobtrusively as they arrived. And so we wait in anticipation of their arrival for another year and imagine how the former inhabitants of the house might have similarly. For it must have been wonderful to have been able to wander around these winter gardens equally freely, indulging in such a beautiful snow-like spectacle. I am very happy that the National Trust allows us to do the same.

(2012)

Seatown

Walking on the clifftops above Seatown, I see the landscape stretching away to an infinite horizon. We feel as if we are on top of the world, away from another which dictates so much of what we do. Up here we are free, and for a blissful few hours we can forget money, timetables and schedules, for here is timeless and I look out over a landscape which seems unchanged through the centuries, an area of outstanding natural beauty- and yet, is it so natural? The terrain is indeed beautiful; sunlight and shadows playing smoothly across its soft, undulating surfaces so that colours constantly change. Yet this landscape's ever-changing face is furrowed with ploughed fields; man's mark. As graffiti etches rock, man also asserts his dominance by marking the surface of the soil, leaving lasting impressions above and below. Despite their function, there is an art to these fields, a perhaps unconscious sense of aesthetic as they crisscross into natural clefts and folds. The iconic landmark of Colmer's Hill rises above them changing, chameleon-like from heathery purple to peat brown through to golden orange as sunlight and shadows shift. And yet it is the trees crowning its summit which make it stand out; trees deliberately planted there.

From the opposite aspect is the sea. We watch the coastline stretch away, the colour of its cliffs the same as the walls of Chideock's cottages, a colour which perhaps gives its name to adjacent Golden Cap. It is so silent here, no traffic, the only sound being the breaking of the sea on the beach below; a sleepy dreamy sea, so soft that its innocuous surface seems like silk; a gentle swell constantly riding its surface in a never-ending forward flowing stream as if someone took a silk sheet, lifted it and lowered it again. Yet this demure face changes at the shore where it lets out a cavernous roar, which would seem to echo the recesses of the earth itself.

We choose to follow unofficial, imperceptible paths, ghost trails where grass has been compressed by the steps of the few who strode out and upwards before. These paths seem less slippery than the coast path marked along the base of the ridge; sticky and muddy from the deeply trodden footprints there. Yet it seems as if this coast path is the most popular, perhaps because it does not climb. It is not always prudent to follow the herd, but to take a new course in a different direction. Setting our hopes higher, we thus begin to climb out of the mud and mire, following the thin trails of flattened grass; the hill before us seeming vertical, too challenging, yet as we climb, it is easier than we thought, and definitely not insurmountable. We hardly stop to catch our breath; even a runner is taking the same challenge.

Walking back towards Seatown, a traditional fishing hamlet comprising a comfortable cluster of old cottages nestling in an inlet along this impressively rugged Jurassic coastline, I wonder how many smugglers came ashore here under the command of 'the colonel', who organised the local smuggling ring [53]. The hamlet, not a town at all as the name suggests, but a 'farm by the sea', according to the old English meaning [52], now seems to be a backwater, reformed and languishing in a lazy retirement from all the action of its notorious past. Its location remains secluded, a sweet escape, and neighbouring Chideock, quiet and unassuming, was once its biggest partner in crime. From up here, Chideock's old cottages crowding around the church tower seem so quintessentially picturesque that I wonder about man's changing sense of aesthetic. In one sense, he can build to enhance the landscape, to blend into it and add interest, in other instances he builds something to scream at natural surrounds such as the ugly lines of caravans which blot the landscape in shimmering rows like gleaming white teeth. As the sea and the landscape are fickle, surprising, ever-changing, so is man's sense of aesthetic unreliable.

Up here though, none of this really seems to matter as we are on top of the world, away from technology (it doesn't work here). We feel fresh, exhilarated, the chill wind racing around our ears and blowing our cares way out across the sea.

(2015)

Holt Heath

Holt Heath has regenerated after the dank and dismal days which made it look merely mottled brown. With the return of the sun after so much rain, a whole new life is born with colours, textures and diversity. Large pools of water accumulated at the fringes of the heath reflect, in their lucid depths, the languid clarity of a carefree sky coursed with bubbling white clouds. Over this blue backdrop, crystal clear images are played back in sharp definition: The dark twigs of naked foliage, the sun-touched trunk of a silver birch, silky, suave. Around the watery wash grow grasses; cream brushes which stroke the sky reflected in the floodwaters. A gentle breeze moves through them, causing their individual 'bristles' to stir in sympathy; a horse's tail turned upwards.

The heath itself remains brown but blushes as the sunlight strikes its shadowy surface. Layers take form; behind thick fringes of grass, the landscape is punctuated with slender silver birch, pine and gorse, which is beginning to flower. Branches brushing each other above our heads clack and rasp together; hollow, wooden, twiggy in the rising breeze. Sometimes they squeak and we hope that they will not fall.

I have failed to appreciate the fullness of the heath, inclined to regard it as monotonous, brooding and almost hostile, but that is my ignorance. For today it breathes deeply, exhaling a freedom and radiance. Having shaken off its dismal winter cloak, like sorrow giving way to joy, it emerges fresh- faced, a new image unveiled. It is as if the sunlight has sparked a revelation allowing it to step out of itself onto the threshold of something new, and from the melancholy of its darker, wintery life, it can move on in the hope of what new life might bring.

(2014)

Dorchester Roman Townhouse

It is thought that the Romans arrived at the port of Hamworthy in around 43AD and began a progressive and systematic conquest of the

Durotrige people. These people inhabited the area which the Roman conquerors named as their civitas of Durotrigum (comprising Dorset, South Wiltshire, South Somerset and East Devon.) Dorchester, or Durnovaria, became the capital of this new civitas, and today, still the county town, it continues to reveal the secrets of its Roman past as it has done throughout the centuries. Hardy, who experienced the uncovering of Roman burials when his house Max Gate was built in the late nineteenth century, states in *The Mayor of Casterbridge* (Casterbridge being his name for Dorchester)

> Casterbridge announced old Rome, in every street, alley, and precinct. It looked Roman, bespoke the art of Rome, concealed dead men of Rome. It was impossible to dig more than a foot or two deep about the town fields and gardens without coming upon some tall soldier or other of the Empire, who had lain there in his silent unobtrusive rest for a space of fifteen hundred years.

The most exciting find, to my mind, is the fourth- century Roman townhouse at Colliton Park, discovered by chance in about 1937. Its extensive foundations not only reveal the size of the house, (a total of fourteen to fifteen rooms built over time from about AD 307) but the ingenuity that the Romans had in engineering and art; the presence of a hypocaust (a heating system running under suspended floors) confirming the former, and mosaics in a suite of about eight rooms the latter. The beautiful execution of these mosaics reveals the Roman's attention to the decorative and aesthetic. In them one can appreciate a subtlety of colour and tone along with an intricacy and symmetry of design, a fluidity of weaving lines contrasting the more geometric. It is amazing that anything so apparently delicate would ever survive at all; two thousand years or more below the earth. Many other such mosaics have not been so lucky; being photographed and built over or perhaps already found damaged. The originality of works of art not only ensures their value but also their vulnerability, for if they are defaced, they are lost forever. These mosaics are now protected by a modern glass building, which has been erected above the broken line of original Roman wall and suggest that this house was a one-storey edifice, as was apparently commonplace. It would have probably had a roof tiled in stone and it is also possible that the exterior, as well as the interior of the house, would have been plastered and perhaps painted dark red [32].

Another part of the building is left in foundation form only- grids of stone peering up through the grass, a column still standing, and what looks like a well. On this grey, drizzly day in February, I wonder how the original Romans of 43AD would have felt living in Britannia, an alien and hostile land. If the inhabitants of this townhouse had themselves come from what is now Italy, they must have missed the warmth and sunshine in their native land. No wonder they required a hypocaust! Of course, the inhabitants of this townhouse would most very probably have been wealthy Britons (Celts) living like Romans in the Roman Empire, as many of them were encouraged to do, and did so readily, realising that such a life brought with it further prosperity and prestige. These conquered Celtic nobles and chiefs often became *Decuriones*, members of the town council and responsible for the everyday governance of the town, which the Romans helped them to build [58]. I imagine that for the Romans, this would have been a cheap and effective way to win over the majority of the population and to avoid unnecessary conflicts. It also might have meant that a system of law could be instigated quickly and more successfully as people would have been more likely to trust one of their own. I imagine also that these Durotrige nobles would have originally had to have learned Latin and would therefore initially have been an invaluable and essential medium of communication between the Romans and the normal population of Britons who continued farming and trading in much the same way as they had done before the Roman invasion.

The public arena was mostly a man's world, although in Pompeii, a very few women are known to have worked or run businesses [19]. It was also virtually impossible to find women as governors or in positions of power. Men exhibited their power by impressing and entertaining their guests, flaunting their wealth and hosting enormous, lavish feasts at their villas, often hiring prostitutes. In Pompeii, rich houses such as this one would have also employed slaves. These young boys or girls could come from any land within the empire [19]. Although in Britannia, the Decurions had gained, through their office, a higher position of privilege and were usually the owners of such rich houses boasting expensive mosaic floors, frescoed walls, dining rooms, bath suites, a kitchen and gardens, I wonder whether they adopted entirely the same lifestyle as the people of Pompeii who were established Roman citizens and would therefore probably not have been partially influenced by any other culture which had once been part of their identity. Those in Pompeii also lived three hundred years prior to the inhabitants of this Roman town house, and lifestyles change through centuries. By the fourth century AD, Christianity was the established Roman religion and many of the burials and mosaics found in Dorset from this time, suggest that the people had adopted it. I will never forget being in the British Museum as a teenager and marvelling at the large floor mosaic from a villa in Hinton St Mary. In the centre of this mosaic a circle contains the Greek letters Chi and Rho, the first two letters of Christ's name, and an early symbol for Christ, along with pomegranates, symbols of eternal life, and the image of a man, who is thought to be Christ Himself [61].

Durnovaria would have no doubt contained many of the essential elements of a Roman town. There is evidence that it was built on a grid system, as was the normal pattern. The Neolithic henge of Maumbury Rings was adapted in Roman times to make an amphitheatre, used perhaps for events such as acrobatics and other circus-type entertainments. There is also evidence of a forum and a large public baths. Certainly in big Roman cities, such as Pompeii, there were many communal baths as well as bars, brothels, shops and temples but there is little evidence of what else was constructed in Dorchester [32].

In contrast to the men, Roman women generally inhabited more of the private sphere. Wealthy women, such as those who resided in this townhouse, would have enjoyed paying attention to their appearance; wearing beautiful jewellery and clothes and pinning up their hair, yet I wonder how, confined to the home, these women would have passed the hours as a wife and mother, perhaps with slaves to wait on them while they languished in a provincial town which existed in one of the farthest flung extremities of the Roman world. Although Durnovaria was the Roman's chosen capital for the civitas, it seems to have lacked the sophistication and variety of many of the larger, more important cities of the empire. As I watch the mizzle trailing down, I wonder what the women did on days like this, shut in their private domain, away from the outside world, watching through windows from their comfortable, heated interiors out onto the damp streets.

(2012)

Ghost Train

The old woman at the bus stop has lived here all her life. On this bright sunny February morning she recounts tales of how all the village children used to walk across the fields of West Parley to school. Now the fields cry out beneath smart brick houses and smooth tarmac roads. She talks of the train, now only a ghost train. As children we were sure we could detect a faint whiff of steam drifting through the trees at Delph Woods or pretend to hear the impending, frantic panting puff of the ghost train bearing down on us, chasing us into stifling, claustrophobic tunnels and even making us jump with its shrill whistle so that we cowered together under the old railway bridge below the Willett. Such is the power of make-believe, for I had a very lively imagination, perhaps stimulated by reading *The Railway Children*.

The ghost train has come alive at last when the old lady tells me how she travelled in it, clattering up what is now the Castleman Trailway from Wimborne to Broadstone, where she and her family climbed out to eat 'faggots and peas.' It is fascinating to hear how times have changed. The railway was closed in the 1960s. The sleepers of the track were still laid when I was a child and we would walk, my family and I, from Merley to Broadstone to do shopping; small, ungainly feet trying to neatly balance, one in front of the other along the eerie metal rail track, tripping over sleepers, stones and lumps of coal which sank hard into fallen arches. I imagined the ghost train. Now the sleepers are gone and a smooth trailway presides. All that is left of the railway is the bridge and perhaps the exhilaration of travelling by train, the smuts, the sulphur-steam smell and the shrill whistle remaining as memories in the minds of those who own them.

Epilogue

I have learnt a lot from writing this book. Researching it has been a pleasure, not just in the reading but in the joy of discovery. History, both natural and manmade, can be found everywhere, the manmade having become so natural that I would have never before imagined the extent to which Dorset's open air museum of hills and valleys reveals human history, man's omnipresent legacy lying dormant in the land. For Dorset tells us of how our ancestors lived and died, how they inhabited their environment, buried their dead, used and tilled the soil, managed forests, maintained pastures and downland through keeping livestock, built and destroyed, forging an identity through the marks they made and the places they named. Their actions were determined by tradition and belief, social, political and demographic upheavals, the steady increase in knowledge with the development of technology, and by geography. We are all a part of that process. Today we appreciate the beauty of the countryside for escape and recreation as well as being an important provider of food. We perhaps understand and appreciate wildlife more because it is becoming scarcer.

Through observation, I have come to see how the countryside, so often regarded as natural and unchanged, is almost always entirely manmade; a wilderness tamed and constantly manipulated to suit human needs. Yet at the same time, when done responsibly, much of this manipulation, such as forest management, hedge laying and grazing, can benefit wildlife habitats. By reading the landscape, it is evident that the present is so shaped by the past that the two seem to fuse in a perpetual motion as time's ticking pendulum swings through the ages, and the seasons pass. Our nostalgic perception of unchanging tradition is therefore perhaps relative, for it depends how far back along history's timeline we are looking. It seems that we search for connections with the past, drawing on its shared experiences, in order to enable us to gain a better understanding of time and our place within it, to make sense of ourselves.

Although man mastered his landscape, making his mark in previous generations, Dorset's landscape also shows that the natural world can reclaim, recover and conquer. Villages long gone, lost to the land, and paths, overgrown and impassable, testify to this. For the past century or more, however, man has been making an indelible mark which causes change at unprecedented levels. Industrialisation along with rampant urbanisation, are probably two of the most significant threats to the landscape and soundscape, as well as the climate. This consequently affects our experience of the natural world. It seems almost hypocritical to say that we want to protect nature and the countryside yet at the same time use our car to visit it. But we are all caught up in the world in which we live, and it is hard to totally stand against it.

Although nothing lasts forever, we should do our best to protect what we have inherited through the generations. While technology has threatened nature, it can now also be used to conserve it like never before. I am so grateful to charities such as The Dorset Wildlife Trust, the RSPB, The Woodland Trust, The National Trust and English Heritage, the Dorset Historic Church Trust, Churches Conservation Trust and the Historic Houses Association, to name but a few, which help to fight this battle through caring for both nature and culture in the beautiful county which is Dorset, and preserving its centuries- long story for future generations to enjoy. Proceeds from this book will go to the Dorset Wildlife Trust.

> '...whatever is pure, whatever is lovely............think about such things.'
>
> (Philippians 4:8)

Select Bibliography

1. Abbotsbury Tourism., nd. *Abbotsbury Swannery* [online].http://abbotsbury-tourism.co.uk/swannery
2. Atwooll, M., 1998. *Shipwrecks*. Stanbridge: The Dovecote press.
3. Ayres, K., 2014. Sandford Orcas. *Dorset Life magazine* [online] http://www.dorsetlife.co.uk/2014/02/sandford-orcas/
4. Baldock, J., 1990. *The elements of Christian symbolism*. Shaftesbury: Element.
5. Bankes, V., 1986. *A Kingston Lacy Childhood*. Stanbridge: The Dovecote press.
6. Bankes, V., 1986. *A Dorset Heritage, The story of Kingston Lacy*. London: Anthony Mott Limited.
7. Barnes, W. 1878. *The Outline of English Speechcraft*. Reproduced by Kessinger Publishing 2008.
8. Barnes, W., 1893. *Poems of rural life in the Dorset dialect.* London: Kegan Paul, Trench, Trubner and co, ltd. https://ia800207.us.archive.org/19/items/poemsrurallifein00barn/poemsrurallifein-00barn.pdf
9. Billett, M., 2002. *Farmhouses and Cottages*. Stanbridge: The Dovecote Press.
10. Bond, L., 1984. *Tyneham, A lost heritage*. Stanbridge: The Dovecote press.
11. Booton, P., 2012. Peter Booton in Symondsbury. *Dorset Life magazine* [online] http://www.dorsetlife.co.uk/2012/07/booton-foot-trails-peter-booton-in-symondsbury/
12. British History Online., 2017. Cerne Abbas, in *An Inventory of the Historical Monuments in Dorset, Volume 1, West* (London, 1952), pp. 74-85. *British History Online* http://www.british-history.ac.uk/rchme/dorset/vol1/pp74-85.
13. British History Online., 2017. Cranborne, in *An Inventory of the Historical Monuments in Dorset, Volume 5, East* (London, 1975), pp. 4-16. *British History Online* http://www.british-history.ac.uk/rchme/dorset/vol5/pp4-16.
14. British History Online., 2017. Sturminster Newton, in *An Inventory of the Historical Monuments in Dorset, Volume 3, Central*

(London, 1970), pp. 269-286. *British History Online* http://www.british-history.ac.uk/rchme/dorset/vol3/pp269-286.

15. British History Online., 2017. Weymouth, in *An Inventory of the Historical Monuments in Dorset, Volume 2, South east* (London, 1970), pp. 330-374. *British History Online* http://www.british-history.ac.uk/rchme/dorset/vol2/pp330-374.

16. British History Online., 2017. Whitchurch Canonicorum, in *An Inventory of the Historical Monuments in Dorset, Volume 1, West* (London, 1952), pp. 260-265. *British History Online* http://www.british-history.ac.uk/rchme/dorset/vol1/pp260-265.

17. British History Online., 2017. Whitcombe, in *An Inventory of the Historical Monuments in Dorset, Volume 2, South east* (London, 1970), pp. 374-376. *British History Online* http://www.british-history.ac.uk/rchme/dorset/vol2/pp374-376.

18. British History Online., 2017. Worth Matravers, in *An Inventory of the Historical Monuments in Dorset, Volume 2, South east* (London, 1970), pp. 410-416. *British History Online* http://www.british-history.ac.uk/rchme/dorset/vol2/pp410-416.

19. Butterworth, A & Laurence, R., 2006. *Pompeii the Living City*. London: Phoenix.

20. Cecil, D., 1985. *Some Dorset Country Houses*. Stanbridge: The Dovecote press.

21. The Churches Conservation Trust., 2017. http://www.visitchurches.org.uk/Ourchurches/Completelistofchurches/The-Church-no-dedication-Whitcombe-Dorset/

22. The Churches Conservation Trust., 2017. http://www.visitchurches.org.uk/Ourchurches/Completelistofchurches/St-Peters-Church-Winterborne-Came-Dorset/

23. The Churches Conservation Trust., 2017. https://www.visitchurches.org.uk/visit/church-listing/st-andrew-winterborne-tomson.html

24. The Churches Conservation Trust https://www.visitchurches.org.uk/visit/church-listing/st-mary-tarrant-crawford.html

25. Clementi society, *Clementi's life and work*. http://clementisociety.com/clementis-life-and-work/#Father

26. Comrie, J and Burnett, D., 1991. *Dorset the county in colour*. Stanbridge: The Dovecote Press.

27. Defoe, D., 1724-27. *A tour through the whole island of Great Britain.* Reproduced by Penguin Classics
28. Dickens, C., 1853. *The Long Voyage.* Reproduced by Starling and Black.
29. Dorset Historic Churches Trust, nd. *Whitcombe.* http://www.dorsethistoricchurchestrust.co.uk/whitcombe.htm
30. Dorset Historic Churches Trust., nd. *Nethercerne.* http://www.dorsethistoricchurchestrust.co.uk/nether_cerne.htm
31. Draper, J., 2000. *Regency, Riot and Reform.* Stanbridge: The Dovecote press.
32. Draper, J., 2001. *Dorchester past.* Chichester: Phillimore.
33. Edwards, A., 2000. *Waterside walks in Dorset.* Newbury: Countryside books.
34. Endecott, V., 2002. *The Dorset days of Enid Blyton.* Lytchett Matravers: Ginger Pop Promotions.
35. English Heritage., nd. *Winterborne Poorlot Barrows.* http://www.English-heritage.org.uk/daysout/properties/winterbourne-poorlot-barrows.
36. Fincham, T., 2011. About Hardy. Thomas Hardy society [online]. http://www.hardysociety.org/about-hardy
37. Faulkner, J.M., 1898. *Moonfleet.* Reproduced by Feedbooks.
38. Fowles, J. *The French Lieutenants Woman.* Jonathan Cape. Reprinted by permission of the Random House Group Limited.
39. Gutteridge, R., 2007. *Cutt Mill.* Dorset Life [online] http://www.dorsetlife.co.uk/2007/11/cut-mill/
40. Hardy,T., 1878 *The Return of the Native.* Reproduced by Wordsworth Classics.
41. Historic England, 2015. *Weymouth's Seaside Heritage.* Swindon: Historic England.
42. Holden, P and Cleeves, T., 2011. *RSPB Handbook of British Birds* 3rd edition. London: Helm.
43. Holt, J., 2000. *Follies.* Stanbridge: The Dovecote press.
44. Horsfall, A, 2003. *Woodlands.* Stanbridge: The Dovecote press.
45. Jones, S., 1985. *The Cambridge Introduction to Art-* The Eighteenth Century. Cambridge: Cambridge University Press

46. Joyce, H.S., nd. *A Country Childhood*. Bournemouth: Red Post Books 2000
47. Legg, R., 2007. *Cerne Abbas*. Dorset life [online] http://www.dorsetlife.co.uk/2007/09/cerne-abbas/
48. Marsh, J and Greenaway, K., 1978. *The illuminated language of flowers*. London: Macdonald and Jane's.
49. Massingham, H.J., 1936. *English Downland*. Reproduced with kind permission of B.T.Batsford, part of Pavilion Books Company Limited.
50. McFarlane, R., 2015. *Landmarks*. Hamish Hamilton.
51. McFetrich, D and Parsons, J., 1998. *Bridges*. Stanbridge: The Dovecote press.
52. Mills, A.D., 2008. *Discover Dorset place names*. Stanbridge: The Dovecote press.
53. Morley, G., 1983. *Smuggling in Hampshire and Dorset 1700-1850*. Newbury: Countryside books.
54. Natural England., 2010. *Axminster to Lyme Regis*. naturalengland.org.uk/publications (visitor leaflet.) https://www.gov.uk/government/publications/devons-national-nature-reserves/devons-national-nature-reserves#axmouth-to-lyme-regis-undercliffs
55. The National Trust. *Cerne giant* [online] https://www.nationaltrust.org.uk/cerne-giant#Overview
56. The National Trust. *Hardy Monument* [online] https://www.nationaltrust.org.uk/hardy-monument
57. Osborn, G., 1987. *Dorset Curiosities*, Stanbridge: The Dovecote Press.
58. Papworth, M., 2011. *The search for the Durotriges, Dorset and the West Country in the Late Iron Age*. Stroud: The History Press.
59. Pollard, A and Brawn, E.,2009. *The Great Trees of Dorset*, Stanbridge: The Dovecote press.
60. Psalm 19
61. Putnam, B., 1984. *Roman Britain*. Stanbridge: The Dovecote press.
62. RSPB. *Kingfisher* http://www.rspb.org.uk/discoverandenjoynature/discoverandlearn/birdguide/name/k/kingfisher/legal_protection.aspx

63. Russell U, and Grindrod, A., 2007. *The Manor Houses of Dorset*, Stanbridge: The Dovecote Press.
64. Stevenson, R.L., 1885. *A Child's Garden of Verses*. Reproduced by Feedbooks.
65. Stokes, J and Rodger, D., 2004. *The Heritage Trees of Britain and Northern Ireland*. London: Constable.
66. Viner, D., 2007. *Roads, tracks and turnpikes*. Stanbridge: The Dovecote press.
67. Viner, L., 2002. *Lost villages*. Stanbridge: The Dovecote Press.
68. Watton R, cited Wallace, M., 1985. *St Aldelm's chapel at St Aldelm's head* (visitor's guide 10th edition June 2012)
69. The Wildlife Trusts. *Lowland calcareous grassland* http://www.wildlifetrusts.org/wildlife/habitats/lowland-calcareous-grassland
70. The Woodland Trust. 2009. *The Remedy Oak*. http://www.ancient-tree-hunt.org.uk/discoveries/newdiscoveries/2009/The+Remedy+Oak
71. Westwood, R., 2007. *Smuggler's Dorset*. Inspiring places publishing.

Disclaimer

The purpose of this book is not a guide; therefore the factual content is only correct to the best of my knowledge. Where I have relied on word of mouth from locals, I have reported what they have said, in order to remain more authentic. While I have tried my upmost to contact the publishers of all sources used regarding permissions, I give my sincerest apologies to any who might have been missed.

Acknowledgements

My sincere thanks to the following for allowing me to use their materials in my work: B.T.Batsford, The Churches Conservation Trust, Clementi society, Countryside books, The Dovecote Press, Dorset Life magazine, Gaynor Burrett, Historic England , Natural England, Random House, Red Post books, The National Trust, The Woodland Trust, Robert Westwood

A special thank you to my wonderful husband: for all your patience and support, for sharing many of these experiences and for making me so happy. Also thank you to my mum and to all the friends who took time to read parts of this manuscript. Thank you all for your advice and encouragement.

Paintings by the author:

Kingfisher on the Stour
Shrimping at Kimmeridge
Wimborne Minster floodlit
Kingston Lacy

Photographs taken in Dorset by the author:

Landscape
Holloway
Poppy field near Wimborne
Abbotsbury
Eggardon Hill
A sheep near Kingston

Flowers
Snowdrops at Kingston Lacy
Bee orchid
Wildflower meadow
Bluebell wood
A sea of wood garlic

Seascapes
Arne
Near Lulworth
Seatown
Kimmeridge
Studland beach

Wildlife
Blue Adonis
Dragon fly
Little egret
Brimstone
Orange tip

Other aspects of Dorset
Two coastal scenes
Café in Kimmeridge
Cows at Hambledon hill
Street in Worth Matravers